Good Day Sunshine State

UNIVERSITY PRESS OF FLORIDA

Florida A&M University, Tallahassee
Florida Atlantic University, Boca Raton
Florida Gulf Coast University, Ft. Myers
Florida International University, Miami
Florida State University, Tallahassee
New College of Florida, Sarasota
University of Central Florida, Orlando
University of Florida, Gainesville
University of North Florida, Jacksonville
University of South Florida, Tampa
University of West Florida, Pensacola

GOOD DAY SUNSHINE STATE

How the Beatles Rocked Florida

Bob Kealing

University Press of Florida

Gainesville · Tallahassee · Tampa · Boca Raton
Pensacola · Orlando · Miami · Jacksonville · Ft. Myers · Sarasota

Funding for this publication was provided through a grant from Florida Humanities with funds from the National Endowment for the Humanities. Any views, findings, conclusions or recommendations expressed in this publication do not necessarily represent those of Florida Humanities or the National Endowment for the Humanities. As the non-profit, state affiliate of the National Endowment for the Humanities, Florida Humanities supports programs and resources that explore the history and culture of Florida and encourage a lifelong appreciation of literature, literacy, and learning.

Frontispiece, top: A ticket from the Jacksonville show the Beatles played at the Gator Bowl Stadium, September 11, 1964; *bottom*: An autographed record sleeve dated "9/11/64."
Page vi: The iconic autographs of the four Beatles band members, signed for their limo driver on the way to the Deauville Hotel.
Page viii: A limo receipt from the company that took the band to the Deauville Hotel on February 13, 1964. Notice the band's name misspelled as "Beetles."

28 27 26 25 24 23   6 5 4 3 2 1

Library of Congress Control Number: 2022944701
ISBN 978-0-8130-6893-0 (pbk)

The University Press of Florida is the scholarly publishing agency for the State University System of Florida, comprising Florida A&M University, Florida Atlantic University, Florida Gulf Coast University, Florida International University, Florida State University, New College of Florida, University of Central Florida, University of Florida, University of North Florida, University of South Florida, and University of West Florida.

University Press of Florida
2046 NE Waldo Road
Suite 2100
Gainesville, FL 32609
http://upress.ufl.edu

Dedicated to the memory of Louis "Buddy" Dresner

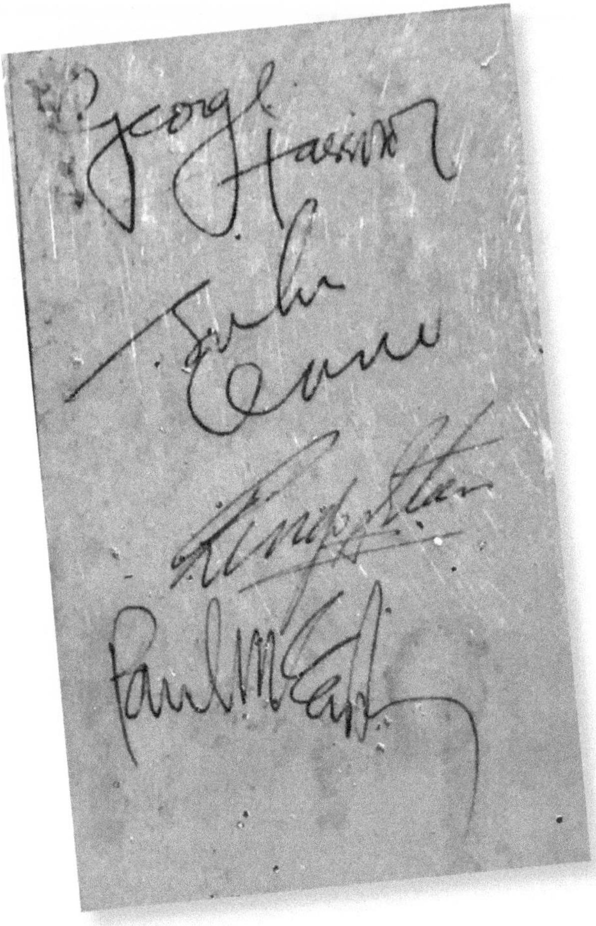

The Beatles were relaxed, glad to be in Miami . . . definitely a vibe to the Miami appearance. More of the Beatles' personality was actually communicated in Miami than New York.

—Rob Precht, Ed Sullivan's grandson

DATE	PICK-UP TIME	FLIGHT TIME	
13 FEB. 64	3 55 P.m.	M.I.A.D.	

NAME			
THE BEETLES From ENGLAND			

ADDRESS
DEAVILLE HOTEL

TOUR COMPANY	CALLED BY
NATIONAL AIRLINES	DISPATCHER

Contents

1

Sparks amid the Darkness

Close your eyes, take a breath, tune out the tech noise, and fly. Imagine yourself aboard a whirring drone scanning the deep night sky, soaring over a deserted stretch of highway from a distant place and time. Here, on the outskirts of suburban Chicago, it's Christmas, 1963. Fat, wind-whipped snowflakes descend through incisor-rattling cold. A pristine blanket of snow—four inches and counting—gives the open country-side along the empty highway a peaceful, ethereal crown. Even in a remote place like this, the magic about to happen in one young man's life remains a marker etched into his soul.

A monthlong period of mourning America's dashing young president has given way to nationwide malaise with the loss of so much hope Camelot represented. Floridians were just getting over nagging anxiety from the year previous: the existential threat of annihilation via Soviet missiles staged in Cuba, at zero lot-line proximity to Key West. That sunny mid-November, who could have imagined, when Floridians feted forty-seven-year-old JFK in Palm Beach, Tampa, Cape Canaveral, and Miami Beach, that this was his *farewell*?

At MacDill Air Force Base in Tampa, Kennedy met with Monsi-gnor Michael Gannon, who briefed him on St. Augustine's upcoming four-hundredth anniversary celebration. The nation's only Catholic president, Kennedy showed a keen interest in Gannon's field of ex-pertise: Catholicism in Spanish Colonial Florida. Gannon shared with

President John F. Kennedy campaigning in Miami Beach, November 18, 1963, four days prior to his assassination. Courtesy of State Archives of Florida, Florida Memory.

Kennedy a beautifully framed photographic copy of the oldest written record of American origin, a marriage certificate dating from 1594. The Chamber of Commerce was hoping the gift might entice the president to return for what was sure to be a magnificent celebration. "As he left he said, 'I'll keep in touch,'" Gannon recalled. "Four days later he was dead."

At the conclusion of his successful trip to the Sunshine State, the president was already laying groundwork for the 1964 election. Kennedy told an aide he dreaded going to Texas; he'd had a chilling premonition about the ease with which someone could fire at the motorcade with a high-powered rifle. And then it happened. A national nightmare of the highest magnitude, the assassination of a president, was captured on film in horrifying detail. Two days later, the nation witnessed his assassin's murder on live television. It was all so dark and *surreal*. With the holidays approaching, snow descending along the Illinois countryside, Americans everywhere struggled, yearned to find some sense of relief.

Along the darkened outskirts of Homewood, Illinois, a 1957 Buick, the long and rangy, gas-guzzling kind with the sleek lines, barreled down the interstate. All alone behind the wheel, a young, crewcut navy man nursed a healthy beer buzz and hauled ass. John Trusty was in transit, having just finished hospital corpsman school in San Diego. In the midst of thirty days home leave near the Windy City, Trusty was preparing to head south to Florida and his assignment at the Naval Air Station hospital in Key West. To pass the time, stay awake, and keep his brother-in-law's car from ending up in a snowy ditch, he switched on the radio to 89 WLS-AM, the bright sound of Chicago radio. In the wee hours of this frigid night, an urgent, unfamiliar beat hit him like a blast of wind: "*Oh ya I, tell you somethin', I think you'll understand.*"

At this heavy and uncertain time in American history, the Beatles had arrived, musically at least. The timing could not have been better. Stateside, popular music had been churning along at a low ebb. In March 1963 country music suffered a crushing loss when superstar-to-be Patsy Cline died in a plane crash coming home from a charity show in Kansas City, Kansas. The one-time King of Rock and Roll Elvis Presley was imprisoned by his manager's desire to develop more middle-of-the-road appeal. Presley's latest single, the jaunty "Bossa Nova Baby," hit the charts and sank like a stone. There was Sam Cooke, whose soulful voice flowed like honey. Keith Richards once said that soul singers who try to measure up to Sam Cooke should "go back to pumping gas." Vanilla crooners like Bobby Vinton and Jack Jones mined the Great American Songbook.

But not these new guys. The music blasting from Trusty's car radio that frigid night was akin to an awakening. During this saddest of holiday seasons, dear God, could we dare say it was *joyous*? Hearing "I Want to Hold Your Hand" for the first time on that deserted, snow-blown stretch of interstate, John Trusty picked up on the vibe immediately. And then, he did something stupid. "I actually started doing donuts on the four-lane highway, I was so happy," he marveled. "I don't know, I can't say why . . . I heard it and just—*wow*. This shit is *good*." In this dream flight of time and imagination, we're witnessing a youth's visceral reaction to music of his generation. Watching from a drone's

John Trusty. Courtesy of John Trusty.

eye above, two tons of American steel on four wheels swirl round and round, just like an old-school 45 RPM single on kid's portable record player. At a pivotal moment in time musically, culturally, and politically, America's youth were meeting the Beatles, their new North Stars, one DJ, one radio, one record player at a time.

In 1964, John Trusty was destined to get much closer to the Beatles than most. Even as a hospital corpsman assigned to an out-of-the-way, end-of-the-road military outpost in tropical Florida, closer to Castro's Cuba than Miami or anywhere else on the mainland. But that's where it happened, thanks to fate and a devastating hurricane.

A thousand miles from the frosty, ivory-blanketed Midwest, sixteen-year-old Kitty Oliver's love affair with the Beatles began to blossom as soon as her mom drifted off to sleep. In the clandestine late-night hours, she clicked on her hand-held transistor radio to WAPE-AM, the Mighty 690, the "white" radio station in rigidly segregated Jacksonville, Florida. At the end of 1963, Jim Crow laws and segregation were still strictly observed there. In June of that year, when Kitty showed up to march in protest of the murder of Medgar Evers, local Klan

Kitty Oliver. Courtesy of Kitty Oliver.

members watched and jeered, foreshadowing greater turmoil in 1964. Kitty, an only child living within the recesses of a Blacks-only Westside neighborhood, knew since early childhood where she could and could not go. There were zones of uncertainty if you were Black, potentially unsafe places for no other reason than the color of your skin. Kitty might as well have been invisible; she was expected to accept lesser prospects and lower horizons like generations of marginalized urban youth before her. "I describe it as being very similar to apartheid," she remembered. "The only white person I ever saw was an insurance man from time to time, and I mean rarely."

Then along came the four Brits whose driving beat and soaring harmonies reminded Kitty of songs from girl groups like the Ronettes. The Beatles sprang from working-class roots and wore their hair long, drawing immediate derision from the establishment. As Kitty saw it, they didn't seem to care. But there was something else about them: early photos featured them alongside Black artists like Little Richard. That was unusual, and it caught her eye. After hearing them on the radio, Kitty and her best friend bought and danced to early Beatles singles on a portable record player; her friend chose Paul as favorite; Kitty opted for shy-but-smiling Ringo. In teen magazine photos, it was unusual to see a drummer staged dramatically up on a riser, bashing away. Most were hidden behind the front men, but not Ringo. That subtle difference gave him more star status, an equal to the guys on guitar.

It was not lost on Kitty that when they started chasing rock-star dreams, the Beatles were nobodies with nothing to lose. She could relate. They shrugged off questions about their appearance, maintained an unflappable certainty of purpose and an all-for-one, one-for-all ethos. To an isolated teenaged girl in a deeply divided corner of the American South, the Beatles' music meant far more than a danceable beat and harmonies she found so appealing; it meant hope. To Kitty, the music playing up and down the eastern seaboard in the late-night hours courtesy of a station nicknamed, "WAPE The Big Ape" represented light in her darkness, an inkling of better days. "It made me think that even with the prejudice and segregation," Kitty recalled, "there was some other part of the world that wasn't like that."

In 1964, the two most important cultural forces driving change in America, civil rights and Beatlemania, converged in Kitty Oliver's hometown. To begin that climactic summer, Martin Luther King Jr. (MLK) himself was held in solitary confinement at the Duval County Jail in downtown Jacksonville. Like the Beatles, he had demanded equality for people of color. Unlike the Fab Four, he was arrested, humiliated, and jailed. Thanks to King's relentless, nonviolent push for equality in Florida; the courage of many locals who held signs and took beatings; and thanks to a forward-thinking federal judge who came down on the side of King and protesters, integration and equality ensued. Later that summer, the Beatles followed MLK's footsteps, walking in his shadow in Northeast Florida. By summer's end, city leaders had no choice but to acquiesce to the Beatles' demand for integrated seating at the Gator Bowl. By then myriad pivotal figures had made a mark in 1964 Florida: the Beatles, MLK, Malcolm X, Cassius Clay, Sonny Liston, Sam Cooke, Jim Brown, a courageous Florida reporter named Mabel Norris Chesley, Jackie Robinson, and Ed Sullivan, among others.

In town after town, the Beatles ignited America's nascent youth culture, set the standard for cool, and spawned widespread interest in making and performing rock music. Keith Harben from Gainesville, home of the University of Florida, remembered the day his best ninth-grade buddy, Tommy, stopped by his house on Northeast Sixth Terrace and told him it was imperative they go to the local "Teen Time" dance that Friday night: "They're gonna play a new record tonight,"

Tommy insisted. "We've *gotta* go hear it." To this day, Keith isn't sure how Tommy knew the disc jockey at the dance was going to play "I Want to Hold Your Hand," with the equally pulsating American B side, "I Saw Her Standing There." That night, at the Gainesville Recreation Center on Northeast Second Avenue, Keith Harben witnessed the life-altering effect the record had on his best friend, thirteen-year-old future Rock and Roll Hall-of-Famer and beloved Florida-born icon Tom Petty. "The Beatles were the key spark to really lighting Tom on fire," Harben said. "Tom got excited and wanted to have a band himself." Thanks to the Beatles and the ensuing British Invasion, the entirety of Florida's peninsula was poised to explode with garage bands, long hair, Beatle boots, and rock star dreams.

As the calendar flipped to 1964, long-term American success for the Beatles was hardly a foregone conclusion. Usually, if they were lucky, bands might have two or three hit singles before they faded into obscurity. Every British artist before the Beatles, even with loads of success in England, had failed to move the needle in America, their Holy Grail market. When Cliff Richard toured America with his group, the Shadows, young people barely noticed. It remained to be seen what chance a Liverpudlian band of four, with no defined front man, would have. In September 1963 the youngest of them, twenty-year-old George Harrison, had taken a vacation to the small midwestern town of Benton, Illinois, where his sister Louise and her husband had relocated. It was the first stateside trip by any of the Beatles. By that time, they had already hit number one in England with their single "Please Please Me." To George's dismay, it was clear from this visit that both he and the Beatles were unknown.

What the Beatles did have, however, was a secret weapon: their manager, Brian Epstein. "Eppy," as they liked to call him, guided the Beatles out of the dank and dreadful basement confines of Liverpool's Cavern Club, where he'd first seen them performing: leather-clad ruffians who smoked, drank, and swore onstage. At this crucial juncture in history, Epstein explained the commonality that brought them together: "They, like me, were becoming bored because they could see no great progress in their lives." Despite being a novice in the world of music management, the urbane and well-dressed Epstein thought of the boys as family and dedicated the rest of his abbreviated life to their success. Beatlemania would not have happened in America without their songs, *those songs*, but early on, Epstein's ability to recognize and act on serendipitous timing had just as much to do with it.

At great effort and expense, Epstein endured one rejection after another from the London music label honchos. The first of these came from a Decca records executive who informed him that guitar groups were on the way out. "You must be out of your mind," Epstein shot back. "These boys are going to explode. I am completely confident that one day they will be bigger than Elvis Presley." When Epstein finally succeeded in securing a recording contract, their less-than-enthused engineer and eventual musical mentor George Martin deemed the Beatles' original drummer, Pete Best, not good enough to record on their first single, "Love Me Do." The dirty work of having to sack one of the group's most popular members was left to Eppy. Then, in August 1962, Epstein orchestrated Ringo Starr's departure from a steady-if-unfulfilling gig with Rory Storm and the Hurricanes to join John, Paul, and George. That series of critical moves set the stage for all the success to come. After all the talk of who was the fifth Beatle, one need look no further than Brian Samuel Epstein.

Another critical moment of serendipity happened when American entertainment mogul Ed Sullivan was passing through Heathrow Airport on October 31, 1963. It was the same day the Beatles were returning home from Sweden, where "Please Please Me" had become a big hit. Upon witnessing all the girls going crazy, Sullivan said he decided to book them on his popular, but Vaudevillian quirky, television show. Two Sullivan talent agents in Europe, however, had already seen the Beatles live at least once earlier that summer, contacted Brian Epstein, and started the momentum toward launching them on Sullivan's show.

In early November, Epstein pounced on this career-making opportunity. He caught a flight to New York and negotiated a ten-thousand-dollar-payment-plus-expenses deal for the Beatles to make *Ed Sullivan Show* appearances in New York and Miami—two live and one taped. By comparison, in 1956 Elvis was paid more than double that amount. Epstein was willing to take less money in exchange for the Beatles being given crucial, prominent billing. After all, as George had seen for himself in September, America didn't know them. Sullivan came to that same realization upon his return stateside and immediately had second thoughts about the booking. "I found out that apparently my wife Sylvia and I were the only people in the country who'd even heard of the Beatles," the host remembered. "I was very worried." Thanks to serendipity and Epstein closing the deal, the Beatles' coming-out party in America would be as big as it could possibly be.

Building on that momentum, Epstein met with Capitol Records and convinced their public relations people to mount an all-out blitz to promote the Beatles' upcoming US appearances. All of that came just before "I Want to Hold Your Hand" was loosed on the youth of America at Christmastime. Young people like John Trusty, Kitty Oliver, and Tommy Petty were already looking for something to get excited about. With Epstein pulling the strings, the Beatles were set to appear before a larger audience—more than seventy million viewers—than most of their contemporaries would have in their entire careers. Then they had the great fortune to have the same massive television audiences for their second and third appearances.

The historic events included a Beatle residency in Florida as performers, then as tourists. Once their professional obligations were over, they devoured all the trappings of beach life in winter: sun, sand, women, celebrities, convertibles, fantastic yachts, and opulent homes. For a group of skinny, pale, mop-topped, chain-smoking Brits from working-class Liverpool who'd paid plenty of dues to reach this new career threshold, it was their awakening to all America had to offer. It was also a rare opportunity to spend quality time in one place, sunny Florida, time they would not have anywhere else in America that year, as their careers skyrocketed and they embarked on an unprecedented North American tour. That remarkable tour would bring the Beatles back to Florida for an unscheduled visit to Key West, then on to Northeast Florida, where weeks earlier, MLK's ideology of nonviolent protest had been put to a severe test. By then the Beatles, too, were doing their part to ensure social justice prevailed.

At the start of a year like no other for the Beatles and fans who fell in love with them, John, Paul, George, and Ringo needed to achieve one more goal they'd set, before meeting their American destiny. In 1964, Floridians bore witness to three stages of the Beatles' remarkable impact: innocence, influence, and activism.

2

Toppermost of the Poppermost

Thirty-eight-year-old Louis "Buddy" Dresner had just drifted off to sleep, or so it seemed, when banging at the front door of his North Miami Beach home rattled him awake. When you do that to someone who works overnight and covets sleep like a precious commodity, you'd better have a *damn* good reason. Dresner came to with a full head of steam, groused out of bed, and flung open the door of his cinder-block, single-story, working cop's home on North 160th Street. "God Damnit, this better be good!" he barked at the young police officer standing at the door. Remaining on task, the young cop told him, "Captain Stewart has been trying to reach you, and you apparently have the phone off the hook."

Of course he did; it's what you *had* to do when you slept days like a vampire. But now the captain was summoning Dresner, a sergeant on the Miami Beach Police force, after he'd already worked his usual overnight shift. That meant whatever he wanted had to be a big deal. Dresner made peace with the officer, sent him on his way, picked up the family's rotary-dial phone, and called headquarters. "We just assigned you to take care of the Beatles," Captain Stewart informed his sleep-deprived subordinate. "They're coming to Miami Beach to be on the *Ed Sullivan Show.*" Dresner, who'd become the department's go-to guy for high-profile security details, was stumped: "What the hell is the Beatles?" he asked himself. "What have I got to do with Beatles?"

Miami Beach Police Sgt. Buddy Dresner, in charge of the Beatles' security during their Miami visit. Courtesy of Barry Dresner.

Of all the big shots Dresner had looked after, never before had he been assigned to a rock-and-roll act.

Those who knew him say Dresner was the perfect guy for the job: straightforward, no-nonsense, cool under pressure, with an engaging sense of humor. Not out for glory or fame himself, Dresner was a cop's cop who wasn't shy about giving direction to celebrities. His other off-duty job was manning the front door at Joe's Stone Crab Restaurant, a South Beach landmark since 1913. More PR than policing, it was Dresner's mission to make sure tourists on a long waiting list didn't get out of order. Not one security detail prior to this, President John F. Kennedy included, could have prepared him for the Beatle mayhem-to-come. Buddy was a seasoned pro, but this would be unlike anything he had ever seen.

Carol Lee Gallagher had a keen awareness of who the Beatles were. Ever since the day Miami's highest-profile disc jockey, Rick Shaw, pulled his copy of "I Want to Hold Your Hand" out of the Capitol Records Special Delivery envelope and slapped it on the air at WQAM, it immediately became part of Shaw's formidable legend in South Florida radio. He would always be known there as the first disc jockey to play the Beatles' American breakthrough single. Thirty seconds in, Shaw said, "the phones exploded" with listeners wanting to know more about the song, who sang it, and, could they hear it again? The song swept across America in a flash, permeating and igniting youth culture. "It was just explosive. I still remember the first time I heard 'I Want to Hold Your Hand,'" said *Rolling Stone* contributing editor and musicologist Anthony DeCurtis, just twelve when the earliest wave of Beatlemania overtook him. "It was providing a jolt of energy into the culture. It was electric. It really was."

Meanwhile Gallagher, a blond twenty-two-year-old South Florida beauty, was already part of the working world, much older than the legion of teens beginning to be smitten with the Beatles. That didn't matter, she confessed. "I was in love with them." There was more exciting news in store for her; Gallagher was about to cross paths with the Beatles in a very public way. Driving home from the beach, Gallagher heard on the radio that the Beatles' first US appearances would include a live televised performance originating from the Deauville Hotel on Miami Beach. Knowing how insatiable Beatle fans were, Shaw, and his rivals from Miami station WFUN, managed to get information on the Beatles' travel itinerary. Their ten-day American trip, more of a visit than a proper tour, would include only three stops: New York and Washington, DC, before the final leg in Miami. They'd be arriving in Florida mid-February via National Airlines. Wait, *National Airlines*? That last bit of news left Gallagher thunderstruck. A National Airlines flight attendant, she worked the New York–Miami route all the time. "Oh my God," Gallagher realized, "That's my flight."

Capitol Records launched a fifty-thousand-dollar ad blitz to promote the Beatles stateside, ten times more than any previous artist. The results were immediate and overwhelming. By January 10, 1964, the initial shipment of one million copies of "I Want to Hold Your Hand" sold out. The label ordered a rush repressing. After all their previous singles, released in America on the tiny Swan label—"From Me to You," "Please Please Me," and "She Loves You"—had flopped, the Beatles finally had their breakthrough. The trio of earlier records carried the same buoyant spirit and Beatles beat, and, after the onset of Beatlemania, all three, rereleased later, topped the American charts. The difference was the lack of promotional dollars laying a necessary foundation for success. Still, it was something more. "The 1950s saw the invention of the American teenager," said DeCurtis. "By the 1960s they were a discernible group with their own marketing power and their own cultural power." Adults, too, were starting to take notice and take the Beatles seriously. That hadn't happened with rock-and-roll acts in the 1950s. The Beatles were on the cusp of becoming a cultural phenomenon; kids, music, marketing—everything was impacted.

John, Paul, George, and Ringo spent much of mid- and late January performing a run of shows at the Olympia Theater in Paris. The chic environs of the Hotel George V became the five-star backdrop for news that shook them to their very core. The usually prim and reserved Brian Epstein came running into their hotel room with a telegram exclaiming, "Hey, look. You are number one in America!" In early February, "I Want to Hold Your Hand" hit music's highest of heights, every musician's fever dream come true. "There can be nothing more important than this," Epstein said to John Lennon. "Can there?" This was the goal they had all wanted to achieve before setting off to conquer the States. Despite his unshakeable confidence in the Beatles, privately Epstein doubted the day would ever come. Beatle music would have a residency of its own, dominating the US charts that spring like never, ever before. In time, it should be noted, influential female artists like Dusty Springfield, Lulu, and Marianne Faithful cashed in on the British Invasion bonanza alongside male-dominated guitar bands: the Rolling Stones, the Dave Clark Five, Gerry and the Pacemakers, the Hollies, the Kinks, and the Zombies.

For the four young men from Liverpool, Epstein's news came as sweet, hard-earned affirmation. Said Paul McCartney, "We didn't come down for a week." Ringo described the melee that followed: "We all started acting like people from Texas hollering and shouting, 'Yahoo!'" How far they had come from those long and miserable nights in Hamburg, when the boys would get depressed and start questioning if they had a future. That's when it was up to John, their unquestioned leader, to pull them back up. He recounted his pep talks: "I'd say, 'Where are we going fellas?' And they'd go, 'To the top Johnny!' And I'd say, 'Where's *that,* fellas?' And they'd say, 'To the toppermost of the poppermost, Johnny!' And I'd say, 'Riiiight!' And we'd all sort of cheer up."

At first, photographer Harry Benson scoffed at having to cover the Beatles—until he met them. "I took myself for a serious journalist and I didn't want to cover a rock 'n roll story," he reflected. "I was so close to not being there." Because he was, Benson captured the quintessential image of the band celebrating that success with an epic Parisian pillow fight. Paul is at the top of the cascade, pillow in hand, one foot on the bed, another in the air; John is caught in the middle of the scrum looking like he's about to absorb an elbow from Ringo, who is smiling at George lying on his back, trying to defend himself from all three. The genuinely joyful smile on Harrison's face is a testament to the importance of the moment and achievement, given how reserved he usually was. When it came time for the Beatles to cross the Atlantic, Benson was with them, filled with a new conviction he'd been on the right story all along.

Miami newsman Larry Kane, the twenty-one-year-old news director at a string of small radio stations including WFUN, "Fun in the Sun" radio, was not convinced the Beatles would be anything more than a fluff story, a passing fad. His was a serious newsman's world of national and international stories playing out in his backyard. Flying above the Florida Straits, he witnessed wave after wave of desperate humanity trying to make their way to the Florida coastline. "Cuban exiles coming over," Kane remembered. "I went out with the Coast Guard to watch the boats. Some of which were made out of cardboard. It was just amazing to see this armada." In the first fifteen years after Fidel Castro seized power on January 1, 1959, an estimated five hundred thousand Cuban exiles, many well-educated businesspeople and property owners, fled the island, hoping to return once Castro's regime was over.

Kane circled other controversial stories including civil rights protests by African Americans and those sympathetic to their cause, and the growing US intervention in Vietnam. At a gym three blocks from his radio station, he had already met a brash but largely unknown boxer named Cassius Clay, who'd won a gold medal in the Light Heavyweight division at the 1960 Rome Olympics. He'd come to Miami to train for his upcoming world championship fight against Sonny Liston, to be staged at the Miami Convention Center in late February. Until the station bosses told him otherwise, Kane had no intention of covering the Beatles' visit to South Beach. Miami was filled with genuine entertainment big shots like Jackie Gleason, Judy Garland, and Frank Sinatra. What made these teenyboppers so special?

Like Harry Benson, Kane soon realized what a generational story the Beatles' visit America was. As a testament to his own hard work and enterprising nature, he ended up alongside the Beatles again and again, asking probing questions the quartet came to appreciate and answer with frankness and honesty. They came to respect and reward him for bothering to tap into their intelligence and developing worldview, the intellectual curiosity each of them possessed, John Lennon especially. That mutual respect ended up in a friendship between Kane and Lennon, the most controversial member of the Beatles. Unlike most media who focused on superficial jabs at the Beatles' appearance, interviewing one titillated teenager after another, in time, the intuitive Kane internalized the revolutionary aspects of what it all meant. He was among the first to witness the dangers also associated with Beatlemania. Often, due to Kane's probing questions, the Beatles became the first rock-and-roll band to speak out on controversial topics and start to be taken more seriously by adults.

Decades later, with the help of a much longer view of that era, the veteran newsman and author drew a parallel between Lennon, whom he called "unpredictable," and Donald Trump, the narcissistic tycoon Lennon never lived to see ascend to the presidency. "Both said in public what they thought in private," Kane observed. "Which can be very, very endearing and very, very damaging." With his travels alongside the Beatles, Kane experienced his own coming of age—and challenges of which he never could have dreamed. His access to the Beatles became the envy of any reporter who lived to chase the Big Story. In 1964, there was no bigger story than Beatlemania enveloping America. The battle over civil rights in the South, destined to boil over in Northeast Florida, came in a close second.

Still, no one, not one American, population 191 million, got to know the Beatles on that first visit as well as Sgt. Buddy Dresner. He guarded their safety, kept them on schedule, arranged for entertainment, roomed with them, dispensed fatherly advice, played tour guide, taught, laughed, argued, helped a couple of them with a very personal problem, chewed them out, even had them over to his modest house in North Miami Beach for their first home-cooked meal in America. Along the way, he earned their enduring affection, friendship, and gratitude.

It's apt to think of Buddy Dresner as South Florida's answer to Forrest Gump; an ever-present witness to the rush of history playing out just beyond the beach. Often dressed in his long-sleeved police uniform, hat, and Wayfarer sunglasses, Dresner ran the security detail for President John F. Kennedy a week before his assassination, became the overlord and protector of the Beatles during their initial visit stateside, and watched over Cassius Clay when he beat Sonny Listen to win boxing's World Heavyweight Championship. In exactly ninety-nine days, Buddy Dresner, the cop's cop who worked nights and slept days, witnessed Camelot in its twilight, the dawning of Beatlemania, and the birth of Muhammad Ali.

3

On to Miami

From the moment the Beatles' flight touched down in New York on February 7, 1964, it was borderline chaos thanks to the thousands of fans there to greet them. Gail Cameron, a twentysomething reporter for prestigious *Life* magazine, got caught in the churning surge of fans following each Beatle to the four limos hired by Capitol Records. The company also allowed a member of the press to ride in each limo. There were crowds, Cameron learned, and then there were *Beatle* crowds.

In the melee, a policeman spotted her press credential and "literally lifted me up and hurled me in to the limo," she recalled. "My shoes flew off as Ringo was hurled on top of me." Before they knew what was happening, the policeman barked to the driver, "Get out of here buddy if you want to get out alive!" Being jettisoned right out of her fashionable high heels was Gail Cameron's introduction to the early vestiges of Beatlemania in America. Once Cameron's shoes were somehow retrieved, during the limo ride to the Plaza Hotel, Starr told her how exciting and unexpected this American reception was. On the plane ride over, the Beatles had no idea how they would be received. Now, Ringo was smiling and calling out the window to kids chasing them in their own cars to the hotel.

So many decades later, Cameron admitted that she and the usually hard-nosed members of the New York press were immediately caught up in what she called "the contagious joy . . . [T]he Beatles too, were sharing the same joy." During the days of Camelot, she'd had close access to JFK and First Lady Jackie Kennedy. After the assassination, Cameron was enveloped in a numbness necessary to grind out three weeks of post-JFK coverage, of a nation adrift in grief and shock. With the coming of the Beatles, Cameron said, "It's like everyone began laughing again, throughout the country." The palpable sense of America's immediate, collective crush on this new group instilled in Cameron and her editors at *Life* the sense that this initial Beatles' visit was the "world-shaking" event history has since affirmed it to be.

For so many young Americans, just *hearing* Beatle records became a transformative, life-altering event. To *see and hear* the Beatles perform live on the *Ed Sullivan Show* took that nationwide fascination into the stratosphere. In so many one-television families around the country on February 9, 1964, children had to *beg* their skeptical or disapproving parents to tune in to *Sullivan* and watch the Beatles perform live for the first time in America. For the Lilleys of Orlando, Florida, however, that scenario was reversed. On that momentous Sunday, ten-year-old Susan Lilley and her younger brothers were horrified when their parents informed them they would not be watching *The Wonderful World of Disney* that night. "Listen you all, we must watch the Ed Sullivan Show," their father informed them. "Something big is going to happen tonight." Sullivan? The young siblings roared with disapproval, remembering his usual assemblage of puppets, jugglers, and comedians whose ethos didn't trickle down to preteens. Their mother wouldn't budge: "I'm not going to miss it. And neither are you." To preserve family harmony, their parents plied the Lilley children with ice cream and Hershey's chocolate syrup.

Skeptical Susan, who had threatened to keep her nose in a Nancy Drew mystery book before being persuaded with ice cream to pay attention, was rendered speechless watching the first Beatle song, "All My Loving." By the time they played their megahit "I Want to Hold Your Hand," she'd somehow been transformed. "I had unconsciously, but thoroughly, made the leap from bookish little girl to pre-teen romantic," she recalled. "All in one hour." It took some time for the full impact of what she'd seen to sink in. Susan Lilley and a generation of young girls were soon beset with Beatlemania, a swooning sensation at the mere thought of Paul, John, George, and Ringo. She recalled,

"It wasn't just the star crush factor. The music hit kids my age with a perfect-storm wallop as adolescence began to rev up." Kid-to-kid, family-to-family, city-to-city, state-to-state, that was the "world-shaking" impact Gail Cameron and her prescient team at *Life* perceived once America beheld the amped-up Beatle phenomenon gathered round the family television.

Editors at *Life* gave Cameron another assignment: "Get on the plane going to Miami with the Beatles," her editor ordered. "We want to take a picture of them in a swimming pool." Not just any picture, she soon learned, a cover shot. From that moment, the pressure was on. A pool? What pool, where? The logistics of it were *her* problem. She had forty-eight hours or less to make it all happen; it was Gail Cameron's new mission and the source of considerable anxiety: find a pool somewhere in Miami, with privacy, suitable for a *Life* shoot, and do it ASAP. Then, somehow, convince all four Beatles to get in it, for the coveted *Life* cover.

Joe Monteleone was working at JFK airport Thursday, February 13, the morning the Beatles left New York to fly to Miami. To be sure, he wanted nothing, nothing at all, to do with the silly-looking, "mop-headed" guys who'd caused a near-riot when they arrived. At the time, the Florida retiree was a twenty-two-year-old National Airlines ramp agent whose job was to load all the mail, freight, and luggage prior to departure. To escape the mere thought of screaming teens and chaos, Joe and a coworker took refuge by Gate 1B; the long, thin blockhouse, away from gate 1A where passengers on the Miami-bound flight would line up to walk out and board the plane. In 1964, rain or shine, you went up a portable staircase to the aircraft.

Dressed in their all-white uniforms, Joe and coworker George Moreno took a seat in the deserted, tranquil preboarding area. After a few minutes, the blockhouse door opened, a security guard peeked his head in, looked around, and told someone out of view the coast was clear. With that, the guard disappeared. Suddenly, four young guys all dressed in coats and ties were ushered in and took seats just down the blockhouse from Joe and George. Contrary to the squeals of delight or rush for an autograph their presence would have prompted from the majority of people at the airport that day, John, Paul, George, and Ringo drew nothing of the sort here. So there they all sat, the new toasts of the American music scene, in the quiet blockhouse where Joe and George were waiting to get to work.

To pass the time, Paul pulled out his camera and started taking pictures: the floor, the wall, the dirty window looking out to the airfield and their National Airlines jetliner. "Being a Brooklyn guy, I always spoke my mind," Monteleone remembered. "So I asked him, what the hell are you taking pictures of?" Continuing to click away, Paul replied, "In case this bubble bursts tomorrow, I want to remember every step of it." Ringo, too, was a constant shutterbug throughout their two weeks in America.

That was enough to break the ice between the young men, all in their early twenties. Joe walked up next to Ringo, whom he recalled was the friendliest. The Beatles spoke of their excitement to get out of the New York City cold and for the first time visit Miami, where it was sunny and a balmy 72 degrees. Despite having appeared before a record-shattering television audience of seventy-three million people on the *Ed Sullivan Show*, followed by capacity concerts in Washington, DC, and Carnegie Hall, where Brian Epstein was so proud of his boys he was moved to tears, here they were at JFK thinking their popularity might not last.

After a few minutes of small talk, it was time for Joe and George to go out on to the airfield and prepare the Beatles' plane for departure. "Can we go with you?" Ringo asked.

With that, in what would most assuredly be a major security breach today, the two workers slid open the metal door leading out to the airfield and escorted the Beatles across from the relative peace and quiet at Gate 1B, to the jetliner and crowd of people waiting at Gate 1A. Flight attendant Carol Lee Gallagher, whose instincts were correct that the Beatles would be on her flight, had thrust into her hands a large, heart-shaped box of candy to give to Ringo for a Valentine's Day photo-op. Dutifully, Ringo stood on portable stairs up to the plane, near Carol, who'd been a stranger to him until that moment, while photographers snapped away. The very instant the Beatles had come into her orbit, there was Carol Lee Gallagher now making history with them through that memorable image.

For Gallagher, it was like a shot of adrenaline. "I was just stunned. They were just the most gorgeous, fabulous men I'd seen in my life.

They didn't call them the Fab Four for nothing," Gallagher recounted. Around the side of the plane, Joe and George set about doing their jobs loading baggage and freight while passengers boarded for the two-hour flight. Once the doors were closed, the stairs pulled back, and the plane turned around to head for the runway, the coworkers now heading back to the blockhouse witnessed something odd: "I noticed the pilot looking out and waving," Joe said. "He had this Beatles head of hair on him. That was funny." The Fab Four had stormed the Northeast, and now they and their cheeky, mop-topped, wig-wearing pilot headed for one more remarkable stop of their first trip to America: Miami Beach, Florida.

Gail Cameron had accomplished the first step of her new mission; she'd managed to get on board with the Beatles. That turned out to be the easy part. "On the plane," she said, "all I remember is my anxiety about getting this message to Brian Epstein. We need to get the Beatles to a house with a pool. Arranging that was like a World War II campaign." She would have to make her appeal to the unquestioned leader of the band, John Lennon himself. And Cameron didn't have much time to manage it.

Carol Gallagher had to get over the shock and still do her job, even on this most unusual and memorable flight. She could not take her eyes off the Beatles. "Do you think anyone will be in Miami to meet us?" Paul asked her, with complete sincerity. George and Ringo spent a good deal of time autographing a stack of photos. John was more subdued, sitting in the back of the plane next to his radiant, blond wife, Cynthia. Not one to seek celebrity in her husband's reflected limelight, Cynthia preferred to stay low-key. To be sure though, she is far more than a mere footnote in the Beatles saga. She had met John when both were art school students and, at one point, broke up with him after he hit her in a fit of jealous rage. Often relegated to the shadows, this was Cynthia's chance to enjoy the spoils of success after many lonely stretches while her husband was away somewhere performing.

The band was due to arrive in Miami Beach that afternoon, participate in a press conference, then hold Friday and Saturday rehearsals leading up to the live *Sullivan Show* broadcast Sunday at 8:00 p.m. from the Deauville Hotel's Napoleon Ballroom. "Public statements have been made that this group will vacation at the Deauville for a week following the TV show," a police memo stated. "This is incorrect, as they are scheduled to depart at about noon Monday." Sgt. Buddy Dresner's security assignment, which at that point involved a long weekend of obligations to the Beatles, meant he would spend another Valentine's Day away from his wife, Dorothy, nicknamed "Dottie," mother of their three children. As soon as the Beatles left, he promised her, the two would have the long-overdue date night she deserved. His working nights, her working days at a local school, all the while raising a son and two daughters ages six to twelve, left little time for them as a couple. From a practical standpoint, the extra three dollars an hour he was due to earn as head of Beatle security would help the family make ends meet—another constant challenge on a policeman's salary.

Dresner pondered how many men he should have for the upcoming assignment. For championship fights, like the one coming up between Cassius Clay and Sonny Liston, he usually employed a security contingent of ten men. For the Beatles, his initial plan was to go with four: two men outside the group's door, one at each end of the hallway. As laughable as it sounds, initially, Dresner planned to employ just *four men* to guard the Beatles during their first visit to his hometown. That all changed, however, when he witnessed news footage of their arrival in New York City, the heaving masses of screaming teenagers, and the gravity of what that meant.

"How many men did they use in New York?" a stunned Dresner asked the Deauville's manager. "Hundreds," he replied. Incredulous, Dresner told him, "We don't have hundreds of officers here."

The entire Miami Beach Police Department numbered sixty men. Word went out to any officer willing to join the Beatles' security contingent at the Deauville. From that uneasy point, Dresner was as ready as he could be. A supervisor suggested the Beatles be brought in via the Deauville's south service elevator, "the same one used by President Kennedy during his last visit." Thursday afternoon, February 13, in a scene reminiscent of the screaming throngs that welcomed the Beatles in New York, as many as seven thousand youngsters descended on Miami International Airport. If a similar mob scene developed on Collins Avenue, along the narrow beachfront strip surrounding the Deauville Hotel, it could be chaos. It was up to Dresner and his team, whose

Thousands descend upon Miami International Airport to greet the Beatles on their arrival, February 13, 1964. Photo by Charles Trainor.

numbers were growing by the hour, to somehow, some way, make sure that didn't happen.

The National Airlines 707 started its descent into Florida. Ringo, now worried, made an odd request. "Ringo insisted on putting on a life jacket and looking out for the sharks," said Gallagher. The Beatles' afternoon arrival gave thousands of kids who hadn't already skipped school time to get out and race to Miami International. Larry Kane, who stood on the tarmac waiting to cover the fevered goings-on for WFUN radio, soon realized the story was not just the mop-topped musicians; a melee was developing inside the terminal. All the jockeying by fans waiting for a view put tremendous pressure on the jalousie windows. The Beatles weren't even out of their plane yet when Kane started to hear loud crashing: "Glass started falling from windows on to the tarmac," he remembered. "I was astounded by this."

The site of the airliner touching down sparked a series of roars, growing louder as the plane made a slow taxi from the runway. Sixteen-year-old Becky Pierce, a Coral Gables High Junior, watched one girl so overwrought with excitement, screaming so intensely, she feared the young fan was about to was about fling herself off the terminal's top deck. When the madness hit a crescendo and the kids could take no more, mercifully, the plane came to a stop. The stairs were rolled in place for the Beatles' arrival in Florida. "The door opened," Pierce remembered of the much-anticipated moment, "and an old lady walked out. This can be very frustrating when you're a kid and expecting the Beatles."

Chants of, "We want the Beatles! We want the Beatles!" arose from the impatient crowd. Out of the plane came photographers and a stream of others clearly not John, Paul, George, or Ringo. Kids were starting to feel let down, tricked even. "Then it happened," Pierce recounted, "A mophead was seen, and then another. Everybody was shrieking and I felt a tingle inside. We were all so happy because we had waited so long." In the early 1960s, this kind of emotionally charged public behavior, with a strong undercurrent of sexuality brought on by the Beatles, was not at all the norm for young women in America. It foreshadowed the coming of age many of them would experience later in the decade, when they would put on more public displays against the Vietnam War and in favor of women's rights.

At this juncture, their happiness was short-lived. The Beatles descended the staircase and were whisked right into limousines and taken away. From the safe cocoon of the National Airlines jetliner, Carol Gallagher watched it all unfold, sympathetic to the thousands of young people who had waited so long to witness so little. Gallagher, on the other hand, had gotten to interact with all the Beatles and get a feel for their personalities: polite and humble Paul; John and Cynthia excited but low-key, holed up in the back of the plane; Ringo and George excited to escape the cold. "It took me about three days to simmer down," Gallagher confessed. "I was very excited about it for a long, long time."

Kane documented those who suffered serious cuts from breaking glass, along with thousands of dollars of damage inside Terminal B. One newspaper detailed the "smashing" welcome fans had given the Beatles: "smashed doors, smashed windows, smashed furniture, a smashed auto roof and one badly cut teen-ager." Photos showed one young man climbing out a broken window. Another teen, detained by a local policeman, appears to be trying to explain what happened.

Unwilling to admit they'd been caught off guard by the enormity of response to the Beatles, airport officials blamed the damage and injuries on those responsible for all the hype. "This wouldn't have happened if those radio stations and news media hadn't stirred those kids up," complained the airport's director. One newspaper gave its own assessment, noting radio stations like WFUN and WQAM "belabor their listeners with Beatle records night and day."

Meanwhile, the same newspaper featured prominent paid ads announcing: "Beatlemania Hits Burdines!" Teens could snap up Beatle Wigs, Beatle T-shirts, Beatle Bug jewelry, and Beatle pens for autographs. "The Beatle invasion is on and what teen can resist it?" the ad reads. "Stock up on all essential paraphernalia—before your best friends scoop up everything." Sears bought a banner headline advertising for sale, at $2.22, the Fab Four's new album, *Meet the Beatles*. While the paper's editorial board complained about early Beatlemania, they were all too willing to let the ad department cash in.

On the Beatles' first day in Miami, Larry Kane witnessed the different sides of nascent Beatlemania; its unprecedented effects on young people, and their reaction to these charismatic new artists. Still, he said, "It hadn't really blossomed yet." After getting only a look but no access to the Beatles, Kane made a dash for the Deauville Hotel. Dangerously close at times, young fans were doing their best to chase the band's motorcade to the beach.

4

The Deauville Hotel

Longtime Beatle photographer Dezo Hoffman witnessed all the madness in their convoy. The young people giving chase for most of the twelve-mile trip from the airport to Miami Beach. "Looking back it seems funny," Hoffman recalled, "but at the time it was frightening how close they got." Gail Cameron had a different take. Now out of yet another crush of Beatle fans at the airport, the *Life* team cruised along with the motorcade whisking them off to a glamorous beachside resort. Their plans to at least *try* to get a cover photo of all four Beatles bobbing in a Florida pool was now starting to get off the ground. There, in that fast-moving line of cars, came the moment of clarity for Cameron; her time with the Beatles would become a career milestone. "We're in the middle of it, and I'm thinking how lucky is this? This front row seat we have," Cameron recalled. "I still remember that feeling; it was amazing." Policemen on motorcycles escorted the Beatle motorcade up the hotel driveway at 6701 Collins Avenue. For the young lads from Liverpool, just pulling in under the Deauville Hotel's dramatic porte-cochere roof, with its elegant-yet-dramatic parabolic curves, made it a memorable entrance.

The man with the burden of assuring everyone's safety in Miami Beach, Sgt. Buddy Dresner, was all business for the first of many complicated Beatle comings-and-goings. He counted at least two dozen people outside the entrance and watched the lobby filling up with curious fans. He decided against bringing the group through the back loading area as they had with JFK, opting to station an officer in a hotel elevator, holding it for the Beatles and their entourage. Car doors opened, and the Beatles' prematurely balding, bespectacled public relations man, Brian Sommerville, got out first. After minimal greetings, Dresner gave instructions to the new visitors, to whom he'd not yet been introduced.

"The hotel lobby was starting to pack," Dresner remembered, "so I told them, just don't stop." The formalities would have to wait. Dresner's men formed a wedge through the crowd, and without a word John and Cynthia, Paul, George, and Ringo made their way through the hotel lobby and into the elevator. Ringo spied a lady friend from their inner circle in New York and managed to pull her, midstride, into their group. Another unplanned visitor to the Beatles' inner sanctum was disc jockey Murray Kaufman. Known to listeners of New York City radio station WINS as Murray the K, he'd championed the group's music and knew his continuing association with them would be ratings gold. Teens loved Murray the K's rapid-fire, near-hysterical on-air patter that included an array of startling sound effects. In New York, he convinced the fetching lead singer of the Ronettes, Ronnie Spector, to help get him into the Beatles' suite for an interview. John soon became smitten with her. In those days, songs, singers, and groups could rise or fall on an influential disc jockey's opinion. Despite his pushiness, the boys appreciated all Murray was doing to help their careers and weren't about to dampen his enthusiasm. So yes, there he was, still with them in Miami.

The unexpected crowd of tourists, police, and press put a temporary crimp in vacation plans for Morty and Nonny Schrager of Fairlawn, New Jersey. Every year during their kids' spring break, the couple brought their daughters, eleven-year-old Barbara and twelve-year-old Gale, to South Beach. Upon checking in, the front-desk clerk informed the family the adjoining rooms they booked were no longer available. Another was being readied. They made their way through a growing crowd in the lobby and headed up the elevator. At their appointed floor, they were greeted by a policeman who told them no one was to get out. When the Schragers produced their twelfth-floor room keys,

Schrager's snapshot of the Beatles being led to their twelfth-floor rooms at the Deauville Hotel. Courtesy of Barbara Glass.

they were allowed off and were immediately stopped again. Just at that moment, the Beatles and their entourage were making their way down the hallway toward them. Only eleven-year-old Barbara knew who they were and urged her father to get out his camera and take a picture. Morty Schrager's snapshot shows the boys in suits and ties being led down the hallway by Buddy Dresner's security contingent. As usual, Cynthia Lennon was mostly out of sight.

The Beatles were shown to their rooms: 1211 for John and Cynthia, 1219 for Paul and Ringo. That meant odd-man-out George, in 1218, was stuck rooming with wild man Murray the K. "I've often wondered how Murray could barge into a room and hang out with us for the entire trip," Harrison reflected in his typical deadpan. "It's funny really." When the coast was sufficiently clear, the Schragers were shown to their replacement room, right next door to Paul and Ringo. Flabbergasted by their good fortune, Barbara and her sister took a pair of stools from the bar in their suite, placed them strategically in the doorway to be there for the possibility of up-close Beatle encounters, and there they remained for most of their vacation.

Happy to be safely ensconced with relative ease in the luxury hotel, the Beatles started to joke around and unpack. Relieved that round one with the crowds went well, Dresner allowed a few moments to get acquainted with the boys. He assigned officers just outside their doors, stairwells, and elevators. Brian Epstein, impeccably dressed as usual, introduced himself. It was time to get back to business, before the Beatles headed back downstairs for a news conference. After calling all of them into George's room, Dresner laid out the gospel according to Buddy: "I don't want anything to happen to you. If it does I'll be working midnights until I'm a hundred," quipped Dresner. "I don't really know what you do, but I'm sure you do it well. There has to be some ground rules and I set them. I'm going to be like your father and your older brother rolled into one. You don't do anything or go anywhere unless I tell you."

The Beatles agreed, assuring him they were there to have a good time. Besides, they'd already experienced enough stampeding crowds in America and back home to know their days of coming and going as they pleased were over—at least while their records were selling. Photos taken of Dresner interacting with the Beatles in their hotel room include another VIP who had joined them upstairs. Singer Del Shannon, whose haunting 1961 single "Runaway" had topped the charts, became the first American artist to cover the Beatles. In 1963, his version of "From Me to You" became a minor hit. By 1964, Shannon's career was headed in the opposite direction of the Fab Four; fame was fading.

Also along on this leg of the trip, filmmaker Albert Maysles captured the "innocents abroad" nature of the Beatles' coming to America. Paul, with a transistor radio in his ear; Ringo, on the train between New York and the Beatles' first American concert in Washington, DC, willing to sign an autograph for a curious child; George, having rallied from his sore throat, climbed into a luggage rack for fun; and John, thrilled to hear the sound of his own voice when the documentarians let him borrow their headset. Albert's brother David Maysles left before Miami to fly back to England and hammer out a distribution deal for their film. Albert was still there, getting footage of the boys standing on the twelfth-floor balcony, waving and shouting to girls on the beach who'd written messages to them in the sand.

Paul reflected on how enamored they were: "Miami was like paradise. We'd never been anywhere where there were palm trees." The Maysles' documentary became a kind of primer for the groundbreaking, amped-up film of their marginally fictionalized day-to-day lives shot later that spring, A Hard Day's Night. In another prescient move, Epstein had made the deal for the Beatles to make the film, months before success came in America.

Life magazine's twentysomething reporter Michael Durham, newly stationed in the Miami Bureau along with his wife, Martha, nicknamed Mardy, received a call from a New York editor. Time was short, and he had some specific requests, "Mardy, please find us a pool, and there needs to be security around the pool." They also wanted it heated. "I thought, 'That doesn't sound hard,'" Mardy Durham recalled. Then again, the editor, who had already dreamed up the photo in his head from the safe confines of his New York offices, wasn't done with his list of demands. "He told me, get a picture of them in the pool . . . with their hair wet," recalled Michael Durham. Life's Miami bureau guy wasn't happy to hear that a New York–based reporter and two photographers were flying down with the Beatles. It was even worse with some editor wanting to micromanage the assignment from 1,300 miles away. Wet hair?

As soon as the Beatles were ensconced in their rooms, Buddy Dresner's next assignment called for a Beatle press conference with hotel big shots. Intrepid reporter Ian Glass from the Miami News, who two years earlier had gotten into Cuba to cover the Bay of Pigs invasion, struggled to make his way through a bevy of excited girls hoping to get in to the interview room. "They were yelling, 'Daddy Daddy take me in with you,' tearfully pleading that I pick one of them as a pretend daughter," Glass reported. "Once I got away from the teenagers, however, I found the Beatles enormously witty. When the craze for their singing dies down, the mop-top youngsters could do a marvelous comedy act." Larry Kane, surprised that he had much less hassle getting into the press conference than trying to get a word with them at the airport, found the group similarly disarming.

"What do you boys plan to do after all this?" one reporter asked.

"What else is there to do?" Ringo responded. Based on his demeanor during the Miami stay, Ringo was genuinely concerned that this first American visit had to be the pinnacle and success would soon run out. To amplify the feeling, the *Fort Lauderdale News* the following day reported a Beatle "setback." For the first time in eleven months, the group failed to have a single in the top ten in England. "Can Beatlemania really be dying?" asked a columnist for Britain's *Financial Times.* Hardly. The Beatles' domination of the English charts started a year earlier than their US success. This was only a respite until they could get back in to the studio later that month. By then, the same singles that caught fire in England in 1963 started shooting up the charts stateside. Epstein, given the here-today-gone-tomorrow nature of popular music, pressured Lennon and McCartney for new songs.

"Do you date much?" reporter Sheila Moran from the *Fort Lauderdale Times* asked Paul McCartney. "Sure," the twenty-one-year-old shot back, never one to miss an opportunity to charm a woman. "What are you doing tonight?" From that opening, the enterprising reporter started to smell a scoop. After all the typical Beatle news conference banter died down, Moran cozied up to Paul. "Still serious about that offer? I'd love to buy you a drink," she told him. "We can't have it down here," he responded, clearly trying to put her off. Not about to lose an opportunity, Moran pressed him, "Well, then, upstairs?" The cute one now cornered, Paul gave in. "Sure," he told her. "Buzz the room." The Beatles were off to buy some swimwear on their manager's tab, leaving Moran needing one more vital piece of information: Paul never told her his room number.

Moran approached the front desk, but hotel staff was forbidden from sharing information about their famous guests. Undeterred, she located a fellow reporter willing to give up the critical number. Up the elevator, Moran made it down the hallway until she ran into two policemen guarding the door. "I'm here to see the Beatle Paul," she informed him. "Just tell him the girl from the press conference in the yellow suit." The policeman disappeared into the room, and soon Moran was face-to-face with Paul in the doorway, still holding his new swimming suit. "Well, we were thinking about taking a shower. Resting. You know, cooling it," he told her, clearly hoping Moran would get the hint and go away. She just stared back, using the silence as leverage.

"Well then," McCartney relented, "come on in."

Moran navigated the fine line between persistent and pushy to gain entrée in to the Beatles' lair. She described the scene: "the three other fagged out Beatles, two females, a policeman, and a New York radio station disc jockey, plus an assortment of unopened gift baskets of fruit." Silence descended while the group watched a television interview with two fighters soon to compete for the World Heavyweight Boxing crown at the Miami Convention Center: the current titleholder, Sonny Liston, an intimidating, man-of-few-words brawler with hands of stone, and his brash young challenger, Cassius Clay, who was everything Liston was not: loud and confident—to some, annoyingly so—and handsome to the point that Clay often referred to himself as "pretty." Clay had a home in a working-class section of Miami while training at the 5th St. Gym in Miami Beach. In their room, his new cultural counterparts, the Beatles, discussed whether he had any chance against Liston. The general consensus was, no.

Moran dialed up the front desk and ordered a glass of Scotch for the Beatles' room. Within ten minutes came a knock on the door. The waiter stood there, tray and drink in hand, with numerous other checks to be signed. "No one produced a cent," Moran noted. Keeping to her word, she paid $1.10 plus tip and handed the drink to Paul. Then it was down to business, a little one-on-one time with him. He forecast "more composing" in the near future and defended their long hair: "We wear it this way because we like it." Moran found out one of the women, named Kitty—the one Ringo had spied in the lobby and pulled into the elevator with them—was a singer he'd met during their tour of Sweden. The other was an unemployed New York actress who declined to give her name.

Buddy Dresner allowed discreet visits from adult women in the Beatles' coterie, but each had to be vetted. They were careful not to intentionally court scandal by having underage fans in their rooms. After forty-five minutes, Brian Epstein appeared at the door and asked Moran to come see him. "You know," he confided, "you'd better go now, some of the press downstairs have threatened to write bad things about the Beatles." Whether or not that was true, Moran had gotten what she came for, a little alone time with Paul. She'd gotten a glimpse of what their lives, if you could call them that, were like on the road. It made for a nice scoop in her Fort Lauderdale newspaper the following day. The boys had other plans, including the next test for their body guard and protector.

5

In the Water, on the Town

Once the Beatles had disposed of formalities: news conference, meeting the hotel brass, getting rid of the reporter who'd made it up to their room, unpacking, drinking, and eating, they asked about exploring the ocean. They'd waited long enough to meet their lovely fans on the beach. "No, no, no, I can control you better in the pool than the ocean," Dresner insisted. The Deauville's expansive pool and high dive bordered the beach. The Beatles saw that as a fine alternative, and down they all went. To Dresner's considerable relief, the photographers were few and the number of curious fans manageable. The boys relaxed, splashed around, and then, after such a tumultuous week in America so far, relaxed poolside.

It was a time you'd think Dresner might allow himself to exhale; with his young charges snoozing by the pool, all seemed fine. Or was it? One long look at the fair-skinned foursome sounded the alarm in Dresner's head. "You gotta be cool with the sun," he implored, afraid they were starting to bake. "Our sun is different; it'll burn the hell out of you." Dresner helped slather on whatever then passed for sun block. By this time, the affable street cop and family man was becoming aware of the enormity of his job. Just as he couldn't keep the boys away from burning their skin in the Florida sun, in public places, he couldn't keep fans and photographers away either. Brian Epstein didn't want him to. You never turn away free publicity, but it had to be managed; and that was never a guarantee. Dresner walked a nerve-wracking tightrope of allowing the Beatles small stretches of freedom, until it became an unmanageable scrum of fans enveloping each of them. He had to know when to draw the line and get them out. If any accidents or injuries should befall them, which might hinder or—God forbid—prevent their Sunday-night live performance on *Ed Sullivan,* it was his ass. Buddy Dresner had good reason to be stressed-out.

From the pool, he led the Beatles back up to the room for a quick shower to wash off the chlorine. Ruth Regina, makeup artist for *The Jackie Gleason Show,* filmed on location in Miami Beach, then coiffed the four mop-tops. With Beatlemania now impacting South Beach like a rogue wave, Regina recalled the Beatles' unassuming reaction to it all: a shared innocence. Taking care of hair and makeup duties in their rooms, Regina observed the boys walking over to the balcony to see fans still waiting a dozen floors below. "They were sweet about it," she said. "They were very much not aware of just how popular they were." At this point in their tumultuous initial week in America, it's hard to believe the Beatles weren't aware of their impact; evidence of it was in their faces everywhere they looked. Regina became aware of it when fans asked if she would give them used Beatle makeup tissues as souvenirs. She refused.

Even in mundane things like ordering a meal via room service, the Beatles discovered something new and uniquely American: grilled cheese.

"They said, 'let's try it,' and went crazy over it," Buddy Dresner recalled. Soon it became their go-to order along with Scotch and Coke, and Marlboro cigarettes. A crazy milieu swirled around them: Some fans tried to sneak onto the floor on room-service carts; another produced a phony letter of introduction entitling her to a meet-and-greet, and a few tried to pose as hotel employees. Competing radio stations played their songs over and over to meet listener demand; gas station employees dressed in mop-top wigs, hoping the faux-four look would attract free publicity. All kinds of store honchos looked to stoke and capitalize on demand. The owner of a local car dealership loaned each of the Beatles a flashy sports car to use while in town. Envious, Brian Epstein arranged to have one for himself, a red MG two-seater.

And then there was Gail Cameron and her *Life* magazine mission. At the beginning, when the Beatles found out what *Life* wanted, they were against it. They believed that the Miami leg of the trip would involve more holiday and less work. Given *Life's* emphasis on high-quality, one-of-a-kind photographs, if the Beatles refused to pose in the pool, then the whole assignment was a bust. Cameron was feeling the pressure. She had one big advantage, though, over most of the other journalists on South Beach—familiarity. During the Beatles' visits to New York and Washington, DC, and surely because Brian Epstein and company were well aware of her employer's prestige and influence, Cameron was welcome in the Beatles' inner circle. Once you gained access, formality fell away. To Cameron, the first part of her week with the Beatles had been disarmingly informal. It didn't hurt that she was still her twenties and had a good-humored way about her.

At the Miami Bureau, Mardy Durham reached out to former recording artist Jerri Pollak, who sung in Big Bands with Duke Ellington and Count Basie. Along with her husband, Paul Pollak, owner of a string of South Florida motels including the Thunderbird, Jerri often threw lavish parties at their home on North Bay Road, overlooking Biscayne Bay. The couple once hosted a party for Frank Sinatra, who flew in his private chef from New York. Jerri said she'd "be delighted to host the Beatles," with one caveat: their pool wasn't heated. That meant the Fab Four, should they agree to the shoot, would be wading into frigid water, at least by South Florida standards. The gated home had a regal look about it, with high walls for privacy and the exclusivity the magazine required. With the private pool home now secured, it was up to Gail Cameron to convince the Beatles to do it.

Cameron made her way up to the twelfth floor at the Deauville, planning to state her case to John Lennon, the one man whose opinion mattered as much, if not more, than Brian Epstein's. "I thought John was incredibly interesting and complicated," Cameron said. Lennon also recognized that appearing on the cover of *Life* could be as important for career advancement and record sales as the *Sullivan Show* itself. Miami reporter Michael Durham had been making a similar pitch to Epstein and Sommerville. In the hallway, finally alone with Lennon, Cameron made her best pitch. To her immense relief, Lennon uttered the magic words: "Okay, love, we'll do it."

That evening the Beatles, lone Beatle-wife Cynthia Lennon, and their number-one sycophant, wired and chatty Murray the K, took in some South Beach nightspots. Ringo insisted on seeing one of his favorite American acts, the Coasters, of "Yakety Yak," "Charlie Brown," and "Young Blood" fame, appearing live at the Mau Mau Lounge. "It was a thrill to see American artists, *in America*," he recalled. But that thrill turned to disgust as the nightclub crowd just kept on dancing instead of giving their full attention to the American hit makers whom Ringo considered "rock and roll gods."

At the Peppermint Lounge, home of "The Twist," a dance popularized by Chubby Checker, and Joey Dee and the Starlighters, the Beatles stayed away from the dance floor, opting to stay at a table in the dark, listening to their own music being played, having drinks, and signing autographs. Earlier that week, the boys had made the scene at the original, mobbed-up Peppermint Lounge in New York City. Footage of Ringo dancing there would later be included in their *A Hard Day's Night* film. Now at the club's South Florida location, a reporter noted the "imposing figure of burly" bodyguard Buddy Dresner, from whom he managed to get the first public comment about what it was like being in charge of Beatle security: "I like them," Dresner told the reporter. "They're nice kids."

At this still-early stage in their careers, the Beatles provided a cogent analysis for their likeability—even with hardened police officers and the most cynical reporters. Paul McCartney and George Harrison explained what made them different. "We used to play at a club called The Cavern in Liverpool," twenty-year-old Harrison said. "It had a relaxed atmosphere and we just talked to the people naturally." McCartney drilled down on that ethos: "We tried to keep being friends of the people. You know why? Because we're just a projection of the people. Some like a star-audience relationship, but most of them don't and we don't. We broke down the barrier between performer and audience. It's like actors in a play, we establish audience contact." The same held true of their relationship with Buddy Dresner; they never saw him as one-dimensional authority figure, and he responded warmly to their good-natured, intellectual curiosity about all things American.

The Beatles enjoyed a pair of bands: Hank Ballard and the Midnighters, followed by a rocking six-piece unit known as the B.G. Ramblers.

"B.G." stood for Bowling Green, Ohio, where several members of the band had met while students at Bowling Green University. Having noticed the VIPs at a back table, the band broke into their own version of the nation's number-one single, "I Want to Hold Your Hand," and its flipside, "I Saw Her Standing There." The Beatles appreciated the gesture and later posed for photos with the group. It wasn't the Ramblers' first brush with the big time. Jackie Gleason, festooned with a carnation in his lapel, once strode in with cast members from his television show, *The Honeymooners*. On another memorable night, Johnny Cash joined them onstage for a few numbers.

Once things started to get too hectic inside the Peppermint Lounge, Dresner pulled the plug. The Beatles and their entourage departed en route to the kitschy, Tahitian-themed Wreck Bar of the Castaways Motel, at 16375 Collins Avenue, "followed by a statuesque blond and comely brunette in a white sedan," one newspaper reported. After going full-throttle all week since their arrival in New York—the electrifying, first *Sullivan* appearance, followed by concerts at Carnegie Hall and at the Coliseum in Washington, DC—by contrast, the Beatles spent their first day and night in Florida as tourists: swimming, hitting nightspots, and enjoying toast-of-the-town status. What would the record executives in London who had rejected them again and again think of them now? Their dream of becoming superstars just as famous Elvis was coming true, just as Eppy had told those bastards it would.

After 1:00 a.m., the group arrived back at the Deauville. Day one had gone as well as it could have. Once the Beatles and their entourage were back in their rooms, Dresner posted guards in the hallway and made sure to put chairs under the stairwell doors. His idea was simple and effective; if they opened, the chairs would fall onto the tile floor, make a racket, and alert security to a possible intruder. Finally, it was time for him to grab a bite to eat, fill out timesheets for his security team, and head home: north on Collins Avenue, east across the 163rd Street Causeway, then a jog south to his home at 815 Northeast 160th Street in North Miami Beach.

"I got home around 2:00 o'clock, showered, and before you know it, I have to be back at 5:30 or 6:00," Dresner remembered. To his kids,

Dresner was like a ghost. The added duty spilled down to Dottie also: managing the house, feeding the kids, making sure the chores and homework were done. For Buddy and Dottie, the following day, Valentine's Day, with all the sentiment, with the requisite flowers, cards, and maybe a little romance, would have to wait.

Grace Kelly and
a Third-Rate Photograph

For the bedraggled policeman who'd only made it back to his home three hours earlier, Valentine's Day began with an unwelcome 5:30 a.m. alarm. Buddy Dresner rose for day two as protector of the number-one rock-and-roll band in America. "I'm going to start calling you 'Daddy,'" Ringo had joked. Instead, the nicknames "Boody" or "Bood" stuck. As he'd mentioned to the newspaper reporter the night previous, Dresner and the Beatles' mutual affection was growing. That aside, the crazy hours Buddy and Dottie worked every day to support their children, now exacerbated by Buddy's all-encompassing special assignment, left little time for them as a couple. Dresner departed for work in the early-morning darkness, without the luxury of time to even leave his wife a Valentine's Day card.

Things were far less subdued at the North Bay Road home of fifteen-year-old Linda Pollak. Jerri had informed daughter Linda and her three brothers that they would not be going to school that day, and, to add to the intrigue, the phone would be off-limits until Friday night. They were expecting visitors who needed to use the backyard pool for a photo shoot and were to be given privacy. Then, Jerri dropped the bomb: "The Beatles are coming over tomorrow." The children's screams reverberated throughout the family home, just across Biscayne Bay from Collins Avenue and the Deauville Hotel. "What? You've gotta be kidding!" they exclaimed. "This is the biggest thing in history!" Jerri added a not-so-great admonishment; she forbade her children from spreading the incredible news. Still, this kind of cloak-and-dagger, hush-hush happening involving someone famous was not all that unusual at the Pollak home.

In March 1962 John F. Kennedy docked his presidential yacht, the *Honey Fitz*, behind their home. To help kick off the reelection campaign of Florida senator George Smathers, JFK sailed to Miami Beach to attend a Smathers fundraiser at the Fontainebleau Hotel, the most famous and swanky hotel on South Beach. During his visit, the president was guest of honor at the mansion next door. The ninety-three-foot yacht, named in honor of the president's maternal grandfather, John F. Fitzgerald, was so large that it occupied two docks, including the Pollaks'. For the next few days, photographers and reporters camped out at their home, using their second-story sun deck to monitor activities next door. On March 10, Kennedy delivered his address at the fundraiser. Full of charisma, effortless humor, and optimism, the president promised Florida would boom in the growing Space Race and claim a prominent place in JFK's vision for America, his "New Frontier."

In 1964, with Camelot fading into history, the Pollaks were eager to greet their next world-famous visitors. Once John Lennon had assured Gail Cameron that he and his bandmates were game for the *Life* shoot, the next hurdle was to figure out how to spirit them out of the hotel. From the moment *Life*'s Miami Bureau man Michael Durham was introduced to them, it was apparent the Beatles were not enthused about doing the session. "My impression the day of the shoot was, the Beatles were at the point where they had decided it was really not fun to be famous," Durham recalled. "They were negative about the whole thing." Durham drove the lead car; Dresner and the Beatles followed them across the causeway and down winding Bay Road to the Pollak home. Despite trying to make a stealthy exit, they were spotted by other reporters, who got in their own cars and pursued. As was the case any time the Beatles rode anywhere in America so far, getting from point A to point B proved to be nerve-wracking.

At 10:00 a.m. the entourage arrived. High gates to the family drive-way were closed behind them, leaving the trailing press shut out. *Life* photographers Bob Gomel and John Loengard wasted no time set-ting up equipment in the walled-off backyard by the family's modest swimming pool on Biscayne Bay. Just three months earlier, Gomel had taken, from the top of the United States Capitol dome, a striking im-age of the assassinated young president's coffin, his body lying in state. The year previous, Loengard photographed the widow of civil rights activist and World War II veteran Medgar Evers as she tried to com-fort their son after his murder. Now, Gomel and Loengard were in the midst of another unforgettable photo session.

For the Beatles shoot, "I had in mind the Howell Conant photo of Grace Kelly," Loengard recalled. That 1955 image featured the twenty-five-year-old ingénue actress, bare-shouldered in water, staring at the lens. The photograph became an early archetype of "natural glamour," without all the Hollywood artifice. For Loengard, anything resembling a re-creation would be a high bar to achieve with four pasty-skinned young men as subjects. He turned to Gail Cameron, "They look re-ally scruffy, what can you do about it?" Given everything she'd been through just to get them all here, Cameron was exasperated, "Every photographer on this planet would love to be where you are with all four Beatles, taking this picture." One lucky teenaged girl, Linda Pol-lak, could attest to that.

"Then, in came the Beatles," Linda Pollak remembered. "Their man-ager Brian Epstein introduced us. They were quite impressed with the house and the photos of my parents with their friends." John needed to change from his long pants and the dark sweatshirt he'd gotten from a Washington, DC, radio station. The others were already in swim gear. George and Ringo sported "Submarine Race Watchers" sweatshirts given to them by George's temporary roommate, Murray the K, pro-moting his 1962 album. To brighten the Fab Four's attitude, Jerri pro-vided a tray of Scotch to which they all helped themselves.

When it came time to get down to business, for all of their usual good nature, the Beatles did grouse about wading in to the cold pool. Epstein was having none of it: "Get in," the no-nonsense manager told them. "*Life* is supporting you." With iconic photojournalism its main selling point and the magazine oversized to best present its images, at its peak *Life* sold 13.5 million copies per week. When it arrived, American siblings would compete, fight even, to get their hands on it first. For that kind of publicity, Brian Epstein might well have ordered the Beatles to jump into a pool of molten lava.

Loengard felt the only way to get his subjects focused on something other than freezing was to ask them to sing. The tune was "I Want to Hold Your Hand," the chart-topping success that had carried them all the way to this rich family's backyard pool in Miami Beach. In the image that ended up running in the magazine, John, singing with eyes closed, bobs closest to the camera. Next in line is Paul, eyes open, animated, and, as always, smiling right at the lens. Ringo is the only one grimacing, presumably still reacting to the water temperature. Zen master George, the youngest of all four, smiles and sings in the background, taking on a resemblance to Paul. John Loengard succeeded in creating one of the quintessential images of the young Beatles in America, retaining their unaffected, down-to-earth personalities. So what if it proved to be nothing like the shimmering, icy sex appeal Grace Kelly exuded in the photo that inspired the Beatles shoot? What did it matter if the Beatles ended up preferring to pose for the cover shot with *dry* hair? Cameron stood poolside next to Loengard, reporter notebook in hand, beaming. Barely seventy-two hours after she was told to get on the plane to Miami, with the help of Mardy and Michael Durham, she'd accomplished her mission. It was all up to New York to decide what to run and where.

"I remember Paul screaming how cold the water was when he dunked his head in," said Bob Gomel, assigned to get black-and-white action photos of the Beatles and the hysteria surrounding them, in case the magazine opted to do a companion story to the cover photo. Beyond the obvious impression of seeing the four young men clearly out of their element, Gomel was moved when they told him they'd never seen palm trees before. Florida's tropical environs, in February, were a radical change from austere winters in England and Germany. "These were four very polite guys considering that they had already achieved stardom," Gomel said. "I told them, just go in and have fun." One photo from the series catches John cannonballing into the pool between Paul and Ringo. It was the kind of frolic the Beatles hadn't had time to enjoy since the Paris free-for-all upon learning they were number one in America.

After the shoot, Jerri offered the boys robes. They took in some sun on lounge chairs to warm up. Dresner hovered, again urging them to put on lotion. Cynthia quietly assumed her place in the background. To consider how far they'd come, in 1962, two years previous to that very day, the Beatles were unknowns playing their first evening show in Liverpool's Cavern Club.

During the buffet lunch of assorted meats, lox, and bagels, Paul inquired of his hostess, "We've heard about this lox and bago. Could you tell us which is the bago and which is the lox?" On another occasion, Dresner delighted in telling the boys about a Jewish cuisine staple, gefilte fish, which they tried and loved. During all this, Linda Pollak had gotten to be a Beatle stand-in before the pool shoot, rub elbows with them, and pinch herself to be sure she was actually having this experience. The only thing she couldn't do was share the news with her friends. As the Beatles finished lunch and prepared to head off to rehearsal and spend part of the afternoon relaxing on a private yacht, a crowd had gathered outside the gates.

Jerri told the group how much she had enjoyed their company and left them an open invitation to return during their stay. As the Beatles were leaving, Linda could hear Ringo scream, "Ow, me 'ead" after someone had gotten close enough to their car to tug on his hair. The Beatles were gone, but not for long. The next morning, while her three brothers were at the movies and her mom at the beauty salon, Linda had just gotten out of the shower when she heard the doorbell ring. The maid came rushing up to tell Linda her famous new friends were back. She recoiled, "That's impossible! I've got wet hair!" Thinking fast, Linda put on her swimsuit, and at Brian Epstein's request, called her mom and asked permission for the Beatles to have another visit.

Since this time it was purely social, the Beatles didn't require total privacy. Linda and her brothers, when they got home from the movies, were able to call up a few friends and blow their minds. "Don't let it get out of hand," Jerri admonished. Linda's brothers William and John asked a couple friends to bring guitars for an impromptu jam session. They played basketball with the youngest Pollak brother, Richard. As a personal favor, Paul walked around the side of the house to say hello to one of Richard's friends who didn't believe the Beatles were really there. Linda and George engaged in a conversation about his growing interest in India. There was poolside dancing and another lunchtime buffet. When it was over, the grateful guests invited the entire Pollak family to attend their live *Sullivan Show* appearance.

"We had a wonderful day," Linda Pollak wrote. "I never heard from the Beatles again. I was never a Beatles maniac, maybe because I was somewhat jaded from being around them and other celebrities. But I was moved by their music like everyone else." Those impromptu visits by the Beatles also moved Linda to pursue her career in public relations, promotions, and event planning. Any time she heard someone mention the Beatles, it became a tempting trigger to retell her story. Mardy Durham was the hero, in particular, for finding and securing a pool home with walls and a front gate.

For the Pollak siblings, memories of those dreamlike days on North Bay Road—playing host to world-famous celebrities like the Beatles, and loaning their dock to JFK during the heyday of his presidency—are bittersweet. Jerri and Paul Pollak's marriage ended in divorce within a year of the Beatles' visit, splitting the family for good. Fifteen years after Linda Pollak wrote about her unforgettable experiences with the Beatles for her hometown newspaper, the *Chicago Tribune,* she died in a diving accident. In 2014, local media reported that the latest owner of the home where so much history took place planned to tear it down. "It's like another piece of Miami history gone to the wrecking ball," lamented a real estate agent who grew up a couple blocks away and had a photo of his brother hanging out with Ringo.

The following week, the magazine's fill-in editor decided John Loengard's now iconic Beatle image was too frivolous to be on *Life*'s cover, instead relegating it to the back page. At the time, Loengard wasn't surprised. He felt his attempt to emulate Conant's Grace Kelly image, or rival Harry Benson's photos of the Beatles' ecstatic French pillow fight upon hearing they were number one in America, had come up short. More than a half century later, Loengard remained unimpressed with his photo: "All sorts of reasons why it didn't work as well in my mind, that's why I thought of it as a third-rate picture and I still do."

Eventually, the bobbing Beatles' image did make *Life*'s cover, in a

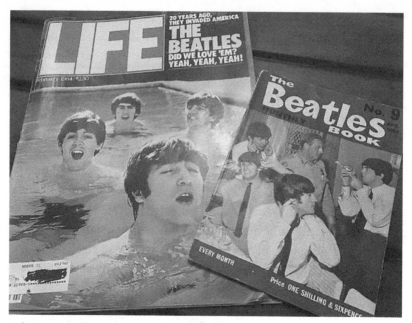

John Loengard's iconic image of the Beatles in the Pollak family pool (*left*) did not appear on the magazine cover until this twenty-year commemorative edition of the Beatles' first US visit. The *Beatles Book Monthly* fan magazine (*right*) features the Fab Four having fun with Buddy Dresner. Courtesy of the author.

1984 Beatles commemorative issue. Cameron, who'd helped orchestrate getting John, Paul, George, and Ringo in a private backyard pool on very short notice, said that at first they were furious their photo didn't end up on the cover. "Understandably," said Cameron. "They'd gone to a lot of trouble." One of the suits from the executive suite, filling in as editor for that 1964 issue had made the call, and that was that. Despite the Durhams' disappointment that they didn't get the cover story and photo, when Michael Durham tells people that he worked for *Life,* all they want to hear about is the Beatles. "The most important thing in my life is that I met the Beatles," he chuckled. "I find that very irritating."

That iconic *Life* photo endures because it evokes a time of innocence in the band; discovering all the wondrous things Miami had to offer a group of guys from an industrial town in England. They were falling in love with America every bit as much as Americans were falling for them. John Loengard realized the enduring significance of his photo when a friend's fourteen-year-old daughter wanted to touch his hand merely because it had been *close* to the Beatles and had taken the *Life* photo.

He reflected, "Maybe it had some quality I was overlooking."

7

Fatherly Advice

Upon the Beatles' return to the Deauville, Buddy Dresner could no longer put off their desire to explore the beach, ocean, and suntanned beauties they'd been viewing like love-starved prisoners from their twelfth-floor perch. When it came to a photo op of the Beatles romping in the ocean on Miami Beach and getting to know their female fans, Brian Epstein never tried to avoid photographers and the free publicity. It was up to Dresner to decide where to accomplish the mission without the Beatles being overwhelmed by the throng hanging out near the hotel. Dresner chose a quiet oceanfront approach around Eighty-Fifth Street, eighteen blocks north of the hotel.

Seventeen-year-old Diane Levine and three friends from Miami Beach High were relaxing in the surf after taking college exams when they saw the cars arrive. To their astonishment, some guys who looked like the Beatles piled out of a Miami Beach police cruiser. All at once, photographers, fans, everyone seemed to converge. Levine and her friends, who'd been there before all the madness, looked on in disbelief. "They were white, blue white, skinny," said Levine. "I backed up. I was totally blown out." As she stood in the surf, some girls chased Paul in her direction. She held out her hand and assured him, "I don't want to rape you, I just want to shake your hand and welcome you to the United States." Impressed, McCartney shook Levine's hand and told her, "Come with me." Paul managed to get Diane over to an area the entourage had carved out as their own, where he could get to know her better.

Among photographers there to document the ocean romp, Charles Trainor of the *Miami News* and longtime Beatle photographer Robert Freeman snapped away at them running, splashing, and mingling with fans, some of whom grabbed and kissed them. Trainor, an intrepid deadline photojournalist in South Florida, also took what have become iconic pictures of Elvis onstage at Miami's Olympia Theater in August 1956. A dogged military veteran, he would do whatever was necessary to get the images he wanted. In 1962, Trainor took what has become a signature portrait of President John F. Kennedy while in Miami Beach for the Smathers fundraiser.

Robert Freeman, who, like Dezo Hoffman, had been with the Beatles since the early days, made history photographing them for each of their album covers of the touring era, 1963–66. Many of the iconic photographs, including the stretched *Rubber Soul* cover, are the product of Freeman's innovative eye; often taken without a lot of time or lighting. In a golden era of photojournalism, the Beatles benefited from the work of many notable pros whose images are now defining: Trainor, Dezo Hoffman, Robert Freeman, Leslie Bryce, Harry Benson, Curt Gunther, Bob Gomel, and John Loengard.

After about forty-five minutes surfside with the cute Beatle, Diane Levine said, "I really felt at home with Paul, we really clicked." For the time being, that's as far as it could go. Buddy Dresner became uncomfortable with the crowd and announced the shoot was over. After Paul had climbed back in the police cruiser, he called out to his new lady friend, "Come see the show!" The Beatle coterie headed for the next stop, one they hoped would have nothing to do with PR shoots or screaming girls. Bernard Castro, a local millionaire who'd put his own distinct stamp on mid-twentieth-century American culture with the Castro Convertible sofa, agreed to let the Beatles come to his lavish home. They were also welcome to use his gorgeous ninety-three-foot yacht, complete with onboard crew and fully stocked galley kitchen, for a private voyage around Biscayne Bay. At long last, for team Beatles, they savored a chance to relax and enjoy South Florida like well-heeled locals.

Built in 1926 by shipbuilder John Trumpy, Castro's yacht named *Southern Trail*, with its long, sleek hull painted white and honey brown, possessed a great deal of Old World charm and character. It resembled another, more famous yacht upon which Trumpy also put his imprint, the *Honey Fitz*, JFK's presidential yacht. The Beatles boarded, still in their swim trucks and promotional sweatshirts, and set out. John found Scotch in the *Southern Trail's* bar and helped himself. Paul, delighted to discover a piano, played a few bars of the new song he was still working on, "Can't Buy Me Love." Cynthia, in dark dress and sunglasses, took her place on deck, seated behind her husband. Dresner took an immediate liking to her Old World manners and understated charm, describing her to a reporter as "the sweetest, nicest lady."

Fifteen minutes out, Paul greeted a man he assumed was a crew member making himself a sandwich in the galley. Oddly, the stranger retreated and started taking pictures, which Paul gladly accommodated. When George came in, however, he perceived the stranger to be a stowaway and contacted Brian Sommerville, who insisted on going back to port and getting rid of him. If this interloper looked familiar, he should have: shortly before the Beatles had boarded, the ever-enterprising *Miami News* photographer Charles Trainor parlayed his connections to land an invitation from Bernard Castro to go aboard his yacht, then proceeded to conceal himself from the Beatles until just the right moment.

Trainor remembered: "Everything went well for a while. Then George Harrison came down and wanted to know who I was. I said I was a guest of the owner. He started getting obnoxious about the whole thing." Trainor asked the captain where the boat was headed. Once deposited back on land, Trainor hauled ass to the Seventy-Ninth Street Causeway in time to capture exclusive photos of the Beatles on their borrowed yacht, passing directly underneath.

This kind of subterfuge wasn't unusual for Trainor. Three years earlier, he rented a boat to get to the secluded location near Crystal River where Elvis Presley was filming *Follow That Dream*. Presley's manager, Tom Parker, was infuriated but powerless; Trainor found a perfect perch on a small bridge to get the exclusive photos of Presley on the movie set below.

After being asked to leave the Castro yacht, photographer Charles Trainor took this image of the boat passing beneath the Seventy-Ninth Street Causeway. Photo by Charles Trainor.

The group cruised around Biscayne Bay. The sun appeared, and warmer temperatures made the water more inviting for a relaxed group swim. The son of a merchant seaman, John especially loved swims in open water. Given the more relaxed environs, Buddy Dresner took advantage of an opportunity to have a deeper conversation with the Beatles about their future. "Americans are funny, one minute you're hot, the next, they don't know you," Dresner opined. "You guys are real nice kids. Save your money. Get a real nice, smart, attorney. Put it away, you're not going to last, it's a novelty." With no real precedent to indicate otherwise, the Beatles, not at all taken aback by Dresner's frankness, accepted their guardian's advice with smiles: "You're right, we'll put it away." Dresner had earned the gravitas with them to dole out advice and give orders like a father figure, but disarmed it all with patience, humor, and open-mindedness the Beatles found appealing.

In advance of the *Sullivan Show*, to be broadcast live Sunday night from the Deauville's Napoleon Ballroom, the band held informal rehearsals in what Dezo Hoffman called the "cool room." He photographed Paul, George, and Ringo still dressed in swim trunks, and John with a dark sweatshirt, dark pants, and sunglasses. John often wore sunglasses indoors, even at nightclubs, but it was not all affectation. Cynthia explained that shielding his eyes from the public was one way John could retain a small bit of privacy once fame began to overwhelm them.

One place you would expect the Beatles to have near total privacy was on the twelfth floor of their chic, oceanfront environs at the Deauville. That wasn't the case. Their young neighbors, the Schrager sisters, spent a lot of time perched on their matching stools not wanting to miss a chance to see the Fab Four. Barbara remembered, "Every night my sister and I heard them playing guitars through the wall as we lay in bed trying to fall asleep. At night it was loud." The next morning, the two would assume their spot in the doorway. Paul greeted them with a friendly hello and a smile. "One morning," said Barbara, "he asked us if their music had been too loud. He said they were rehearsing for the show." As a goodwill gesture, McCartney gave the young sisters a signed picture and tickets to their dress rehearsal. If the second *Sullivan Show* was anywhere near as successful as the first, the Beatles could expect one out of every three Americans to tune in, a staggering audience of seventy million people; that's twenty-five million *more* viewers than the entire population of England.

It's been reported that Dresner took the Beatles home to have dinner with his family that night, Valentine's Day evening. According to son Barry, his dad didn't see the family at all that day, and later he sought to make that up to Dottie with a little help from his young friends. At this point, he was still keeping his Beatles assignment a secret from his children, especially Jeri, his oldest daughter, who was in junior high. That night Morris Lansburgh, the owner of the Deauville, invited the Beatles to join him in the hotel nightclub, the Musketeer Room, where comedian Don Rickles was appearing. With his scorched-earth, take-no-prisoners patter, Rickles made a point of ripping his audience to shreds. Dresner had seen him many times and hoped, by some miracle, the Beatles could stay out of the line of fire.

Hardly. Lansburgh made sure the Beatles received VIP treatment, seating them right down in front. Dresner, still in his police uniform, was there with them, of course, seated in plain view, right in Rickles's crosshairs. "I'd rather be in Omaha, I kept staring down," Dresner recalled. Out came Rickles, mop in hand, eyes already glaring laser beams at the VIP table: "Here, here's another one of your group you MOP HEADS! You have your own policeman? People out getting raped and robbed," and with a flourish, Rickles bellowed, "Why don't you get a job cop?" Don Rickles's line resonated between Buddy and the Beatles. That zinger became another indelible moment Lennon and McCartney commemorated five years later, in lyrics to their song, "She Came in through the Bathroom Window": *And so I quit the police department / And got myself a steady job.*

During Director Peter Jackson's 2021 docuseries *Get Back,* the Fab Four do a rollicking, joyous version of the song. Paul exclaims, "Got myself a proper job." John being John, goes over the top in response, "Bloody 'bout time, too, if ya ask me!" *Rolling Stone* magazine later called this jam, "One of the countless perfect moments in *Get Back.*" Most viewers will never know this moment in Beatle recording history would not have happened without Don Rickles and long-suffering Miami Beach Police Sgt. Buddy Dresner.

At the time, the Beatles didn't take to Rickles's firebrand comedy. "We were not amused, very cutting," McCartney remembered. "At first he was a bit of a shock." After a long day, culminating with getting skewered by Don Rickles, the Beatles decided to leave early. After the Fab Four vacated the Musketeer Room, most of the audience followed.

Finally back upstairs, Dresner saw to it that they were all in for the night, doubled up his men's presence on their floor, tallied up his time sheet and those of his expanding security team. For the second night, Dresner didn't arrive home until 2:00 a.m. and would have to be back at the Deauville no later than 6:00 a.m. Something had to change. The next day Dresner informed the youngest Beatle what he'd decided: "George, you're getting a roommate."

8

The Day Before

On Saturday February 15, 1964, the Beatles received dramatic news: their album *Meet the Beatles*, had hit number one on the *Billboard* charts. "I Want to Hold Your Hand," the single that started this fantasy run stateside, remained at number one for the third week. Every sales report brought further validation. And yet, this was but a glimpse of what was in store for the Beatles post-Miami. That spring and summer, Beatlemania erupted in America with a historic domination of the *Billboard* singles chart like no artist before them: claiming all five spots on the singles chart, and two more number-one albums.

At the Deauville, John took delivery of one of his most iconic guitars: a small, black Rickenbacker 325 c64 he nicknamed, "Miami." A photo of the Beatles walking through the hotel lobby shows John carrying his new prize in a guitar case. Lennon's famous "Miami" guitar made its debut in rehearsal that Saturday before the *Sullivan Show*. Other historic Beatle guitars, including the twelve-string Rickenbacker George snapped up the week previous in New York for the first *Sullivan Show*, defined their sound. As the Beatles' influence grew, a legion of other would-be lead guitarists took note of the instruments behind so much success. It was no accident, the following year, that Roger McGuinn of the Byrds played a blond Rickenbacker twelve-string on "Mr. Tambourine Man," a number-one smash that defined the so-called "California Sound."

Beatles rehearsal includes John's new Rickenbacker guitar, which he nick-named "Miami." Photo by Charles Trainor.

For their South Florida fans, the first weekend day since the Beatles began their residency meant more of them could swarm the Deauville property, hoping for a glimpse of their heroes. Some wrote messages in the sand using logs, visible from the Beatles' twelfth-floor rooms—at least until the tide washed them away. Though Dresner had more men at his disposal, there were times the Beatlemaniacs still caught him shorthanded. At one calm juncture, a newspaperman had asked for permission to come up, which Buddy granted. As the two spoke, Dresner heard the sound of the chair he left propped under a stair-way door, falling to the tile floor. That could only mean one thing: a fan had snuck in. No, he was wrong. A stampede of fans, perhaps emboldened by the writer gaining access to the Beatle floor, charged toward Buddy, standing there with no backup. What the hell would he do now?

"Fifteen or twenty started running down the hall, and I'm sitting there with this writer," Dresner remembered. Acting on instinct, the outnumbered cop held his ground and raised his arms. "I said, 'Okay, that's it, you're all under arrest, get their names, no one move, up against the wall.'" That may have been the only thing anyone could have said to get the stampeding, determined young fans to reverse course and disappear back down the stairwell. With a chuckle that his bluff worked, Buddy won that round, but the battle was constant and fans were always coming up with new schemes. Some succeeded.

George welcomed the chance to have Buddy as a roommate and distance himself from motormouth Murray the K, who wasn't about to give up access to the Beatles. The band still felt they owed him, due to Murray's playing their music with an evangelist's fervor on his highly rated New York City radio show. Once Buddy moved in, George tuned into the strain this assignment was putting on Buddy's home life. During the rush of getting the Beatles from one place to another, Buddy realized it had slipped his mind to send his wife flowers for Valentine's Day. He called her up to smooth things over. George and Paul picked up another extension and begged forgiveness: "Hey, don't be mad at him!" they implored. The two Beatles called downstairs and ordered flowers be sent to her.

That day, Dick Clark had a phone interview scheduled with the Fab Four. Clark, whose afternoon television show out of Philadelphia, *American Bandstand*, had become required viewing for teenagers intent on getting hip to new songs, dances, and style. Clark, with his coiffed black hair, youthful appearance, friendly smile, and easygoing, unflappable personality, seemed to be everything the more rigid and aging Ed Sullivan was not. There was no denying, however, that Sullivan and his team had seen something in the Beatles that Clark had not. For all of his acumen when it came to recognizing the Next Big Thing, Clark, the man often credited with creating the marriage between music, television, and video, missed out on getting them to perform on his show or promote them on concert tours.

In 1963, on *Bandstand*'s rate-a-record segment, young fans gave a lukewarm 73 rating to the Beatles' single "She Loves You." Then, when Clark showed them a photo of the group, some snickered at the way they looked. Without a premier launching vehicle like *The Ed Sullivan Show*, "She Loves You," released in September 1963 on the tiny Swan label, sold fewer than a thousand copies in the United States. The song many mistakenly believe broke the Beatles big in the United States had actually bombed. Had it not been for the convergence of Sullivan and Epstein, it's likely that the Beatles also would have never seen the slightest hint of success in America. Upon rerelease by Capitol in 1964, with Beatlemania on high heat, "She Loves You" soared to the top of the charts. In 1963, though, that early *Bandstand* flop may have been a signal to Clark that the Beatles didn't have much of a future. It's reminiscent of October 2, 1954, the only time Elvis Presley played the Grand Ol' Opry. Not knowing what to make of him, the traditional country crowd gave Presley such a lukewarm reception that the manager told him not to quit his day job. Presley never played there again.

Local radio stations battled for whatever Beatle exclusives they could claim. In a phone interview with Miami station WQAM, twenty-year-old George Harrison showed off his quick wit with DJ Charlie Murdock. "Can you account personally for the Beatles popularity?" Murdock asked. "I don't know. It's hard to say," Harrison offered. "As we said at the airport, if we did know we'd probably form another group and we'd be the managers."

Murdock chuckled, "Very good." Upon being asked where the name *Beatles* came from, George credited John with settling on a double entendre referring to the insect and then also, "B-e-a-t, on the beat. We all liked the name and we kept it," Harrison explained.

During downtime, Buddy and the Beatles watched television. In one memorable episode of an eerie, ahead-of-its-time science fiction cartoon called *The Outer Limits*, a ray gun is used to make the bad guys disappear. Buddy picked up on the notion of having a magic weapon to wipe out all the lawbreakers: "I'd be like Captain Marvel zapping all the bad guys," he remarked. "Zap, goodbye Mr. Bank Robber. Zap, goodbye Mr. Murderer. Hold it right there or I'll zap you right between the eyes, Zap!" Lennon and McCartney summoned that memory years later, for the lyrics to their 1968 song "Bungalow Bill" on *The White Album*: "*Deep in the jungle where the mighty tiger lies / Bill and his elephants were taken by surprise / So Captain Marvel zapped him right between the eyes.*"

As the next *Sullivan* appearance loomed, the Beatles ramped up rehearsals. If you didn't know better, you'd think they were just away on holiday. Ringo and George are in swim trunks and short-sleeved cabana clothes. John and Paul appear in dark jeans but otherwise casually dressed. Tables and chairs have been pushed to the side, clearing plenty of space on the tile floor, inside the plain, cinder-block "cool room." "It was ideal for them," Dezo Hoffman explained, "because they could come straight in from the pool, pick up their instruments, and get to work."

In one Hoffman photo, Buddy Dresner is an equally cool customer controlling the entryway, leaning on what appears to be a luggage cart. In sunglasses and police uniform including long sleeves and a tie, he had to be exhausted. Rehearsals then moved to the Napoleon Ballroom, where the live show would take place the next night. Judging from advance coverage by old-school, nationally syndicated columnist Harvey Pack, far more pressure was on the shoulders of the Deauville's owner, Morris Lansburgh. In all the excitement of bringing Sullivan to South Beach, Lansburgh had forgotten one crucial detail about this day, Saturday, February 15. "For the past year the couple has been planning their son's bar mitzvah for today," Pack noted. "Now the room would be occupied by an *Ed Sullivan* rehearsal." In his preview article, which ran in newspapers nationwide, Pack devoted more attention to the show's top-billed performer, dancer Mitzi Gaynor.

Bringing the *Sullivan Show* down the East Coast was a massive undertaking. The Deauville's loading dock filled with trucks jammed with all of the necessary electronics, cable, cameras, and assorted ephemera. WTVJ, the local CBS affiliate at the time, chipped in with camera gear and personnel for the broadcast. In 1964, the only network television shows frequently staged live on location were sporting events. Just three networks, CBS, NBC and ABC, dominated the American television landscape. NBC led the way into the future of television, broadcasting half of its schedule, including *The Wonderful World of Disney*, in color. By comparison, CBS was still in black-and-white and getting criticism for its heavy rotation of rural comedies like the *Beverly Hillbillies, Gomer Pyle USMC,* and *Petticoat Junction.* For all he did to move America's youth culture forward by bringing Elvis Presley and the Beatles to American audiences, to many the dowdy Ed Sullivan, with his slicked-back hair and stiff mannerisms, personified the square 1950s. To those who knew him, however, Sullivan had always been comfortable in his own skin and felt no need to try and adopt some phony on-air persona.

Obviously fond of the Fab Four, during rehearsal Sullivan took time to call upon the Beatles to pose for photos with his two grandsons. One of them, nine-year-old Robert Precht, had already witnessed, from an

Paul McCartney and John Lennon with Ed Sullivan in
Miami Beach. Photo by CBS via Getty Images.

intimate vantage point, the weekly grind of churning out a live, nationally televised variety show. His father, Bob Precht, behind the scenes
as producer, and his grandfather in front of the camera were arbiters
of an emerging popular culture. Still, it seemed so commonplace after
a while that young Robert described all the weekly goings-on as "the
family store." Barbara Forster, one of two Sullivan production secretar-
ies who'd made the trip to Miami Beach, said the only word to describe
the workload was "overwhelming." Members of the production team
were operating on four hours of sleep per night, trying to deal with one
issue after another. Precht compared them to Green Berets, dedicated

and highly professional, who'd pulled off remotes from as far away as Moscow.

As Sullivan acted as traffic cop from the Napoleon Ballroom stage, all four Beatles reclined nearby. They were surrounded by camera and microphone equipment, stage managers, lighting directors, assistants with clipboards, all trying to get the production organized. Due to lack of facilities, John, Paul, George, and Ringo were encamped among ballroom chairs getting their makeup done. Without a green room or back stage, it was either there in the swirl of production preparation or in one of their rooms, twelve floors up. In exchange for putting up with all the hysteria surrounding the Beatles, guests at the Deauville were issued free tickets to the *Sullivan Show* live broadcast. In addition, employees of WTVJ had the option of attending the broadcast or the taped dress rehearsal from 2:30 to 3:30. During that early session, Sullivan was irritated that young fans kept screaming over him.

When the time came for Sullivan to call out the Beatles to perform as if it were the next day's live broadcast, his grandson was still standing close to the band, transfixed. At just nine years old, Precht called it a peak moment of his life. "When they started playing 'All My Lovin,' it was the most beautiful sound," he recalled. "The most beautiful sensation of music and sound that I had ever experienced. Then and now. I've never experienced the sense of this magical sound coming from these guys. It still is in my heart and soul."

That afternoon, two enterprising, well-dressed young men were out to make good on their scheme to meet the Beatles. University of Miami Sigma Chi fraternity brothers Bill Marsh and Tom Hill had dreamed up the idea of making the Beatles honorary pledges. The two had a plaque made honoring the Fab Four for their "service to youth." Dressed in sport coats and ties and looking like the epitome of youthful respectability, the fraternity brothers talked their way past a phalanx of police and into the heart of Beatledom. "The Beatles kept telling us how much they liked the attention and fame, but wanted so much just to get away and have some fun," Bill later recounted. So Bill and Tom did what any friendly fraternity brother would do; they invited their new honorary pledges to go waterskiing.

As far-fetched as it sounds, the Beatles were still the same age as many of the students on the University of Miami's tawny Coral Gables campus. Bill and Tom were allowed to hang out long enough to get their photos taken with the Beatles and their plaque designating them as honorary Sigma Chi pledges, standing just a few feet from where Ed Sullivan was preparing for The Big Show. Among the stories of those who made a Beatles pilgrimage to the Deauville Hotel, another exceeds Bill Marsh and Tom Hill's audacity.

9

Ed, the Abstract,
and a Second First

Throughout the Beatles' Deauville residency, all kinds of local businesses hoped to cash in on Beatlemania. Fans at the hotel sent gifts up to their rooms unsolicited, in the hope of making a connection and striking it rich. Twin brothers Doug and Don Spence of Daytona Beach embarked on such a quest to meet and go into business with the Beatles. Unlike so many others, their plan looked like it was going to succeed. It took the Spence brothers more than a half century to find out the truth behind why it didn't.

During downtime at work one day, Don stood on top of a filing cabinet and plopped four drops of black India ink onto a piece of cardboard. Then he tilted it back at a slight angle until the ink ran to the bottom, giving each black blot what appeared to be a pair of long, skinny legs. His wife, Peggy, said, "He didn't have a particular plan for it until co-workers started telling him the artwork looked like the Beatles." Two blots represented Paul and George, of similar height, on the left, a smaller blot toward the back representing Ringo, and a fourth, alone to the right, represented where John stood on stage.

Doug Spence, the twin in charge of marketing, came up with the idea of actually showing it to the Beatles. "We printed about two hundred copies of Don's artwork and, almost as a joke, decided to take

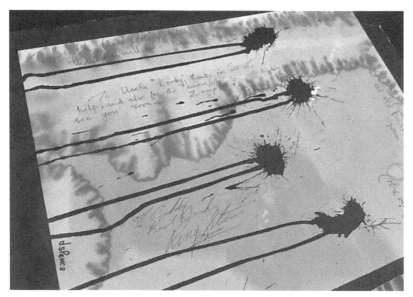

Don Spence's abstract artwork that he gave to the Beatles on February 16, 1964. Courtesy of the author.

them to Miami. Our goal was to meet the Beatles and sell them the artwork," Doug said. The Spences would have to drive four hours and 260 miles to Miami Beach and somehow make their way through Sgt. Buddy Dresner's security gauntlet set up specifically to prevent random strangers like the Spence brothers from getting to the Beatles. As if that didn't require enough audacity, the Spences attempted this scheme on Sunday, February 16, the day the Beatles were set to appear live on *The Ed Sullivan Show*.

In a newspaper interview, Doug Spence described their good fortune upon arrival: "We showed our art to the hotel manager. Word got around quickly," he said. Also intrigued, ever-present Beatle assistant Mal Evans had taken a copy of the inkblot piece to Brian Epstein, who was enamored with the whimsical image and saw marketing potential. Epstein appeared in the lobby and invited them to come up to the Beatles' floor. The Spences could not have dreamed it any better. Before they could grasp the gravity of what they'd already accomplished, the thirty-year-old twins were eye-to-eye with all four Beatles.

"They wore dungarees and smoked cigarettes one after another.

Peggy and Don Spence. Courtesy of Peggy and Don Spence.

When they saw the artwork, they picked themselves out in the abstract," Doug said. Brother Don was awestruck that the Beatles were taking his artwork seriously. "We just couldn't believe ourselves," he said. "They kept looking at Doug and I, twins, 'look-alike, look-alike' and they would laugh. It was so special." Then came the moment they'd been waiting for; Brian Epstein proposed working with their agents in New York to market their art internationally. The Spence brothers had good reason to believe this was the break they were hoping for.

All of this discussion and joking around was a pleasant distraction from a final dress rehearsal and live performance for which fans were already swarming the street and hotel lobby. The Beatles shook hands with the Spences and proceeded to leave the brothers behind, by themselves. It was all so surreal. Doug marveled, "Don and I stayed around answering the telephone and helping ourselves to the bar. You wouldn't believe some of the crazy calls they got."

Unbeknownst to Epstein, the deal he'd already made to market the Beatles with New York–based representatives, and the potential to rake in untold riches, was destined for disaster. Epstein, overwhelmed by the demands of managing the Beatles and a stable of other young artists, hadn't given much thought to this ancillary revenue stream and didn't want to deal with it. Today, it's well known to artists that marketing their likenesses commercially can make as much as recording, streaming, and touring. The Beatles, via their befuddled manager, would find out the awful truth later in the year; it was the biggest and most costly blunder "Eppy" made while managing the Beatles.

After all the preparation, rehearsals, and mayhem, downstairs at the Deauville, it was getting close to showtime. When the demand for lighting and air-conditioning exceeded the hotel generator's ability to power it all, a spare had to be trucked in at the last minute. The security force had swollen to twice the size of the one used for President Kennedy's visit. Outside, the Miami Beach Fire Department staged a hook-and-ladder truck to rescue fans climbing hotel walls to get in.

Excited fans who'd jammed the hotel lobby and spilled out on to Collins Avenue with tickets for the live broadcast were waiting to be allowed into the ballroom. Because of recurring audio problems, rehearsals continued well into the evening—past the allotted time. "The dress rehearsal was not finished until 7:10 p.m., and then we started letting people in for the show as rapidly as possible," recounted Deauville owner Morris Lansburgh. Getting the audience in and seated before the 8:00 p.m. broadcast was problematic. Another challenge became gauging capacity in the three-thousand-seat Napoleon Ballroom due to how much space was occupied by stage, television, and lighting equipment. Time was running out. In the tense atmosphere, show staff made the decision to close the lobby doors, leaving a good number of seats empty. Now shut out, devastated fans still waiting in the lobby got angry. Someone called in a bomb threat.

In the midst of the hustle and bustle, a Miami Beach Police car pulled right up the driveway and parked out front. Out stepped Police Chief Rocky Pomerance, his wife, Hope, and their two sons. At six feet tall and 250 pounds, Pomerance had gotten the name "Rocky" from his days as a boxer. No one in the overflow crowd protested as he and his family were ushered right through a special entryway into the Napoleon Ballroom. While his security team worked the Big Show, Pomerance was directed to VIP seating in the second row. A couple of honored guests, former Heavyweight Boxing Champ Joe Louis, in town for the Liston-Clay fight, and the current champ himself, Sonny Liston, took their seats.

Sullivan's own family, meanwhile, chose to watch the show from the tranquility of their rooms at the Fontainebleau Hotel, blocks away from all the madness. Being there in the audience was "too nerve-wracking," said Sullivan's grandson Rob Precht, too painful. God forbid some calamity happen. Just the thought of it, and all that pressure, was enough for Sullivan's family to stay away. Perhaps that's the same reason why Brian Epstein chose to watch the show on television from his room on the twelfth floor, wearing a novelty "Stamp out the Beatles" sweatshirt produced by some Michigan students as a PR stunt.

On this crucial night, no one felt the pressure more than the Beatles' bodyguard, Buddy Dresner. After dress rehearsal ran late, he and his officers managed to get them back upstairs for makeup and a quick dinner. If Dresner had one job above all else, it was to make damn sure the Beatles were back in the ballroom on time, in place, and ready to take Sullivan's cue. "Dress rehearsal tired them out," Dresner said. Calls started coming from downstairs, where are they? Dresner told his men to grab the elevator and "freeze it" to hasten the Beatles' trip back downstairs. The boys had ordered grilled cheese again and would not budge until they'd eaten. By the time they hit the elevator, it was ten minutes until eight.

Making the situation more urgent, comedian Myron Cohen considered it an insult to go on before the Beatles and refused. Due to the crowd still milling around in the lobby, Dresner and the Beatles made their way through the kitchen and out by the swimming pool. "Get the hell out of the way!" he shouted. To buy time, Sullivan pitched to an iced-tea commercial. At its conclusion, with no time to spare and his boss looking on from the second row, Dresner literally pushed the Beatles up onstage seconds before they were due to go on. They were just finding their places when Sullivan was back on the air before an eager national television audience.

"Ladies and gentlemen, here are four of the nicest youngsters we've ever had on our stage, *The Beatles!*" The introduction brought torrents of screams as the band ripped into "She Loves You." Bandleader Len Dorson, whose job was to hire local musicians to be part of the production, watched teen fans in the audience erupt: "I saw a girl bite the *hair* of a girl in front of her. For no reason except excitement." Despite prime seats in the second row, Chief Pomerance's son, nine-year-old Jimmy, couldn't hear a thing: "Truthfully, the screaming is

The Beatles appearing on *The Ed Sullivan Show* live from the Deauville Hotel's Napoleon Ballroom, February 16, 1964. Photo by Charles Trainor.

Napoleon Ballroom audience. Photo by Charles Trainor.

what I remember more than anything else. To see them onstage was a big deal, but you could barely hear the music," he said. "I remember my brother and I holding our ears, the screaming was so deafening." Adults in the audience were amused as young people went wild. Reporter Larry Kane, initially not at all convinced that these four mop-tops could do justice to their intricate and well-produced recordings, and still just twenty-one himself, saw what America's youth were seeing. Kane said, "Suddenly the stereotype of 'mop-tops' singing meaningless music vanished . . . The Beatles owned the American television audience."

Nowhere did that notion turn out to be truer than in Florida among its nearly six million residents. At the tail end of the Baby Boom, post–World War II suburban homes were filled with impressionable young children. Driving home that night, the Spences, tired but still on an adrenaline high from meeting the Beatles, pulled up to a roadside restaurant in Vero Beach to have a burger and watch the show. Like conquering kings, they beamed as they watched Sullivan announce the Fab Four. "We told some folks, 'we were just with the Beatles earlier today,' Doug recalled. "And they said, 'sure, sure you were.'" It was such a whirlwind that the brothers hadn't thought to ask for a single autograph to show as proof to the skeptical strangers. Maybe it all was just a dream? So they watched, ate, then got back in their car and headed north on US 1 for Daytona Beach, still hopeful about the deal they had discussed with Epstein.

The Beatles performed two live sets and six songs. The main problem you can see during the performances was simple: the height and direction of the microphones. Midsong, John had to crouch and reposition one of the damned things for his lead vocal to be heard. Through it all they gave each other knowing smiles and soldiered on. Gone were the days of flying bottles and drunken toughs threatening to kick their asses during marathon sets along Hamburg's Reeperbahn. Two hundred chairs in the audience were left empty, like undiscovered gold to devastated Beatle fans. One of many who couldn't get in, a young woman, had to be restrained from banging her head on the sidewalk. Miami Beach promoter Hank Meyer, who'd handled negotiations to bring Sullivan and the Beatles to the Deauville, called it a public relations disaster. "It was inexcusable," he fumed. Lansburgh was apologetic, explaining they hadn't had enough time after rehearsals to get so many people seated.

After the show, seventeen-year-old Diane Levine, the high-schooler who'd met up with Paul McCartney during an ocean photoshoot, accepted his invitation up to the Beatles' rooms. John, Paul, George, and Ringo, still wired from a second successful performance on national television, were whisked away to the exclusive after-show party. Diane didn't even have a chance to tell Paul goodbye. Instead, she left him a thank-you note and a couple of phone numbers where she could be reached. Seemingly, that was the end of it. The following day, when she stopped by her father's office, she was shocked when he asked, "Who's this Paul McCartney calling you?"

No one was more relieved the Beatles' second nationally televised show was over than Buddy Dresner. His time with the Beatles had been exhausting, but he was proud of the part he played in making sure they made it to the performance on time, albeit barely. Now he was looking forward to a return to normalcy. He'd developed a genuine affection for the Beatles, Cynthia Lennon, and their appreciative, well-mannered entourage. They all considered him a friend. Chief Rocky Pomerance congratulated Buddy on a job well done and had a chance to meet the Beatles. When the family got back into the car out front, immediately his wife exclaimed, "Oh my God, they're such nice boys."

Still, to many, this landmark show is only a footnote to the first. Stating the obvious, it's for the same reason people remember the order of things, what came first: the first kiss, the first boyfriend or girlfriend, the first Sullivan introduction to the Beatles' first song, live from New York, the greatest city in the world. Consider, however, the greater degree of difficulty in Miami Beach. You can see why Rob Precht's comparison of this crew to Green Berets is apt. Away from the safe confines of the Sullivan Theater, they produced a live, on-location broadcast from a chaotic, working beach resort with a failing power grid, a bomb threat, angry fans, in a ballroom bereft of dressing rooms. For Sullivan's team to have minimal technical difficulties in the midst of such chaos is a testament to their professionalism. From this point of view, both live shows should be seen as firsts: live from the Sullivan Theater and live from the Deauville Hotel; arguably it was the Beatles' most challenging and historic, live remote performance.

At the postparty, celebrities Mitzi Gaynor and the Beatles' Friday-night nemesis Don Rickles feasted on roast beef and lobster. CBS bigwigs all took turns thanking them. The man himself, Ed Sullivan, showed his pride and appreciation. The next Sunday his show would feature yet another Beatles segment, this one already pretaped in New York. After this monumental week, orchestrated by Sullivan and Brian Epstein, these Beatle performances have remained an indelible part of American history, a turning point in popular culture. "In many ways, it was the high point of his career," said Rob Precht of his grandfather Ed Sullivan. "The Beatles, for him, was the ultimate scoop and gave him great satisfaction."

At around midnight, Buddy Dresner escorted the Beatles to their rooms. The most important part of this extraordinary assignment was finished. "Thank God I'm going home tomorrow," Dresner muttered. Just then, the Beatle press man, bespectacled Brian Sommerville, approached: "I've got some news. I don't know how to tell you this, but the boys are not going home." Sommerville had a serious look on his face and was never the type to joke around, but that's how Dresner took it. "Oh ya, they're going home," he replied. "No, they want to stay a few more days," said Sommerville. Incredulous, Dresner finally asked, "Does the hotel know? Somebody has to pay the hotel. And you have half the police department here!"

"Well," Sommerville told him, "We're waiting on Mr. Epstein."

10

Fast Times, Mob Ties, and a Surprise Visit

In the wake of the second *Sullivan Show*, it was clear some critics did not share America's crush on the Beatles. In his one-star review, Percy Shain of the *Boston Globe* wrote that the entire show was one of the biggest bombs of Ed Sullivan's career. Of the Beatles, Shain opined, "They still sound like a group of disorganized amateurs whose voices seem to be fighting each other rather than blending." National publications like *Newsweek* wrote them off: "Musically they're a near disaster . . . Their lyrics are a catastrophe." As the Beatles' success grew, so did hyperbole from critics like conservative blowhard William F. Buckley, who was mystified as to what all the fuss was about. "The Beatles are not merely awful," Buckley wrote. "I would consider it sacrilegious to say anything less than that they are Godawful . . . unbelievably horrible." It was not yet apparent to adults that the Beatles represented the first wave of the British Invasion: musicians writing their own songs, destined to define America's youth culture of the 1960s.

None of that criticism mattered to their growing fan base or to the Beatles themselves. Now veterans of two of the most-watched television shows ever in the United States, they had the rest of the week to step back, work on a few new songs, and take a well-earned South Florida holiday. The days ahead would be remarkable for the intriguing characters with whom they would come into contact. There was also the matter of their bodyguard, Buddy Dresner, who'd found out, in a rather startling way, that his post–*Sullivan Show* life was still not yet his own. There would be no exhaling, not yet anyway.

With the news still fresh, Dresner called Chief Rocky Pomerance for help, advice, anything to ease the shock:

"Rock, we've got a problem; they ain't going home," Dresner moaned.

Equally stunned, his chief replied, "What are they gonna do?"

"Beats the hell out of me," said Dresner. "What do I do with them?"

The only thing Pomerance could give in the way of orders or advice was, "Just keep doin' what you're doing."

Dresner also had to break it to Dottie that their separation would continue for the rest of the week. The notion of being embedded with the Beatles round-the-clock in a posh, oceanfront Miami Beach resort was the stuff of fantasy for their young fans. For a middle-aged policeman, father of three, and sleep-deprived tour guide already missing his family, it was the last place he wanted to be. Sure, he had come to enjoy their company, but hell, enough was enough.

Brian Epstein was no help. He told Dresner, "The boys want to stay." For the Beatles manager, dedicating every waking hour of his life to them was routine; his raison d'être. "I'm sleeping here; I haven't seen my family," Dresner pleaded. "Well," said Epstein, "they appreciate everything you're doing," In a day or two he'd be headed back to England with the money from the *Sullivan* appearances. There was much for Epstein to do while the boys took this short breather. He was considering numerous big-money offers to bring them back to the States for a much more expansive summer tour. Ed Sullivan departed, satisfied that the Miami show was another ratings smash, right up there with America's highest-rated program: *The Beverly Hillbillies*.

Late Monday morning, team Beatles was back to work with their trusted, albeit deflated, policeman and mate. *Life* magazine photographer Bob Gomel had arranged for an exclusive oceanfront shoot with the Beatles. When they arrived, the Beatles, as usual, were soon set upon by teenagers. For Gomel, the photos took on greater intimacy because he had these world-famous subjects all to himself. Sixteen-year-old Ruth Blythe and her friend were among the young bikini-clad women greeting them. To no one's surprise, they moved in on Paul. Other girls latched on to Ringo. To Gomel, Paul was trying to put some distance between himself and his new admirers. Blythe was determined not to let this moment of serendipity pass without giving Paul a kiss on the cheek. That moment, captured on film by Gomel, became more special when he found out what happened after.

"When Ruth got home and told her parents she had just kissed Paul McCartney, they did not believe her," Gomel remembered. When *Life's* editor relegated John Loengard's bobbing Beatles photo to the back page, he also rejected any idea companion story from Gail Cameron. That meant Gomel's assignment, to capture intimate black-and-white photos of the boys frolicking at the Pollaks' and posing at the beach, never appeared in the magazine. It wasn't until 2005, when another publication featured his "lost" photos taken in Miami Beach, that a local television station in Houston, where Gomel lived, ran a feature story on them. That story, picked up by stations across the country, caught the attention of Ruth Blythe's family in Portland. To their astonishment, there was young Ruth, hanging out in the surf with the Beatles and kissing Paul McCartney, just as she had told them. As a bittersweet footnote, Ruth had died a decade previous to these unseen images resurfacing, verifying the claim she'd made to her skeptical family.

After the shoot, Murray the K had arranged for another Beatle boat ride, this one much different than their laid-back Castro yacht cruise. This excursion also brought the Beatles into the orbit of a character who would become legendary in the annals of South Florida Babylon. Don Aronow pioneered offshore racing boat design in the sport's formative years. He'd made millions as a developer in New Jersey, then abruptly retired to Florida. Still only in his thirties, he got bored and started designing and building the archetypical cigarette boat. He also became a champion offshore racer. The ultracompetitive Aronow had rugged, movie-star looks, loved to chase women, and reveled in staring down anyone who dared oppose him in business.

When the Beatles hopped on board the sleek, 435 horsepower, twenty-three-foot craft with no seats, they were about to get an early taste of the live-fast, *Miami Vice*, Cocaine Cowboy culture that permeated South Florida in the 1980s. Aronow fired up the engine and hit the throttle. "I don't think the Beatles knew what they were in for," said Bob DiNesco, who bought and restored the historic 233 Formula racing boat. "John, Paul and George got a little seasick, but Ringo, he had the time of his life." In Dezo Hoffman photos, you could see Murray the K, Cynthia, and even George Martin went along for a ride. After all the stress of the *Sullivan Show* television appearances, this adrenaline-filled speedboat ride gave the Fab Four some wind and water in their faces, South Florida style. Aronow even let Ringo and John take the wheel. After about an hour of riding at high speed, the Beatles were "white as ghosts and almost speechless." Ringo, in particular, loved the fast ride and even tried his hand at steering the boat into shore, a move he regretted when he tried to bring the craft in nose first, slightly damaging it. In retrospect, the excursion itself was also risky; had anything gone wrong at high speed, it could have been disaster.

In most of the stories told about Aronow's accomplished, live-fast life, the time he spent with the Beatles the day after their *Sullivan* appearance barely brings a mention. Rare images taken by Hoffman remain, of the Fab Four roaring around in Aronow's boat without a life jacket in sight. Like the Beatles, Aronow went on to live the kind of life they write movies about. In 1987, outside the business where he'd built his boat racing empire, a stranger pulled up next to his Mercedes and shot him three times, killing him. A business rival and convicted drug smuggler who felt he'd been cheated and humiliated by Aronow had paid a hit man sixty thousand dollars to take him out.

As the Beatles roared around on Aronow's super speedboat, Brian Epstein sat at the dock. Dressed in beachwear similar to that of the Beatles, their manager reviewed the newspaper for coverage of the *Sullivan Show* appearance. In photographs, he looks uncomfortable and out of his element, for once not clad in a Savile Row power suit. Hoffman had also gotten a few frames of Epstein tooling around in the MG he'd insisted on renting. Brian was like that: the shy impresario mimicking the Beatles' status and style, feeding off their fame vicariously. Heaven knows he'd earned the right to do so. Unfortunately, for trusted Beatle inner-circle photographer Dezo Hoffman, one of his photos of John during the boating adventures that day led to a serious rift. "One magazine carried a photo I took of John water-skiing in which his hair was, quite naturally, blown back by the wind," Hoffman recalled. Lennon thought the image made it appear his hairline was receding. "When John saw the picture he was livid," said Hoffman. "He was terribly vain about his hair and insisted it be pictured swept forward covering his forehead."

Cynthia enjoyed being close and relaxed with her husband poolside and on the water, without the demands of a national magazine shoot, swarming girls, or some other distraction. Kids from the neighborhood strained to catch a glimpse of the Beatles enjoying themselves at the walled-off waterfront residence near Surprise Lake. Some of them managed to get a better look by standing on the bridge near Pine Tree Drive and West Fifty-First Street. From a short distance, they could see them fishing off the dock or climbing into a boat to take them to the lake just off Biscayne Bay, where all the local kids water-skied.

Epstein and the Beatles also accepted an invitation for an afternoon barbeque at the home of Sam Cohen, a business partner of Deauville Hotel big shot Morris Lansburgh. The Cohens invited a couple of local girls, Sheri Shepherd and Susan Coolik, seniors at Edison High, to hang out with the Beatles during their impromptu pool party. George Martin recalled an odd encounter with a security guard, cigarette dangling from his mouth, a gun and holster clearly visible, tasked with grilling steaks for them. As Brian was complaining about the poor quality of all the Beatle bootleg records coming out, their cook asked quite seriously, "You want we should take care of them for you, Mr. Epstein?" In his memoir, George Martin called it a "very sinister moment."

The Beatles' 1964 visit came in the midst of high times for hoteliers Cohen and Lansburgh, as evidenced by their opulent lifestyles. When you take time to follow the money, it becomes clear that both men had profitable Mob ties. In 1973, a federal grand jury indicted them along with one of the Mafia's most storied figures, Meyer Lansky, in connection with a scheme from 1960–67 to skim $36 million in profits from the Flamingo Hotel in Las Vegas. The diminutive Lansky, who stood barely over five feet tall, was the Mafioso financial genius who devised the skimming operation to avoid taxes. Despite having untold riches, Lansky lived quietly, often being seen walking his dog along Forty-First Street on Miami Beach. Cohen and Lansburgh pleaded guilty and were sentenced to a year in prison. Cohen's family maintained that the money involved was far less than portrayed by ambitious government prosecutors looking to make a name for themselves. Aged and in failing health, Lansky fought hard and eventually beat the rap. In his 1974 film *Godfather II*, director Francis Ford Coppola based the character Hyman Roth on Lansky.

In the midst enjoying the best of what South Florida and these mobbed-up guys had to offer, the Beatles could see Buddy Dresner was not himself. As much as he'd grown to care for them, he'd confided that all the time away from his wife and family was putting further strain on his marriage. Straightaway, in a show of mutual empathy, the boys came up with a solution, one that could have been the basis for a scene in their upcoming film, A *Hard Day's Night*. They decided to visit Dottie and give her a gentlemanly, collective thank-you for all the sacrifices she and her husband had made on their behalf. "They said, 'let's go to where she is and get you out of the doghouse,'" Buddy's son Barry Dresner recalled. Buddy told them she worked in the front office at North Miami Beach Junior High, recently renamed in honor of President John F. Kennedy. By that time, it was late afternoon. Buddy figured students had already left for the day, and it would be as good a time as any to go see her. They jumped in his cruiser and headed north.

Just the notion of a group of young men, world famous or otherwise, sneaking onto a school campus, any school, anywhere, illustrates what an innocent time this was. In the wake of tragedies in Columbine, Colorado; Sandy Hook, Connecticut; Uvalde, Texas; and at Marjory Stoneman Douglas High in South Florida, American schools are now fortified, patrolled by armed police officers and, out of necessity, protected by fencing, walls, video systems, and panic apps. If anyone pulls up to a school and attempts to sneak onto campus, they can expect to be met by an officer under orders to engage them. Such a world the Beatles could have never fathomed that February afternoon in 1964, when Buddy pulled in to the parking lot of JFK Junior High on Northeast 167th Street.

As anticipated, school had already let out for the day. "It all seems kind of quiet," recounted Barry Dresner. What a scene it must have been: the Beatles piling out of a marked Miami Beach Police car, shutting the doors quietly so as not to raise attention, and padding their way in to a Florida school. "They sneak down the hallway to the registrar's office where my mom was," said Barry. They open the office door about to yell, 'Surprise!'" Simultaneously, another door down the hall opens, and group of students emerge who've just gotten out of band practice. "These are musical kids," Barry emphasized, who knew exactly who the Beatles were and had the shock of their lives seeing them in their own school hallway. The boys shut the office door as quickly as they had opened it, turned around and ran back down the hall toward the exit, the band kids starting to give chase. They piled into Buddy's cruiser and got out of the parking lot, heading back toward the Deauville. They would have to thank Dottie another time.

In the wake of the near meet-and-greet, Buddy decided it was finally time to formally introduce the Beatles to his family. Doing that meant breaking the big secret he'd been keeping from their children, twelve-year-old daughter Teri especially. Barry was much younger, but to his recollection, it happened early in the week after the Beatles appeared on *Ed Sullivan*. So too did a historic meeting between the Beatles and the athlete who went on to as much fame, success, celebrity, and controversy as they did. Their second day off brought them into the orbit of the brash young boxer few were giving any chance of winning his impending World Heavyweight Championship title bout: Cassius Clay.

11

Molding Clay

The morning of Tuesday, February 18, the Beatles were due for a meetup with Cassius Marcellus Clay Jr., the United States' 1960 Olympic Gold Medal winner in light-heavyweight boxing, now just a week from challenging Sonny Liston for the World Heavyweight Championship. Outspoken, brimming with confidence and good looks, at twenty-two, Clay was a year younger than John Lennon, and a year older than Paul McCartney. Had Sonny Liston not thought of the Beatles as "Sissies" and refused to pose for photos with them, this historic meeting of twentieth-century icons might not have happened. On the surface, this appeared to be no more than a throwaway photo-op for the Beatles with their second choice among the fighters they hoped to meet, in one of the most run-down corners of South Beach.

In England the year previous, Clay staged a one-man American Invasion of his own, boxing opposite local favorite Henry Cooper before thirty-five thousand spectators at Wembley Stadium. On June 18, 1963, Clay rented a Rolls Royce to take him to the fight. Fans booed seeing Clay make a grand entrance into the ring wearing a crown. In the fourth round, Cooper—the champion Clay had dismissed as "a bum"—hit Clay with a left hook so forceful it lifted him off his feet and sent him collapsing between the ropes. Embarrassed and lucky to have made it to the next round, Clay unleashed a flurry of punches to Cooper's head that led to the fight being called due to his excessive bleeding. Temporarily humbled, Clay acknowledged he'd survived the fight of his life.

Two months before Clay's victory broke hometown hearts, the Beatles topped the British charts with their second top-five single, "From Me to You." Despite their mutual success in England, by the time they met in Miami Beach, Clay and the Beatles professed to have no knowledge of each other. Always on the hunt for compelling images, British photographer Harry Benson said he had arranged the photo-op at the Dundee Brothers' 5th Street Gym, Clay's training headquarters.

By 1964, Miami had been Clay's home for four years while training with boxing guru Angelo Dundee. When he arrived in Miami on December 19, 1960, the young boxer took a room at the Mary Elizabeth Motel, a run-down "den of thieves," according to his fight doctor, Ferdie Pacheco, who ran a medical clinic in Overtown. Optimistic and dedicated to the pursuit of a world championship, Clay would get up early, put on pants, army boots, and a T-shirt he had made special with his name on it, and run across the MacArthur Causeway to the gym. More than once he was stopped by police for little more than being a young Black man running toward segregated Miami Beach. "The cops would call me and ask, 'You got a tall fighter named Clay?'" Dundee recalled. "He says he trains with you, but it looks to us like he was running from something."

Photographer Flip Schulke was to Clay what Leslie Bryce and Dezo Hoffman were to the Beatles; trusted by the inner circle to capture definitive images of the young boxer, in many ways still an innocent, coming out of a sheltered life in Louisville. In a stunning photo series that later became known as "Ali Underwater," Schulke photographed Clay clad only in boxing shorts working out in a swimming pool and showing off his chiseled physique. His black-and-white photos of the up-and-coming boxer going through his paces inside the 5th St. Gym are defining. "Those were the best, purest years of his life," Dundee said. Schulke was there with his camera to document something seemingly as mundane as Clay shopping for a new dress shirt at Burdines downtown. The clerk would allow Clay to try on sport coats but not a shirt, not a garment that would actually touch his dark skin. While Clay was dismissive about the slight, Schulke fumed at the store manager: "This man won an Olympic Gold Medal for his country!"

Living in segregated Overtown and experiencing how Blacks were treated, Clay took an interest in the separatist message of the Nation of Islam. He started attending meetings at a local Mosque, number 29, where he became aware of the teachings of an influential young minister, Malcolm X, who eschewed Martin Luther King's message of integration through nonviolent demonstration, advocating a separatist Black Power mantra. Given his recent experiences, Clay began to internalize that message. Through hard work and the backing of investors from his hometown, Louisville, in 1963 the Olympic champion moved into a small three-bedroom home at 4610 Northwest Fifteenth Court, west of downtown Miami.

In the runup to his fight with Sonny Liston, Clay befriended Malcolm X, who was ostensibly in South Florida to vacation with his wife and daughters. For Malcolm, it was more than that; getting the ear of the young devotee he believed was about to become the next World Heavyweight Boxing Champion would be a public relations coup. During a prefight prayer session, Malcolm assured Clay it was his destiny to prevail over Liston. Clay also developed a close friendship with suave, velvet-voiced soul singer Sam Cooke, who owned his own music publishing company, rebelled against segregation on southern tours, and spoke out about racial oppression in songs like "A Change Is Gonna Come." For the time being, Clay tried to keep his association with the Nation of Islam on the down-low. The day the Beatles came calling he was a 7–1 underdog to Liston, and any of that kind of talk could damage already sluggish ticket sales.

Civil rights came onto the Beatles' radar during this initial visit to the South. John took time to question Buddy Dresner about race relations in America. One of the more intriguing photos taken during their stay shows the Beatles stopped outside the Montmartre Hotel on Collins Street, Buddy Dresner at the wheel. The car windows are down, and John is sitting in back, Paul in the front, speaking with Black women in maid uniforms sitting at a bus stop. Newspapers carried stories about young African Americans arrested in Jacksonville, demanding to be served at a segregated Morrison's Cafeteria counter. In London, actor Marlon Brando was heckled as a Communist after insisting his contracts include a clause to withhold his films from release in segregated cities.

Robert Lipsyte, a young *New York Times* reporter, was assigned to cover his first heavyweight fight in Miami. Their senior boxing writer had opted out of what he was convinced would be a one-round affair. It was clear the editors agreed. Upon Lipsyte's arrival in South Florida, his instructions were to rent a car, drive to the convention center where the fight would take place, then seek out the nearest hospital, he recalled, "so I could follow Clay into intensive care." Once he'd accomplished those tasks, Lipsyte made his way to the 5th St. Gym to meet the young challenger.

He ascended the creaking set of steps right off the entryway, where an employee stopped him. It would cost fifty cents admission to watch Clay, who had not yet arrived for his morning workout. Just after Lipsyte identified himself as a member of the press, there was a commotion at the bottom of the stairs. "It was our four little friends," Lipsyte recalled. "Dressed alike in terrycloth cabana clothes. Once they heard Cassius wasn't there they went nuts, turned around and walked back down the stairs." Two large security guards started pushing them back up the stairs. Intrigued, Lipsyte was happy to be pushed right along with them into an empty dressing room. The guards locked the door, and there was Lipsyte, alone in this dank space with the Beatles.

Now on the second day of their beach vacation week, the Fab Four started looking at their watches and getting pissed off. "Where's that big mouth who's gonna lose?" Lennon asked. "Fuck it, let's go," Ringo grumbled. The young writer tried to lighten the mood by introducing himself, "Hi, I'm Robert Lipsyte with the *New York Times*, a very important person." Feigning amusement, Lennon replied, "Hi, I'm Ringo." On cue Starr answered back, "I'm George Harrison." He asked them who they thought would win. "Oh Sonny's gonna knock the wanker out," John replied, clearly unhappy that this nobody was keeping them waiting.

After about ten tense minutes the door burst open. Standing there, at six foot three, 200 pounds, towering over all of them, glowing in all his youthful, imposing glory, was Cassius Clay. "We all kind of gasped," said Lipsyte. "He was the most beautiful human being we'd ever seen." Clay leaned in with an inviting smile, "Hey Beatles, let's make some money!" Charmed by his cheeky invite, the Beatles' anger went away, and, now smiling themselves, they trotted out after him.

As soon as Clay and his guests climbed into the ring, the slapstick show started for photographers and reporters. Four Beatles to one Clay, he pretended to punch George with such ferocity that all of them collapsed like bowling pins. As smitten photographers snapped away, the Beatles formed a human pyramid. At one point Clay held Ringo in his arms like a rag doll, shouting, "You ain't as dumb as you look!" John, the one used to giving out jabs, not taking them, shot back, "No, but you are!" Nervous silence ensued before Clay chuckled and kept on: "When Liston reads about the Beatles visiting me, he'll get so mad, I'll knock him out in three!" A photo caption read: *Beatles Turn Out to be Clay Pigeons.*

To Lipsyte, it looked like the entire comedic romp between the Beatles and Clay was choreographed. After fifteen minutes of clowning around and shutters snapping, the Beatles couldn't wait to get out of Clay's lair. Away from the press, John seethed that Clay had made fools out of them. He blamed Harry Benson for setting them up, temporarily ending their chummy relationship. Clay didn't think much of the Beatles either. After the workout, he retired to his dressing room for a rubdown. There on the table, he waved Lipsyte over to speak privately. "He whispers, puts his mouth against my ear," Lipsyte recalled. "'Who were those little f-----s?'" To be able to use the quote in the newspaper, Lipsyte substituted the word "Sissies."

The following Tuesday, with Buddy Dresner and his police force providing security, Cassius Clay stayed on the move, hitting flat-footed brawler Sonny Liston with jab after stinging jab until the champ's head was swollen and he'd had enough. When Liston failed to answer the bell for the seventh round, Clay raised his arms in triumph, knowing the World Heavyweight Boxing title belonged to him. The unlikely underdog, who had ascended to the top of professional boxing, shouted, "I shook up the world!" There were no trips to intensive care for the cocksure new champ. Things started to happen quickly soon after. In Clay's locker room, a group of well-dressed men in jackets and bow ties informed Dresner his security services were no longer needed. In typical Dresner fashion, now four weeks into the most exhausting month of his career, he deadpanned, "Fellas, he's all yours."

That night, at the Hampton House Motel in Liberty City, where Black performers, not allowed to stay on Miami Beach, found accom-

The Beatles clowning around with Cassius Clay, days before he defeated Sonny Liston to win his first World Heavyweight Boxing Championship. Photo by Express Newspapers via AP Images.

modations, Clay and Malcolm X met with the greatest football player alive, Jim Brown, and superstar Sam Cooke. In room 38, theirs was a historic power summit of young, successful cultural leaders ready to chart a new course for Black America. A film based on the historic summit, *One Night in Miami*, was released in 2020. To reporters at the postfight press conference the following morning, the subdued young champ declared, "I don't have to be what you want me to be . . . I'm free to be who I want." Lipsyte used that as the first line of his article the following day in the *New York Times*. He quoted reporters who asked Clay if he was "a card-carrying member of the Black Muslims?"

Outside his modest, single-story, aqua-colored home on NW Fifteenth Court, Clay was mobbed by locals who'd come to know him as the courteous neighbor who boxed with kids in the front yard and had movie nights out back. Standing nearby, bespectacled and overdressed, was his new friend and advisor, Malcolm X. At a packed diner in Liberty City, Clay, dressed in Nation of Islam garb, a suit, and bow tie, held court while an obviously pleased Malcolm X took his picture. Actually standing on the counter above them, to get a better view of the remarkable, historic scene unfolding, was photographer Bob Gomel, who'd been ringside to document Clay's stunning upset. At the time, Clay's unlikely victory and the Beatles coming to America seemed routine. "We didn't appreciate how iconic the 1960s would become," Gomel reflected.

Within days, Clay announced he wanted to be known as Muhammad Ali, a name given to him by Nation of Islam prophet Elijah Mohammad. Ali said he would no longer answer to his former "slave name." In a follow-up interview that week, Ali made it clear he would not be carrying signs and protesting for integration or equality. His new religion did not aspire to imitate and assimilate with white culture. To Lipsyte, Clay was still an innocent who didn't understand the ramifications of aligning himself with the movement; at the time he was merely parroting Nation of Islam dogma. Martin Luther King reacted by suggesting that the new heavyweight champion do less talking and more boxing. "When Cassius Clay joined the Black Muslims he became a champion of racial segregation," said King. "And that is what we are fighting against. I believe in neither black supremacy nor white supremacy. I believe in equality." Malcolm X chided King for urging followers to love white oppressors, who turned dogs and hoses on everyone during peaceful marches, women included. It was also here, while Ali lived just west of downtown Miami, that he became one of the first high-profile American athletes to speak out against the Vietnam War.

In Miami Beach, during that first visit stateside, John Lennon asked Buddy Dresner point-blank about Vietnam: "Why is the United States butting in?" John asked. Dresner rebuffed him, "John, why did we butt in when England was getting their ass whipped in two World Wars? If it wasn't for us, you'd still be walking with the Germans over there. We stick our neck in to save people's asses. Especially the British." Dresner echoed hawkish adults who'd served in Korea and World War II, and he bought into LBJ's pronouncements that US military involvement in Vietnam was necessary to halt the spread of communism in Asia.

In the wake of his decision to refuse induction into the US Army in 1967, Ali was stripped of his championship title and unable to fight. A judge sentenced him to five years in prison for draft evasion. Those who knew him said the times Ali was treated as a second-class citizen set him on a course to as much controversy as achievement. The "Fight Doctor" Ferdie Pacheco reflected, "Cassius Clay was born in Louisville, Kentucky, but Muhammad Ali was born in Miami."

12

Dinner with Uncle Harold

Since the early 1950s, children growing up in the cluster of single-story, concrete-block homes on Northeast 160th Street in Miami Beach felt free to come and go from each other's homes as they pleased. By 1964, the Dresners' eleven-year-old neighbor Debbie Nelson had long been friends with ten-year-old Andrea Dresner, nicknamed Andi, and her big sister, twelve-year-old Jeri. One February afternoon, when the phone rang at the Dresner home, the neighbor girl Debbie thought nothing of answering the phone herself. "A person in a British accent said, 'Who is this?'" Nelson recalled. "I said. 'This is Debbie. Who is this?' And he said, 'Paul McCartney.' I said, 'Paul McCartney of the Beatles?' And he said 'Yes, Paul McCartney of the Beatles.' I said, 'NO, you're kidding!' And at that point Buddy got on the line and said, 'Debbie, either say hello or pass the phone on.' So that's when I realized Buddy was with them."

The next day, the inquisitive neighbor girl was back at the Dresner home watching Dottie Dresner prepare for a formal dinner. For a middle-class family with no dining room, setting up card tables in the living room was as formal as they could get. Like a junior detective, she was starting to figure things out. She got with Andi and asked, "Who is coming to dinner?" Andi replied, "Uncle Harold." Not satisfied, Nelson pulled her young neighbor outside and asked again. This time Andi relented, "The Beatles. But if they come and there are people outside, they're just going to drive by." Thrilled by the news but cautious due Andi's warning, Debbie Nelson waited inside her home, watching for the arrival of the Dresners' famous dinner guests.

Not once since the Beatles landed in America had they had a chance to enjoy some semblance of a home-cooked meal with an average American family. After all the subterfuge surrounding the Beatles visit, Buddy had finally come clean with his children and told them where their dad had been for almost a week. It was time for the Beatles to meet and thank Dottie; time for the Dresner family, and a few lucky neighbors, to have an evening they'd never forget. The Beatles' thank-you gesture also meant a considerable amount of work for Dottie welcoming honored guests—and their sizable entourage—to her home. "She wasn't fazed," Buddy remembered. "She served roast beef, green beans, baked potato and strawberry shortcake. It was a dynamite meal."

Dottie pulled the kids out of school early. They'd settled on Uncle Harold as a ruse to keep their secret from getting out. Barry, who wasn't told who was coming to dinner, assumed it was some sort of Jewish holiday. He thought their extended family would be driving up from the south side of town, and he would have Jess, a cousin his age, to play with. A smaller card table had been set up at the end for the "kiddies." The Dresners had a maid, commonplace for middle-class families of the 1950s and 1960s, who helped with cleaning and cooking. What meal could be more all-American than roast beef and potatoes? Andi and Jeri put on dresses, and Barry a short-sleeved shirt and tie. Thinking his young cousin would soon arrive, Barry watched at the front door for their guests. Having cracked the mystery of who was really coming to dinner, neighbor Debbie Nelson pulsed with excitement, keeping watch from her home.

Late that afternoon, when a limousine and other cars pulled up, Barry shouted, "They're here!" He watched as one man after another he didn't recognize walked up toward him. From Barry's diminutive perspective, at waist-level, he shook hands with each, waiting for cousin Jess to arrive. That never happened; the only person Barry recognized was the last; his father, still wearing his police uniform. Barry recalled his moment of clarity: "Wait a minute," I thought, "This isn't a Jewish holiday. And the Beatles are in my living room." Buddy didn't need to introduce his two daughters, standing there thunderstruck to see John, Paul, George, and Ringo, all of them, right there in the living room. It's as if they had sprung from the TV like magic, and now here there they were, big as life. Buddy had felt especially guilty keeping his secret from twelve-year-old Jeri. "Kind of the biggest betrayal in the history of teenaged girls," Barry joked. His parents thought telling the children would only make Buddy's job harder, and their home potentially besieged by curious fans.

The evening started with cocktail hour. Trusted British press were allowed to memorialize the Beatles' first family dinner in America; special in the sense that they were able to have a glimpse of what life was like in suburbia. Dezo Hoffman was moved by what he was witnessing. "It was a simple, down-to-earth occasion," Hoffman wrote. "For them, it was like being with their own families. The day was not only relaxing, but also educational, because this was a real American family with all the little differences. It gave them their first insight into the way of life of ordinary Americans." Given the boys' endless intellectual curiosity, there was plenty to learn.

Jeri kept telling herself, "Don't say anything stupid." It was almost impossible as the cute one, Paul, came up, introduced himself, and asked about her life. All of them were so approachable and friendly. Images captured that night depict the Dresner children surrounding Paul, who is showing them photos from the *Beatles Monthly Book*, a British fanzine published since August 1963, when their popularity took off in England. The photographer for that publication, also enjoying dinner at the Dresner home, was Leslie Bryce. It was Bryce, even more so than Hoffman, who gained closest Beatle access in their homes, the studio, and on the road; his images reflect that trusted intimacy. Featuring content often written by Beatle confidants like Mal Evans, Neil Aspinall, or Brian Epstein's loyal secretary with the cute, dimpled smile, Freda Kelly, each issue of the *Beatles Book* is a dispatch from the inner circle. A photo of the boys clowning around with Buddy at his home ended up on the cover of issue 9 in April 1964.

It would be understandable if Paul would rather use the time to kick back, relax, and enjoy a stiff drink or two. These charming images show the children, transfixed that Paul McCartney himself is showing them a Beatles picture book. He, in turn, is patiently pointing out each photograph and reading from the captions. "Paul was always like the pied piper to children," Hoffman wrote. "He was a complete slave to them." In another photo, Paul and the Dresner children are seated, while Buddy and Dottie, together finally, stand above them by the window, smiling. John, too, extended kindness to young Barry, by letting him try on his Beatles boots and jacket.

At dinner, all the way down at the kiddie table, Ringo was seated next to Barry, and Jeri next to George. While trying to serve him a baked potato, the awkward utensil was making things difficult. "I dropped it right in George Harrison's lap," said Jeri, her voice still reflecting a preteen girl's shattering embarrassment. "That's one of those heart scars I don't think you ever get rid of." George just laughed it off so Jeri wouldn't feel bad. Ringo obliged Dottie's request to help Barry cut his potato: two strokes across and one down the middle, which made it open up like a flower. Barry gawked at his new friend's rings, festooned with showy stones. "Are those real?" Barry asked. "Yes, but don't tell anybody," Ringo joked. Toward the head of the table, Lennon and McCartney fueled the jocular dinner conversation nonstop.

As the evening went on, there came a knock on the door. Debbie Nelson, who had stayed away until the famous visitors were well into their evening, was hopeful for an introduction or, at the very least, a closer look. Still in the glow of the evening, Buddy cheerfully allowed Debbie, and other starstruck neighbors, to walk past the dinner table, single file and no screaming, to shake hands with the Beatles. Having kept the secret for twenty-four excruciating hours, Debbie Nelson was finally rewarded; she was invited to stay for dessert. "I wish I was older because I would have been able to sit there and do something other than just stare," she recalled. "Here are the Beatles everyone screams about and I'm sitting in a room with them."

The highly rated *Sullivan* appearances ensured that the Beatles had built on the success of their first American No. 1 single. The wave of popularity in America would only get bigger. Dinner at the Dresners was but a brief layover on their eventual march to immortality in America. Said Jeri, "It was just a very relaxing, typical family dinner at my house. The Beatles were superfriendly, supertalkative. Before they

The Beatles and staff at Buddy Dresner's Miami Beach home.
Courtesy of the author.

became who they became. Not snobby. I think they were very appreciative of the role my father played with them. Protecting them."

After strawberry shortcake, the Beatles thanked Dottie for all she was doing while her husband was working with them on South Beach. "They kissed my Mom, and it just kind of patched things up between my Mom and Dad," said Barry. Photographs from that evening commemorate the special bond that had developed between the Beatles, their bodyguard, and his family; genuinely warm smiles, even from dour PR man Brian Sommerville, whose off hours were as minimal as Buddy's. Without Dresner always around, plying his local contacts and being so conscientious about his mission, managing this travelling circus would have fallen to Sommerville and longtime Beatle mate, Neil

Aspinall. "Both Neil and I can never thank you enough for the holiday you gave us, by handling everything so well," Sommerville later wrote to Buddy. As soon as dinner was over, Buddy became tour guide once more. "Have any of you boys ever been to a drive-in movie?" he asked. After all, what could be a more quintessentially American evening, among everyday people, than dinner and a movie? Off they went in Buddy's cruiser, to the North Dade Drive-in off 171st Street.

The marquee would have caught the quartet's eyes immediately: now playing, Elvis Presley starring in *Fun in Acapulco*. While this period of Elvis's career is widely viewed as a low point, his influence on the Beatles was, nevertheless, profound. During bitterly cold nights growing up in Liverpool, John remembered curling up to sleep listening to Elvis via Radio Luxembourg. His family didn't have hot water bottles; to insulate themselves from the cold, they bedded down with a brick, heated in the fireplace. Young John, buried deep under the covers, was alone in the night with the stirring voice of the new King of Rock and Roll. "Elvis was bigger than religion in my life," John remembered. "When I heard 'Heartbreak Hotel' it was so great I couldn't speak." And now his own band was on their way to conquering America, watching the one-time King of Rock and Roll, Lennon's avatar, in one of his many, forgettable, B movies.

After he got out of the army in 1960, Presley traveled to Miami to co-star in a welcome home Frank Sinatra television special filmed at the Fontainebleau Hotel. In the new decade, Presley's manager, tone-deaf huckster Tom Parker, wanted to soften his image to make him palatable to adults. In the Sinatra special, Presley, in a tux with curly hair piled on top of his head, snaps his fingers like Mack the Knife. His considerable talent and charisma notwithstanding, it's difficult to watch him sing such bland songs as "Stuck on You." Presley set off the first tsunami of youth culture in post–World War II America with music geared toward teens, not their parents. No artist came close to matching that level of success—until these lads from Liverpool came along. In the drive-in film, Elvis sings a vapid song about having no room to rhumba in a sports car. This also informed the Beatles about what they were determined *not* to let their careers become.

The boys were having a great time marveling at the drive-in speaker you took from a post and hung inside your car window. Before long, thanks to tag-along Murray the K trying to attract attention, kids walking to the snack bar got a glimpse of Buddy and the Beatles parked in a row just like anyone else. "You started to see them crowding around the car," said Dresner, which was always his signal, no matter how long they'd been somewhere, to haul ass. It wouldn't be long before those same kids on the way to and from the snack bar would be watching the Beatles' own movie at the drive-in.

In a matter of a few hours that night, the Beatles made indelible memories for everyone who'd come in contact with them. Even Dezo Hoffman, who claimed to have taken more photos of the Beatles than anyone else, marveled at this innocent and relatively carefree period of their ascent to superstardom. "Sometimes my adventures with the Beatles in those early days, seem like an amazing once-upon-a-time fairy tale," Hoffman reflected. "I wonder if it all really happened?" Many of those who witnessed the Beatles' first visit to America still ask themselves the same question. This initial trip stateside, and final stop in Florida, proved to be the only chance the Beatles had to slow down and make genuine connections with ordinary Americans. By contrast, their first American tour later that summer came at warp speed, maximum volume, and with over-the-top hysteria.

13

You Can't Do That

During their Miami Beach residency, the Beatles' main songwriters could not take a break from the pressure to produce new songs. "Paul and I enjoyed writing the music for the [*Hard Day's Night*] film, but we honestly thought we'd never get time to write all the material," John Lennon recalled. For that reason, Lennon confirmed, their final days in Florida during this stateside visit were, indeed, a working holiday: "We managed to get a couple finished while we were in Paris, and three more soaking up sun on Miami Beach."

George confirmed one of those songs was John's "You Can't Do That," his bluesy rocker containing lyrical foreshadowing: *I'm gonna let you down, and leave you flat.* Four years later, at the culmination of what Cynthia Lennon called Yoko Ono's "determined pursuit" of her husband, Cynthia and John's decade-long relationship ended in divorce. To be sure, there are photos of them smiling and happy together in America. Cynthia's presence, however, during the Beatles' first American visit, was also a source of consternation to John. In New York, he scolded her for being too "bloody slow" and getting left out of their car in a mad rush of fans. In their fanzine, *Beatles Book Monthly,* writers noted a "nasty moment" for John when his wife showed off outstanding water-skiing prowess before falling into the water. "I thought she was going to show me up," commented her always-competitive husband.

Given the tight time frame between the Beatles' return from the US and when they entered the studio to record the week following, another song likely completed in Miami Beach is the ballad "If I Fell." John wrote the lyrics on the back of a Valentine's Day card, which would correspond to the time period the Beatles were in Florida. When those handwritten lyrics came up for auction years later, it was revealed that John wrote them on an airplane. If that scenario played out, then Cynthia was sitting next to him. What is, arguably, the best early Beatle love ballad is not addressed to Cynthia. In a telling twist, the song John later described as "semi-autobiographical" is sung to someone with whom he is contemplating an affair: *So I hope you see, that I, would love to love you and that she, will cry, when she learns we are two.* Several moody, introspective numbers by John, including "I'll Be Back" and "I'll Cry Instead," are candidates for the third Beatles song composed in Miami Beach, attributed to Lennon and McCartney.

So it went for Cynthia, who always kept a low profile; staying to the rear of Don Aronow's racing boat when the boys went for a joyride; as out of sight as possible on the Castro yacht, and the endless photo shoots, nights out on the town, the *Sullivan Show* rehearsals and live broadcast. This was Cynthia's nature: lovely and demure, willing to cede all of the notoriety to John and the other Beatles. Despite her best efforts, at times she was simply in the way. Miami Beach was crawling with available, eager young women, but John also stayed low-key, assuming the role of dutiful-if-withdrawn husband; he and Cynthia making daily long-distance phone calls to England to check on their ten-month-old son, Julian. For the Beatles' shoot-from-the-hip blunt, emotionally edgy leader, domesticity on the road with Cynthia had to be akin to wearing a straitjacket. He revealed his true self in his lyrics. After all, this is the same John Lennon who went on a two-week drinking holiday to Spain with Brian Epstein, just days after Julian was born. "I wasn't going to miss a holiday for a baby," Lennon recalled. "What a bastard I was."

Paul McCartney, on the other hand, used his well of endless charm to zealously pursue young women. He made no secret about his openness to having sexual encounters, all part of the spoils of success. In many cases, of course, women pursued him. "We felt like trawlers, trawling for sex. Everywhere we went it was on our minds," McCartney said. "They were throwing themselves at you, nothing more and nothing less, and this was very pleasing. I was a young bachelor, I didn't feel ashamed of it. I felt good about it. It felt natural." Cynthia Lennon once referred to Paul as "the town bull," in reference to his willingness to please the ladies. In recent years, McCartney has been candid about the band's frequent assignations with prostitutes.

In Miami Beach, he had a convertible red MG roadster at his disposal to facilitate his escapades. The only issue, he lamented, was the car's size, which made it tough to squire around more than one woman at a time. The warm nights, sun and sand, lovely palm trees and girls, girls, girls, gave McCartney pause to reconsider lyrics to *his* new song, "Can't Buy Me Love," most of which he'd written during their January stay at the Hotel George V in Paris. "You kidding?" he said, "It should have been, '*Can* Buy Me Love.'" There was a girl in a polka dot bikini who gained immediate access to him during their Miami stay. Another young woman named Lucy reportedly slipped past Dresner and his men hidden on a room service food cart. A biographer reported that McCartney ended up drinking champagne in bed with both women in his Deauville Hotel love nest overlooking the Atlantic Ocean. In the never-ending rivalry between Lennon and McCartney, it was as if Paul was flaunting his women to John, always tied down with his devoted wife.

Symbolically, at the very least, this dynamic was the yin and yang behind one of Lennon and McCartney's megahits from that magical spring of 1964. McCartney's "Can't Buy Me Love" as the A-side, and on the B-side, John's rollicking, confrontational Miami Beach homage to Wilson Pickett, "You Can't Do That," perhaps motivated by all the things he himself could not do with his wife always around. Richard Lester later filmed the Beatles performing John's song during the famous concert sequences for *A Hard Day's Night*, but it was not included in the final cut of the film. "Can't Buy Me Love," on the other hand, became a quick-cut, breathless montage showpiece in the film, a video primer two decades before MTV.

Given all the demands of worldwide stardom, the Beatles, nonetheless, kept their juices flowing and the hits coming. Much of it had to do with competition between Lennon and McCartney to see who could write the better, more successful singles. To show how quickly these songs were turned into records, the Beatles took "You Can't Do That" into the studio the week after Lennon wrote it, and on February 25 recorded it as part of a spate of new material for *A Hard Day's Night*. In less than three more weeks, the B-side song was out in the US with the A-Side, "Can't Buy Me Love," spending five weeks at number one.

Part of Buddy Dresner's job was vetting and facilitating Beatle dates without drawing widespread attention. He did the best he could to limit the number of women allowed in the Beatles' rooms, and those who did get in for any extended period of time absolutely had to be of age. As long as consenting adults were involved, the rest was none of his concern. Not long after they arrived, Paul and George approached Dresner with a very personal problem: an accommodating young actress from New York, they suspected, had given them both pubic lice. Could he help them? "I called downstairs and asked if they had Cuprex, which I used in the navy," Dresner remembered. He instructed the two where to apply the "personal insecticide." Then he told them to take turns standing in the shower, running water as hot as they could stand it until both were satisfied the Cuprex had worked. Anyone surprised by this revelation need only read about the boys' Bacchanalian adventures during their unhinged Hamburg days. They had no intention of stopping in America—quite the contrary, as Paul readily admitted.

George, the Beatle to whom Buddy grew closest as his security guard, roommate, fishing buddy, and father figure, only pissed him off one time—the night he violated Buddy's rigid curfew. In a move that would be impossible during frenetic Beatle tours to come, George asked for and was given permission by Buddy to take his loaner, candy-apple-red-with-white-stripe convertible Plymouth Fury on a nighttime drive along South Beach. "It was a hell of a car; George loved it," Dresner recalled. George invited a trusted member of the inner circle, either PR man Derek Taylor or recording guru George Martin, to go with him. "Here's what you do, go up Collins Avenue as far as you want to go, start at Sixty-Seventh Avenue, go down by the water. Just don't speed," Dresner admonished the youngest Beatle. "I want you home by 11:00." "Oh ya, thanks Bud," George replied, in full-cooperation mode.

With that, George disappeared into the South Beach night. When 11:00 p.m. came, the youngest Beatle had not returned . . . then midnight, and then 1:00 a.m. By that time, Dresner was thinking the worst had happened, "I'm in big trouble. Then, finally, the lobby door opens, and George comes strolling in. I chewed him out: 'You son of a bitch. I don't have enough gray hair?'" In his typical low-key demeanor, George replied, "Let me explain." Harrison detailed how he and his travel companion were driving up Collins Avenue, obviously thrilled to have the opportunity for such a warm, glorious experience while back home in England it was the dead of winter. Around Golden Beach, where Collins Avenue becomes Highway A1A, the friends were driving along with their arms around each other's shoulders. Recognizing two men in a public display of affection, police likely pulled them over, Dresner concluded, on suspicion of being homosexuals.

This was still the American South, long before South Beach became a safe haven for gays, lesbians, and transgender people. In 1964, the LGBTQ community still faced harassment and arrest if they dared set foot out of the closet and show public affection. The Beatles knew their manager Brian Epstein was gay; he had told them, and they displayed acceptance that was well ahead of their time. Still, Epstein was tormented by the possibility that he, too, could face public humiliation if caught engaging in the kind of rough trade encounters he was known to seek out. Once Harrison informed the police of who they were and what they were doing, they dropped the investigation and insisted on getting autographs and photos for their kids. That, Harrison explained to his highly relieved bodyguard, is what took so much extra time and forced him to break curfew. The episode serves as a reminder of the endless stress Buddy Dresner faced, sequestered with some of the world's most sought-after musician-celebrities, earning three dollars an hour.

Another time it was John Lennon coming to Buddy with an urgent request: "Look you've got to help me with Cynthia, she feels like she's a prisoner. Would you get her a wig and makeup?" Ever the problem-solver, Dresner employed Ruth Regina to disguise Cynthia so she could venture out for a bit of shopping with George Martin's wife, Judy. Sweet freedom for Cynthia meant slipping past the encamped fans downstairs to enjoy some shopping at a hotel boutique. Her anonymity also facilitated Cynthia's ability to eavesdrop on a couple of middle-aged, overweight fans in Bermuda shorts, caked-on makeup, and faux diamond sunglasses complaining about the Beatles: "Aren't they just too awful? All that hair! I don't know what the kids see in them. They look like something out of a zoo." Cynthia just smiled and slipped back toward the elevator to go upstairs. Because she still had on a disguise and carried no ID, the security guard didn't believe she was Mrs. Cynthia Lennon. "Yeah honey, they all try that one, now get lost," he said. As Cynthia was close to tears, a group of fans recognized her by her British accent and helped convince the guard she was telling the truth.

When Brian Epstein returned to England, he took with him the money from their *Sullivan Show* appearances. That meant for the rest of the Beatles' stay, it was up to Dresner to pay for outings he arranged. Dresner informed PR man Brian Sommerville he'd laid out forty dollars of his own money—no small amount on a policeman's salary—for which he'd not been reimbursed. The Beatles had come to America collectively broke but quite understandably assumed their management would take care of everything. That wasn't the case. By the time he departed the Deauville, McCartney's room 1219 bill, for instance, totaled $579.45. Eddie Liles, the Deauville's tall and gregarious maître d', said they ended up threatening to sue Epstein months later to recover payment for items charged by the Beatles and entourage to their hotel account, including the cabana clothes they're wearing in many of their famous Miami photos. "He loved the Beatles and he loved American money," Liles said of Epstein. "He did not like to part with either." Newspaper articles in 1964 indicated the Beatles' bills, well into thousands of dollars, were finally settled in July of that year to fend off pending legal action.

14

Stars on Star Island

The Fab Four kept the final days of their Florida residency as low-key as possible—shopping for souvenirs and records, fishing, and water-skiing. The silly photo op with Cassius Clay had been enough, and, God knows, they'd already generated enough publicity during this unforgettable trip stateside. Their schedule for the coming weeks was finalized: March through May in England, recording the soundtrack for *Hard Day's Night,* then shooting it. Upon completion of filming, in early June, a world tour starting in Copenhagen, Denmark; the Netherlands; Australia; and New Zealand. After that, Brian Epstein was still devising how to milk the massive cash cow the Beatles' first North American tour was sure to be.

At night, the Beatles ventured out as far as Buddy would allow, visiting clubs and young women they'd met during their stay. Paul reconnected with Diane Levine and accepted a dinner invitation at her home. Dresner, who was always looking to provide inexpensive fun and privacy for the boys, called up a friend on the police force, Malachi Garvey, who, like Dresner, had a jovial personality and was happy to welcome the Beatles to the beautiful home at 2 Star Island he shared with wife, Betty. The Garveys' home became the epicenter of fun and relaxation just beyond the lone bridge that took motorists on and off the picturesque residential island. In later years, original homes were torn down to make way for mansions of the rich and famous: Gloria

Estefan, Shaquille O'Neal, Sean Combs, and Rosie O'Donnell. To get the Beatles there with less hassle, Dresner devised a clandestine transport method.

"I need your truck. I'll be responsible," Dresner assured a friend, "but I want it empty." Wearing a hat and white jacket that said "Ace Parcel Delivery," he backed a box truck into the Deauville's loading dock. Out came three laundry carts with the Beatles and Cynthia Lennon hidden under piles of clothing. Dresner's passengers chided him about their uncomfortable ride to Star Island disguised as dirty laundry. With nothing to hold onto in the back of the truck, when Dresner jerked the wheel sharply to the left and right, the carts slammed into each other. Upon hearing his young charges swearing from the impact, Buddy joked, "You say something bad, this is what happens!" At a stoplight, a guy he knew did a double take at the sight of Buddy driving a truck.

"What the hell are you doing in there?" his friend asked. "I'm working part-time," he smiled.

When Dresner pulled the truck into the Garveys' driveway, his passengers, still battered from the drive, let their amused chauffer know about it. The Garveys' fishing dock was visible to anyone on the bridge to the island, but far enough away to be inaccessible. There are images of Buddy smiling at George while the two are fishing; Ringo was captured peeling apart wet dollar bills after accidentally taking a spill into the water. Buddy could also monitor how many curious onlookers were gathering on the bridge. A time or two, when the Beatles were boating, people actually jumped in the water to try to get to them and had to be fished out. The Beatles took reams of photographs themselves, but it's unclear how many ended up being developed. Once in a while, a photo of gregarious and fun-loving Mal Garvey with the Beatles surfaces online. Decades later, Betty Garvey's obituary mentioned that she had hosted the Beatles at her home. The lack of reportage on the Beatles' stay there is thanks to the Garveys' commitment to giving their star guests the privacy and space they needed.

During one of the Beatles' early romps in the ocean, Ringo became friendly with two local girls, Carol Olesky and Barbara Turchin. According to Turchin, Ringo came to dinner at her house, arriving via Buddy's box truck. Ringo savored another chance to have dinner in

America with an everyday family—another taste of normalcy. Unlike the Dresners, where Ringo was relegated to the kiddie table, at Barbara's house he played piano and entertained Turchin's family. Her grandmother called him "Hugo" and, not believing his mop-top was real, gave it a tug. Years later, during a bawdy interview with Howard Stern, Ringo claimed Florida had been "the best place" to take advantage of his newfound fame and enjoy the company of beautiful young women.

The Beatles granted a few radio interviews with disc jockeys from Detroit, Springfield, and a farewell interview with Jack Milman of WQAM in Miami. "I'd like to thank all the police," said Paul, "but especially Sgt. Buddy Dresner, who took us up to his house for a meal. One of the biggest meals I've ever eaten. But a wonderful one. And his kids." John singled out the University of Miami students who gave them the plaque making them honorary Greeks: "Making us a member of the fraternity. Sorry we didn't get a chance to ski with you." Before it was over, all four thanked the hotel staff, Morris Lansburgh, the ever-present fans out on the beach, Ed Sullivan, and Capitol Records.

The Maysles' documentary footage captured the Beatles packing up for the Friday flight to New York, then home to London. Knowing how much extra work Buddy had put into also keeping Cynthia safe and entertained, John embraced him and shook his hand. "Thank you so much, you're a gentleman," he told Buddy. The other Beatles had nothing appropriate to offer him as a token of their appreciation given all the sacrifices they were aware the entire Dresner family had made. Paul gifted him his electric razor, and George promised to send some British shirts Buddy admired. In the documentary footage, while they're packing, Paul can be seen holding Don Spence's abstract, inkblot artwork. Finally seeing what he thought could be a memorable souvenir, Buddy asked if he could have it. They all agreed and autographed it. Throughout his time guarding the Beatles, always the professional, Buddy had never taken their picture or asked for an autograph until this moment. On a whim, Don Spence's artwork turned out to be Buddy Dresner's most prized souvenir of his service to the Beatles.

John and Paul included Don Rickles's nightclub zinger from the week previous, "get a job cop," in their autographs. Additionally, John signed off as "the married one." George called him "Uncle Boody,"

The Dresner family collection of Beatle memorabilia, featuring Don Spence's inkblot artwork, in the Hard Rock Vault. Courtesy of the author.

thanking him for the home-cooked dinner and putting Dottie to so much trouble. Ringo's was the only pro forma "Best Wishes" autograph. All four picked up on the symbolism and signed next to the appropriate inkblot. John even put an arrow pointing to his—the solo blot on the right. The Spences' big dreams of licensing to the Beatles what one newspaper writer nicknamed the "Beatleful Abstract" never materialized. Still, the twins managed to meet them at the Deauville on the day they performed live on *Ed Sullivan*, something they could look back on and treasure.

One afternoon, in the early 2000s, Doug Spence and his wife, Marlene, were eating lunch at the Hard Rock Café in Orlando. On their way out, Marlene did a double take at something on the wall and asked her husband, "Isn't that your Beatles art?" Somehow, there at the Hard

Rock, was Don's inkblot piece, framed, and autographed by all of the Beatles. But how? Thunderstruck to see the piece emerge after so long, with no idea how it got there, the couple went home and told Don and Peggy the news. "Talk about the thrill of a lifetime," said Peggy. "Don and I drove over and stood in front of the abstract and had our picture taken with our Beatle T-shirts on." Somehow, Don's whimsical art had found a home in the expansive Hard Rock collection. "We were just beside ourselves," Don said. "We couldn't get home soon enough to celebrate." Don didn't find out the full story of how it got there until 2019, when he was eighty-five years old.

For years after the Beatles gifted it to Buddy, the abstract remained on the sun porch of the Dresner home on 160th Street, all but forgotten. It had gotten water-stained thanks to a ceiling leak. When Dottie was sick with cancer in the 1980s, the family sold it at auction, along with photos and thank-you letters the Beatles and their management had written to them. The memorabilia didn't come close to generating the kind of payday it would today, but it did help pay the medical bills. Daughter Jeri had an alternate explanation: Buddy sold the collection to pay for his children's college education. When the Spences found out that was how Hard Rock came to own Don's art, they were okay with it, whatever the explanation.

Another Dresner family keepsake sold to Hard Rock is Paul's four-page thank-you letter to Buddy. Displaying warmth and sincerity, there's also sense of foreboding about difficult times to come. McCartney wrote it after the Beatles' eight-day tour of New Zealand in late June 1964 on stationery from the Hotel St. George in Wellington. "I hope you, your wife and the kids are all ok—give them my love." McCartney wrote. "We'll be out in America soon, that is, if they don't start a war or something. For instance, all this business in Viet Nam. If we're anywhere near you, come along won't you? Yes, you will! Good. See you, Paul, Zaap!"

Brian Sommerville, who would have been saddled with making other arrangements for the Beatles' post-*Sullivan* security had Buddy not agreed to stay on, wrote an effusive thank-you letter to Miami Beach Police Chief Rocky Pomerance. On Deauville Hotel stationery dated February 20, 1964, Sommerville wrote: "We cannot speak too highly of the way our comfort and security has been taken care of by

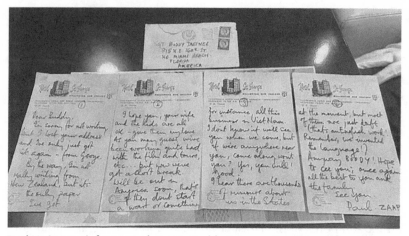

Paul McCartney's four-page letter to Buddy Dresner. Courtesy of the author.

Sergeant Buddy Dresner. He has been a real friend to the boys and their management, advisor and father-confessor and a darned good policeman to boot . . . [A]lthough occasionally he had to be strict with us, our welfare and security have always been his main concern." Sommerville said his letter had come at the Beatles' insistence.

By way of the historic *Sullivan* shows and their extended Florida residency, the Beatles achieved fever-dream-level success in America. Pollinated by a healthy buzz of publicity, by late February, they had sold six million records worldwide, including more than two million copies of "I Want to Hold Your Hand" in the US. Sales of the Beatles debut album, at a time when kids generally concentrated on collecting singles, eclipsed one million in the US. Within a month of their first visit stateside, the Beatles were the undisputed kings of the *Billboard* charts. In February 1964 financial analysts forecasted the sale of merchandise and all Beatlemania-related items to hit a staggering $50 million. In time, that fact became one of the Beatles' biggest frustrations with their wunderkind manager.

Prior to the group's unprecedented success in America, Brian Epstein had entrusted supervision of merchandising requests to his attorney, David Jacobs. Jacobs reached out to a bon vivant named Nicky Byrne, who formed the company Saltaeb—"Beatles" spelled backward—to make marketing deals on the group's behalf. Inexplicably, Epstein signed off on the deal Jacobs presented, which gave away to their new subcontractor Saltaeb 90 percent of Beatle marketing revenues, a colossal blunder that cost the Beatles tens of millions of dollars. Outside Saltaeb's Fifth Avenue offices in New York, Jacobs witnessed the ugly truth: people lining up to pay a one-time twenty-five-thousand-dollar franchising fee to license any number of Beatle-related products—shirts, dolls, wigs, dresses, lunch boxes. Scores of franchises were sold, and to Epstein and his lawyer's despair, they received a pittance of the proceeds, while nouveau riche Nicky Byrne was already living like a king. Epstein sued, becoming embroiled in a three-year court battle. All the chaos explains why the marketing deal Epstein promised to the Spence brothers never came to pass.

After all the excitement of taking care of the Beatles, then working Cassius Clay's stunning upset of Sonny Liston the next week, Buddy Dresner finally went back to the police beat. For a time, the family retained residual fame locally due to their close ties with the Beatles. "My dad had a fan club," Barry Dresner recalled. He has vivid recollections of a teenaged girl who asked for a tour of the Dresner home, "sitting on the toilet screaming" because the Beatles had used it. The first year or two, to mark the anniversary of the Beatles' visit, local radio stations would call the Dresners and put them on the air to reminisce. One time all three kids were on with Rick Shaw, though they were all sick in bed with the flu. Buddy finally got off the night shift and was promoted. Later, when other rock stars came to Miami Beach—Bob Dylan, Herman's Hermits, the Monkees—Dresner was his department's go-to security guy.

On yet another celebrity detail on September 12, 1970, Lieutenant Dresner was alone in a hotel room, sitting across a table from Elvis Presley. After a musical hiatus through much of the 1960s, Presley stormed back in 1968 with his acclaimed NBC comeback special. He topped the US charts the following year with the single "Suspicious Minds." In 1970, the hits were still coming. Presley looked great and was finally back out doing what he loved most, performing. Never one to be intimidated by celebrity or fame, Dresner struck up a conversation. "I saw some of your movies," Dresner told Presley, who immediately shook his head.

"Mr. Wallace wanted to make them as fast as they could," said Presley, of producer Hal Wallace. Even though he was not always proud of his acting, the assembly-line B movies had made Presley a fortune without all the rigors of touring. But by this time his acting days were behind him, and Presley was back on the road where he belonged, performing for his adoring fans. Dresner replied, "I took care of the Beatles and took them to see one of your movies at the drive in. I can't remember which one, but you sang." Presley just smiled.

Buddy Dresner, the cop, confidant, friend, father figure, bodyguard, the constant, had been there for a who's who of twentieth-century icons: JFK, the Beatles, Cassius Clay, Dylan, and, now, Elvis. Dresner was a guy you could talk to, a guy you could trust. When the Beatles wanted to see what America was really like—to cruise the streets of Miami Beach, to have some discreet, adult fun; to go clubbing, boating, to chill out in waterfront mansions, to pose for all the iconic images in the runup to the *Sullivan Show* and after—Buddy made it all happen with aplomb. He had carried an enormous burden and sacrificed his own family time. No one during the Beatles' first visit to America got to know them as well as he did. He came to care for them, and they for him, their good mate "Boody." After nine days during which Buddy and the Beatles were inseparable, on Friday February 21, 1964, the Fab Four parted ways with him as friends.

Through the years, as the Beatle mystique grew, Dresner participated in numerous retrospective articles including *Rolling Stone*'s 1984, twenty-year commemorative issue of the Beatles' first trip stateside. Louis "Buddy" Dresner, husband, father, and beloved grandfather, died on September 27, 2002, at seventy-six years of age. His time spent guarding the Beatles was noted in his obituary.

Weeks later, a signed sympathy card to the Dresners arrived in the mail from Paul McCartney: "He was a lovely man; full of humor, and a big generous heart. I very much enjoyed the moments I spent with him, particularly our visit to your house . . . warm regards, Paul."

In February 1964, none of the Beatles, not even their cocksure leader John Lennon, could have dared to imagine how successful their first visit stateside would be. One man, however, had sensed all of it, every bit of the success now coming to pass. From the first time he saw the Beatles in the dank confines of the Cavern Club, Brian Epstein predicted they would eclipse Elvis's popularity. During the spring of 1964, any doubts about that seemingly foolhardy prediction were gone. "In America, it seemed every American wanted them," Epstein reflected. "It was marvelously exciting, but the strain was immense." Brian Epstein had made mistakes along the way, but no one could doubt that the success of this historic trip was due to his vision and effort.

15

Dreams within Reach

In no time, the flash bomb effect of the Beatles' *Ed Sullivan* appearances manifested itself throughout America. On its release date, March 16, 1964, the Beatles' new single "Can't Buy Me Love," with John's acerbic B-side, "You Can't Do That," rocketed to number one, selling 940,225 copies, breaking all records. On April 4, 1964, the Beatles held all top-five spots on the *Billboard* charts, and fourteen of their songs placed in the top 100. *Meet the Beatles* was the first Beatles album on Capitol to go to number one in the States. Vee-Jay's earlier offering, "Introducing the Beatles," piggy-backed at number two. Fifteen of their records, singles and albums, went platinum that year. In 1964, the Beatles sold twenty-five million records in America. The boys from working-class Liverpool had claimed their own pinnacle of success.

Simultaneously, the Beatles' effect as cultural agents of change permeated youth culture. Girls danced to their music, formed fan clubs, bought Beatle dolls, dresses, lunch boxes, fan zines, and dreamed of dating them. Often in conflict with their parents and teachers, boys grew their hair longer, wore Beatle boots, bought guitars, started bands, and dreamed rock star dreams like never before. Besides Buddy Holly and the Crickets, whom the Beatles themselves emulated, never before had average American kids who didn't look and sound anything like Elvis start to think they could follow this path: form a collective, write and record their own rock songs, with a goal of musical self-determination.

The Beatles provided the template: bass, lead guitar, rhythm guitar, and drums. Teen dreamers didn't realize the convergence of talent, infrastructure, promotion, timing, chemistry, hard work, sacrifices, and serendipity that all fell the Beatles' way.

In Central and North Florida—Gainesville, particularly—a sizable group of young people followed the Beatles' recipe for success, all the way to the Rock and Roll Hall of Fame. "The Beatles were God's gift to guitar players," said Gainesville musicologist Marty Jourard, member of the 1980s hit-making band the Motels. Twentysomething *Gainesville Sun* columnist Jean Carver sided with Beatle bashers: "These barbershop refugees don't even sound like anything that would be remotely acceptable to the most primitive tribes in New Zealand." The motivation to achieve such dramatic heights was something one of the pioneers of country-infused rock, Bernie Leadon, called Gainesville's "cauldron of creativity." Leadon's father, a college professor, relocated his wife and nine children from San Diego to Gainesville in the summer of 1964. It was that blending of cultural and musical sensibilities between outsiders drawn to the University of Florida, and locals like Tom Petty, whose parents, Earl and Katharine "Kitty" Petty, were from the Deep South.

On the surface, there was nothing special at all about Petty, nothing to give the slightest inkling that one day he would become a superstar and his bands, all commercial successes, would go on to sell eighty million records. One day, as impossibly far-fetched as it would have sounded when Petty caught the bug in eighth grade, he would end up bandmates with a Beatle, George Harrison, aka Nelson Wilbury, in a beloved rock-and-roll supergroup, the Traveling Wilburys. His journey began just as soon as he saw them on *Ed Sullivan*.

"I think the whole world was watching that night," Petty recalled of their first *Sullivan Show* appearance. "Everything around you was changing. It was like going from black-and-white to color really. They came out and just flattened me . . . it was electrifying." Petty's musical interests changed just that quickly. "It changed him from being a solid Elvis fan. Then he got super, super interested in what was happening with the Beatles," Petty's childhood friend Keith Harben remembered.

Growing up in Jacksonville, Mike Campbell, the teen destined to become Petty's songwriting soulmate, said his lifelong obsession with music didn't come into full flower, until he, too, saw the Beatles via the *Sullivan Show*. "I saw them and I wanted a guitar," he reflected. "The Beatles showed up when people were ready for some medicine. Some soul medicine. After that, I played guitar from the time I came home from school until I went to bed." Though the two would not meet until the end of the decade, the Beatles and *Sullivan* put Petty and Campbell on the path to convergence and their own indelible impact on rock and roll.

A short time after *Sullivan*, at a teen dance at the American Legion Hall, the Beatles' influence could be seen and heard from the band playing. "They were pretty good," Petty said, "but what knocked me out was their hair—it was already long!" The Escorts, featuring two brothers from Daytona Beach Shores, Duane and Gregg Allman, were all dressed in Beatles-inspired collarless jackets. They had picked up on the transformative effect of the Beatles in sound and fashion, integrating both elements into their earliest live shows. Soon there was a competition among local garage bands to see who could best reproduce Beatles songs.

His passion to pursue music and songwriting now stoked, Petty bought his first guitar for twenty-five dollars and sought out lessons at the center of the music universe in Gainesville: Lipham Music—located at Tenth and Main Streets in the new Gainesville Shopping Plaza. Owner Buster Lipham would become beloved by a constellation of important musicians from a variety of genres. It's where Petty met a local teen named Don Felder, two years his senior, who taught him a few chords on the guitar. "I learned to play because I had to," Petty reflected. "I loved rock 'n' roll and I especially loved being in a band. I was fourteen years old and found a social structure that would sustain me." Petty had seen Felder play surf music at Teen Time with his band the Continentals, whose lineup included another future Rock and Roll Hall-of-Famer, an army brat named Stephen Stills. Felder experienced the similar revelatory effect of Beatlemania when he walked into a high school dance. "'I Want to Hold Your Hand' was blaring in the gymnasium," said Felder. "It was unbelievable. It was rocking, great vocals, and it just really lit me up."

The musician who would one day bring Felder to rock superstardom, Bernie Leadon, had already been in a several bluegrass groups in

Southern California. One of them, the Scottsville Squirrel Barkers, had even made an album. Leadon was a true folkie, strongly influenced by the songwriting and clean-cut showmanship of the Kingston Trio. He aspired to live the singer-songwriter lifestyle. "I decided I was gonna do that when I was thirteen," Leadon recalled. For folkies like Leadon, the Beatles represented a logical progression, playing electric music with a drummer. "Then they were on *Sullivan* and, wow, very dynamic group, very high energy. I got really excited about them," he said. That night, watching the Beatles, was the first time the musical Leadon family saw a band whose guitars were all electrified, not an acoustic in the bunch. It wasn't long before Leadon joined his first rock group, the Pink Panthers.

Leadon, who didn't have a radio of his own, sat in his father's car playing music and running down the battery. By that time the Beatles were so ubiquitous, you could hear them station-to-station every ten minutes or less. Unlike the Felders' house, the Leadon place had central air and a pool. Soon Don would come over to jam for hours in Bernie's bedroom. Leadon and Felder became experts at deconstructing Beatle song parts, lead and rhythm guitar, harmonies, and keyboards when necessary. Bernie's younger brother Tom, already an aspiring musician in his early teens, often sat listening to them, not saying much, but absorbing it all. After Tom started playing in his own bands, like the Epics, "we almost considered the Beatles to be like our gurus, they were the ones bringing the message." In that sense, they were all learning while they listened. From afar, George Harrison was teaching them all how to be rock-and-roll lead guitarists.

After the Beatles hit, like any other devotee, Tom Petty devoured their records, wanting to know what instruments they played and how songs were arranged. "You either had a copy of *Meet the Beatles* or you didn't," Petty remembered. "And if you didn't it was like there was something wrong with you." His ambition to be like the Beatles stoked, Petty formed his first band, the Sundowners, in his living room. Keith Harben's twin sister, Kathy Harben Arce, would urge her brother to help get her in to watch the Sundowners rehearse in a storage room of the Petty home at 1715 Northeast Sixth Terrace. She had a crush on lead guitarist Robert Crawford, who, like Tommy, was shy and reserved when not playing with the band. It became a running joke between

Teenaged Tom Petty plays bass and sings with his first music group, the Sundowners. Courtesy of Kathy Harben Acre.

them when Tommy would repeat to Kathy things Robert said. She would write them down on an ornate cigar box her father gave her. Once the boys were good enough to perform in public, Robert's mom helped outfit the Sundowners with matching pink, collarless jackets.

Tom Petty's road to stardom included early Sundowners gigs at the local Moose club and Howard Bishop Middle School, where he was in eighth grade. It was a bigger deal to load into someone's station wagon for an out-of-town gig at places like the lakeside pavilion at Keystone Beach. Finally, Tommy Petty had something that spurred serious interest, passion even; heaven knows it wasn't school. But Petty's love for music came with a price: all of the trappings of this new obsession increased tensions with his father, Earl Petty—a no-nonsense, bespectacled insurance man. The two got into violent arguments over Tommy growing his hair long. "One day Tommy skipped school and showed up later with a black eye," Kathy Harben Arce recalled. "He was real tense. So I put my hand on his shoulder and said, 'You can come live with us.'" Still embarrassed and upset, he pulled his shoulder away. To adhere to the standards of cool in his band, and in the hope of minimizing his father's wrath at home, Petty invested in a Beatle wig he could take off after gigs.

Bernie Leadon and Don Felder formed their own Beatles-inspired group and chose a name, the Maundy Quintet, because it sounded British. In no time, they were one of the hottest cover bands in town playing Gainesville beer bars, the local rec center, and lucrative fraternity parties on the University of Florida campus. During football season, frat houses hired bands like the Maundy Quintet, Ron and the Starfires, and the Outlaws for two hundred dollars a night. Two gigs a weekend netted each band member from eighty to one hundred dollars, often more than each would make working any normal teen job. Playing in a band could also help shy, nonathletic guys get girls. In that sense, there was nothing else like it.

To Leadon, the most inspiring aftershock of Beatlemania came in 1965, when a new group of Southern California folkies known as the Byrds, hit number one on the *Billboard* charts with an electrified cover of Bob Dylan's "Mr. Tambourine Man." They scored a second chart-topper with their folk-rock version of Pete Seeger's "Turn, Turn, Turn." To Leadon's profound surprise, the quiet young teenager on bass for the so-called "American Beatles" was Chris Hillman, his former Southern California bluegrass bandmate from the Scottsville Squirrel Barkers. "When Chris went to number one, it lit a fire under my butt," Leadon laughed. "The bass player from the Squirrel Barkers now has Beatle hair and is the bass player in the fucking Byrds!" Duly inspired, Leadon wrote and sung the Maundy Quintet's first original songs: "I'm Not Alone," and on the flipside "2's Better than 3," with harmonies so credible that either could have passed as a Byrds' B-side.

Tom Leadon had gotten good enough on guitar to play lead in a succession of Beatle cover bands including the Group, the Essex, and the Epics. It was through the latter Gainesville garage band that the musical trajectory of two notable Toms, Leadon and Petty, merged. After a rehearsal where the two had barely spoken, the next day Leadon walked to Petty's home just across the park from his and knocked on the front door. "I remember how nervous I was, thinking, the guy barely knows me," Leadon recalled. "He looked at me kind of puzzled, then recognized me and invited me in." Petty started playing records in his living room: the Everly Brothers, Little Richard, and Elvis. At this early stage of their on-again-off-again musical journey spanning a half century, Tom Leadon recalled, "Petty kept saying, 'This is where the Beatles got this.' He was really giving me a musical education. He was into the roots of rock and roll from the beginning."

The Epics learned to play Beatle songs like "And I Love Her," "Things We Said Today," and "Nowhere Man." From the outset, Tom Leadon was impressed with Petty's confidence playing bass and singing lead vocals. This was years before he started writing any of his own songs. "He just seemed to be at home onstage," said Leadon. "He was in charge. He looked cool." Every time a new Beatles album came out, the first order of business was to listen to the entire record a couple times, then figure out what songs they could deconstruct and perform. Like the bond Lennon formed with his younger friend Paul McCartney when they were still teenagers, Tom Petty and Tom Leadon grew inseparable through a mutual love of music. "He was the closest friend I ever had," Leadon said. "I never had a friend I was with constantly, like I was for few years with Tom."

During their journey to music stardom, Tom Petty, Don Felder, Bernie Leadon, and Bernie's brother Tom worked at Lipham Music; Bernie in the guitar and amp section, where would-be musicians flocked to the long rows of shiny, high-end guitars. The family store became a focal point of future rock-and-roll royalty because of Lipham's liberal policy of allowing musicians, some of whom were not yet out of high school, to sign promissory notes and walk out with some of the finest gear most teen musicians could only drool over. Bernie and Tom Leadon's father was not happy with an arrangement he didn't believe was legal. Then again, he couldn't argue with Buster Lipham's rationale that with better equipment, the youngsters got higher-paying gigs, were able to pay down their IOUs faster, and develop as musicians. As the 1960s progressed, Gainesville's impressive roster of would-be Rock and Roll Hall-of-Famers, all of them, were poised to live their own Beatle dreams of multiplatinum success and stardom, and none more so than Tom Petty. Once Gainesville had been "bitten very hard" by the British Invasion, Petty wrote, "bands were forming as fast and plentiful as spores on the swamp ferns."

From all over Florida—carports, clubs, farmhouses, and a certain, un-air-conditioned cabin nicknamed "Hell House"—came music that would define a generation. Another group of young musicians, still navigating their way out of hardscrabble childhoods, rented a rural patch of land in Green Cove Springs to practice without getting noise complaints. "After we heard the Beatles, that was it," declared guitarist Gary Rossington, who along with lead singer-songwriter and hellraiser Ronnie Van Zant, became obsessed with making a career in music. "We decided to start up a band like millions of people did." After going through an evolution of names like the Noble Five and the One-Percent, friends who grew up on the tough streets of West Jacksonville settled on the name Lynyrd Skynyrd; a tongue-and-cheek homage to their hard-assed gym teacher Leonard Skinner. Many Skynyrd classics were written during those sweltering days woodshedding in that little red hunting cabin with a fishing dock down along Peters Creek.

As a way to avoid being drafted and sent to Vietnam, Bernie Leadon joined the army reserve and was sent back to California. After completing his military obligations, Leadon seemed to be everywhere in the nascent movement soon to be known as country rock. In 1967, Leadon joined the country- and folk-infused band Hearts and Flowers. The next year he moved on to jam sessions with banjo virtuoso Doug Dillard, who'd fallen in with ex-Byrd and songwriting genius Gene Clark. Leadon provided backup vocals and guitar for the duo's critically acclaimed album *The Fantastic Expedition of Dillard and Clark*. Ready to take on a more prominent role, Leadon was invited to join his former Squirrel Barkers' bandmate Chris Hillman and another notable Floridian, Gram Parsons, in the archetypal, full-on country-rock band the Flying Burrito Brothers. Hillman and Parsons had departed the Byrds after recording one landmark album together, *Sweetheart of the Rodeo*; revered as the first country-rock album by a major rock act. As if all that wasn't enough, Leadon also played on and off in Linda Ronstadt's backup band. For Leadon and his guitar-playing partner in the Maundy Quintet, Don Felder, the 1970s would bring staggering success and music immortality as members of the Eagles. Tom Petty would follow closely behind.

Now graduated from Gainesville High, Petty spent only a year in college in St. Petersburg. After returning to Gainesville, he took odd jobs as a landscaper, food delivery driver, even a gravedigger. Like most free spirits, often referred to as hippies during that era, his hair grew down beyond his shoulders, and he often wore a mustache or goatee. When he stopped by the local tag office where his mother, Kitty, worked, just the sight of him worried friends. "He looked terrible. He was thin, unkempt," remembered neighbor and former classmate Kathy Harben Arce. "I asked my brother, 'Keith, do you think Tommy is on drugs?'"

Tensions at home over his appearance and lack of direction reached a boiling point between Petty and his father. One of their violent clashes was particularly disturbing: "Mr. Petty threatened and chased him out of the house with a gun," said Tom Leadon. "I've never seen Tom so frightened." Leadon, Petty, and Petty's girlfriend, Jane Benyo, drove across town to hide out in Westside Park for the rest of the night. Petty ended up living at Jane's mother's house for the next few months. Through difficult and, in this case, dangerous times at home, Petty still had his de facto family of bandmates and a dream to make it as a musician and songwriter. It was during this uncertain time that Petty found a new home and met his musical brother-in-arms.

In concerts many years later, Tom Petty liked to tell the story, in hilarious detail, of going to a sketchy farmhouse in Alachua County to audition drummer Randall Marsh. It was there that he met a skinny, bookish student who reluctantly joined their jam session with a cheap Japanese guitar Petty claimed cost exactly one dollar. "You could just see their disappointment," Mike Campbell recalled. Every bit of it went away as soon as Campbell ripped into "Johnny B. Goode." Soon the two were jamming for hours every day. Petty moved into that rural property on Northwest Forty-Fifth Avenue, at the end of a dirt driveway, known as "Mudcrutch Farm." It was 1970. Petty and Leadon joined up with Marsh and Campbell, and Jim Lenehan on vocals, in a new group aptly named Mudcrutch.

By the end of the new decade, Petty and Campbell were world-famous rock stars as Tom Petty and the Heartbreakers. Petty went on to multiplatinum success as a solo artist, and, on a lark, joined former Beatle George Harrison, Bob Dylan, Geoff Lynne, and the iconic singer they all admired, Roy Orbison, in a supergroup named the Traveling Wilburys. At the height of all that success, Petty took a dramatic and risky career U-turn, in 2007 deciding to reform Mudcrutch. He wanted to include old friends Tom Leadon and Randall Marsh. When he received Petty's phone call, driving home from the grocery store in

Nashville, Leadon was incredulous. It was like a dream; Tom Petty was calling to ask if he was interested in being bandmates again. At first, Leadon didn't even believe it was really *him*.

"I swear, I'm not kidding. It felt like a lightning bolt hit the top of my head and went down through my body and out through my shoes," Leadon recalled. "I said to Tom, 'Why'? Tom said, 'I just kind of feel like doing it.'" With that one decision from Petty, one act of generosity, and that fateful phone call, Tom Leadon's deferred dream of being a rock star himself would soon be fulfilled. The Mudcrutch reunion, Petty and Leadon side by side just like in their mid-1960s garage band days, spawned two hit studio albums and successful tours.

The Beatles sent a resounding message to aspiring musicians like Tom and Bernie Leadon, Don Felder, Tom Petty, Mike Campbell, Gary Rossington, and Ronnie Van Zant—so many Rock and Roll Hall-of-Famers with deep Florida roots. "They were the first people we could relate to who showed us that your dreams were within reach," said Petty. "That's what I found so liberating about seeing the Beatles."

In the spring and summer of 1964, the Beatles' first tour of North America provided them an opportunity to nurture the dreams of other up-and-coming musicians. The color of their skin, however, became an issue. The reality of race in America—the South in particular—inspired the Beatles to speak out against entrenched practices of segregation. In doing so, it was their first opportunity as activists to promote social and cultural change.

16

Seeds of Change

On the front and back of a rectangular folding postcard, Brian Epstein sketched out an early itinerary for the Beatles' epic 1964 summer tour of North America. Most of the locations he listed ended up on the Beatles' meandering cross-continent trek. In three southern cities he jotted down, however, 1964 Beatle concerts never happened: Montgomery, Alabama; Charlotte, North Carolina; and Houston, Texas. When finalized, Epstein's plan for the Beatles to play six southern dates had shrunk to just three: September 11 in Jacksonville, Florida; September 16 in New Orleans; and September 18 in Dallas. Three cities added later were Boston, Pittsburgh, and Kansas City. One obvious reason why only half the southern dates materialized can be traced to a single line from a rider in the contract that every promoter who wished to bring the Beatles to their city was compelled to sign.

On April 16, 1964, the day the Beatles recorded the title track for their third album and first feature film, *A Hard Day's Night*, broadcaster William Brennan signed on to bring the Beatles back to Florida. Brennan and his brothers ran a southern radio empire including WAPE-AM in Jacksonville. The Brennans also owned radio stations in Montgomery and Birmingham, Alabama. Bill Brennan was the Wall Street savvy business mind in the family, Cyril the engineering whiz, and youngest brother, Dan "the Music Man," educated and urbane, served as a reporter, station manager, and on-air talent for stations in both states. In a shrewd deal struck by Bill, the Beatles would be paid a flat fee of fifty thousand dollars in two twenty-five-thousand-dollar installments with no cut of the gate proceeds. The Beatles were dominating the singles charts like never before, exploding all across America. The Brennans were keen to seal listener loyalty by giving them a chance to see the Beatles live in concert.

On page one of the rider, a common type of contract addendum spelling out specific performer demands, the sixth clause written at the bottom of the page read: "Artists will not be required to perform before a segregated audience." Dan Brennan's daughter, Debbie Brennan-Bartoletti said, "There was no resistance from the family at all" to the sixth clause. Times were changing, and, from a practical standpoint, this was likely their single chance to stage a Beatles show. "They knew they'd never get them back for that money," she added. Just as they could not segregate fans who listened to their stations, the Brennans were intent to sell tickets to whomever wanted one, whatever their skin color.

In April, the silent stand taken in the tour contract signed by Brian Epstein on behalf of the Beatles for every stop on their first North American tour compelled promoters to align with the group's contractual requirement that the shows be integrated. It's more likely this clause originated with Epstein, the man who negotiated the contract, rather than with the Beatles themselves. Regardless, the effect of that one line was profound. In the segregated South, "that was taking a big risk," said Beatles scholar Anthony DeCurtis. "It would have been the easiest thing to gloss over it. To take a stand? That's impressive." Residents in Northeast Florida knew that most events at the city-owned Gator Bowl, where the Beatles were due to perform their first outdoor stadium show in the southeastern United States, had been segregated. There were a few exceptions. Throughout the South, organized sports had already started cracking the color barrier; in 1961 the city of Jacksonville hosted its first integrated Gator Bowl football game. The Brennans, cherished among fans for their sold-out "Shower of Stars" concerts in Alabama and Florida, were committed to staging the Beatles concert at the Gator Bowl. Other forces, however, having nothing to do with segregation, would put them through hell to do it.

By demanding that anyone must be allowed to sit anywhere, the Beatles did, however unwittingly, insert themselves into a simmering, violent, historic battle over racial equality focused in and around the nation's oldest city, St. Augustine, just forty miles south of Jacksonville. In a region of Florida firmly in the grasp of Jim Crow, that perilous undertaking required the help of Dr. Martin Luther King Jr. himself, destined to become America's most revered civil rights martyr. Advocating for civil rights became a little-known nexus between Dr. King and the Beatles that developed in Northeast Florida that spring and summer of 1964.

In previous years, King had been arrested in Albany, Georgia, and Birmingham, Alabama, for challenging local segregation laws in order to bring the struggle for racial equality into the national spotlight. As King found out in 1964, during his many travels throughout the Sunshine State, some Florida officials were more receptive than others. The outcome of his willingness to go to jail yet again in pursuit of racial equality helped pave the way for the Beatles' integration requirements.

In March, King and a delegation of local pastors met with Orlando mayor Bob Carr to discuss why desegregation efforts there had stalled. At the time, King was not yet a household name, but, like the Beatles, his star was rising fast. In a tip of the hat to his "I Have a Dream" speech from the summer of 1963 March on Washington, *Time* magazine named King "Man of the Year" the following January. In recognition of his growing influence, LBJ called King personally from the White House, just three days after JFK's assassination, to assure him he would not let Kennedy's progressive policies, like his proposed civil rights bill, die with him. In a tense meeting, with tough talk about the plight of Blacks in his city, Mayor Carr promised King he would form a biracial committee to facilitate ending segregation.

By committing to concrete action, Carr was able to avoid the possibility of King coming back with demonstrators and, undoubtedly, drawing negative press coverage. Carr was willing to acquiesce to King and avoid any possibility of dampening Walt Disney's secretive plan to use multiple shell companies to buy up tracts of land southwest of Orlando to establish a new entertainment complex. In Anaheim, Disney hated how others were able to cash in on his success by establishing lower-end attractions and motels close to Disneyland's front entrance.

He made sure that would not happen in Orlando by buying up enough land, more than twenty-five thousand acres, to keep any and all other businesses at a considerable distance.

Hours after his meeting with Mayor Carr, King strode to the pitcher's mound at Orlando's Tinker Field baseball stadium. Surrounded by local pastors for security, in a historic baseball venue where Babe Ruth, Stan Musial, and Jackie Robinson competed, King delivered a pro-integration message to two thousand African Americans sitting in the heretofore whites-only section of the grandstands. "Segregation is on its deathbed," King said. "And the only question now is how expensive its funeral will be because of segregationists." He referred to the civil rights bill, currently stalled in the Senate, and encouraged people to call out the southern senators blocking its passage. "Law cannot make a man love me," he declared on that unseasonably cool night in Orlando, "but it can keep him from lynching me." Elsewhere in Florida, local governments were less willing to acquiesce to King, whom they saw as nothing more than an outside agitator intent on upsetting the local rule of law and courting publicity.

America's "unfinished Civil War" started to catch fire in St. Augustine after local Black leaders learned the upcoming four-hundredth birthday celebration would not include African Americans. To finance the Quadricentennial Celebration, lawmakers appropriated $350,000 in public money. Two leaders of the NAACP's local branch, dentist Robert Hayling and a minister, Goldie Eubanks, called for demonstrations against using tax dollars for a segregated celebration. Hayling, a former air force lieutenant whose practice included Blacks and whites, was particularly outspoken. He let it be known to the Ku Klux Klan and others intent on enforcing segregation through violence and intimidation that he was willing to use force in return if he had to. The back-and-forth brought national attention and scrutiny as the celebration plans of the usually quiet tourist city devolved into chaos.

This was the very celebration Father Michael Gannon had told President Kennedy about in November the year previous. In the wake of JFK's assassination, Gannon's hopes were dashed and the president's proposed civil rights bill to mandate desegregation in all public facilities, a fading memory. In Congress, Democratic backers fought to revive it. St. Augustine became ground zero for protests in support of the new law to end the age-old practice, a century after their emancipation, of treating Blacks as second-class, back-door citizens. Local leaders were having none of it. Four teens who participated in a peaceful sit-in at the lunch counter of a St. Augustine Woolworth's were arrested and sent off to reform school.

In April 1964 King held a workshop in Tallahassee on how to stage nonviolent demonstrations. The challenge was not responding in kind when met with jeers, pushing and shoving, and, ultimately, violence. To further the cause, there had to be no question about who was the unlawful aggressor. Under the auspices of his Southern Christian Leadership Conference, headed by a group of idealistic thirtysomething pastors, King promised to personally intervene in St. Augustine and bring segregation down, even if it took all summer: "You can expect scars . . . jail . . . to be called names . . . to lose jobs . . . even death," was King's ominous message to those in the audience in Florida's capital city. "Freedom is never given freely by the oppressor; freedom must be demanded by the oppressed."

To this point in their careers, the Beatles didn't have to make their feelings known about civil rights and racial equality; they lived them. Their progressive attitude on race relations reflected the mores in England and France, where many notable Black American musicians had emigrated to enjoy better treatment as artists and more lucrative career opportunities. From their working-class, at times racially intolerant, roots, the Beatles knew what it was like to be scorned and looked down upon due to nothing more than the station they were born into or how long they wore their hair. As artists, they idolized Little Richard, Fats Domino, and Chuck Berry. They picked African American opening acts for their upcoming tour: the Exciters, a group of bright, talented, and streetwise young women from Queens, New York, and New Orleans blues singer Clarence "Frogman" Henry, whose catchy songs like "Aint Got No Home" often filled the dance floor.

How could any white musician who played rock and roll, rhythm and blues, or jazz maintain any credibility by distancing himself from the Black artists whose culture spawned so much of it? The very notion that a white musician would spurn a Black artist from sharing the stage was ludicrous; to the Beatles it was logical to expect that same fairness reflected in the audiences who bought what were—to any thinking person—integrated records. There was no separation of white and Black in the music, and it was farcical to expect that in audiences. Accepting white artists like the Beatles or Elvis performing music by Black artists like Big Mama Thornton and Chuck Berry amounted to tacit approval of the concept of integration. Still, in places like Miami Beach, the only place Blacks were welcome was onstage to entertain, or in uniform to drive a bus, make beds, or flip burgers.

Other white musicians slated to tour with the Beatles applauded their stance. Reggie Young, the Bill Black Combo's lead guitarist, who worked for years with Black artists all across the South, said, "I thought it was great. I thought it was a strong move on their part." Seeing that integration was such a logical consequence of racially blended music, many hard-liners in the South derisively labeled rhythm and blues as "race music" and preached the danger of the degenerative effects it would have on suburban young people. Given America's developing youth culture with the Beatles replacing Elvis as standard-bearers, those antiquated views were falling away, but, in places like Alabama, Mississippi, and Florida, not without bloodshed and strife, as King predicted. "There are many whites willing to go to jail with us," King told a reporter. "Thus making it a biracial assault against an unjust system."

When the program director of WFUN radio in Miami learned of a tentative Beatles concert date in Florida, he encouraged his news director, Larry Kane, to try to land an interview with them in Jacksonville. Given their unprecedented, ongoing chart success, Kane was starting to realize they were not just the hottest rock stars in America; the Beatles were also a bona fide cultural phenomenon. Kane wrote to Brian Epstein, making a strong pitch for an interview with the Beatles. Epstein's response was stunning: "The Beatles would be pleased to have you join us in our travelling press party during the tour commencing August 19 in San Francisco." Upon reading Epstein's response, Kane's jaw fell open: "I had asked for one interview. In return, I was invited to travel with the band and be granted unimaginable access! Station management was flabbergasted at our good fortune." Kane's business card, which included a string of other, smaller radio stations besides

WFUN, had given Epstein the impression his stories would have a much larger listening audience. That was enough to prompt the invite from Epstein.

For the upcoming tour, Epstein had already turned down mouth-watering, big-money offers to stage shows at Fenway Park; Detroit Tigers Stadium; and the LA Coliseum sponsored by Disney Land; as well as a four-hour musical extravaganza sponsored by Dick Clark, who'd come up short once again in the race to cash in on Beatlemania. A Miami offer would have given the Beatles a second Florida tour stop after Jacksonville. Epstein turned down a lucrative deal to stage a 1964 Shea Stadium show in front of sixty thousand fans, opting for a smaller New York venue, Forest Hills. The Gator Bowl proved to be a rare occasion where Epstein agreed to a stadium show and the possibility of empty seats. Taking a page from manager Tom Parker's playbook when he staged shows for Elvis, Epstein wanted all Beatle concerts to sell out, or come as close as possible, even if it meant smaller venues and profits. After the Gator Bowl, Epstein had initially agreed on another stadium show the following night in front of twenty-six thousand fans at the Crampton Bowl in Montgomery, Alabama. That concert never happened.

When the initial euphoria died down, Epstein's offer to Larry Kane left him conflicted. From a business standpoint, the $2,500 it would cost WFUN to put Kane on road with the Beatles was significant. But there was a far more pressing, personal concern; Kane's mother, Mildred, was suffering from advanced-stage multiple sclerosis. When the young newsman convened with station management to discuss a plan, they decided to sell syndicated reports from each tour stop to stations across North America. "We argued back and forth," Kane remembered. Station disc jockeys, eager to pump up their on-air personas by getting in-person promotional announcements from the Beatles in person, were hot to travel cross-country with them. The general manager nixed that idea, coming down in favor of Kane due to his storytelling prowess. "We need a real news person," he said. "You can't just say, 'they played' and that's it."

In light of having to provide daily syndicated material about a music group that to that point he hadn't done much research on, and the issues surrounding his mother, Kane balked. "I said 'I just can't go,'" he recalled. "And I went home to see my mom and dad." Kane's father told him the Beatles "are a menace" and that covering the tour might be dangerous. His mother had a much different take: "Larry, you should go," she urged. "This could open doors for you. It might even take you to a different town." That singular, intuitive advice from his mother changed Kane's life. In deference to her advice, Kane signed on to the most arduous and historic assignment of his career.

More than forty stations in the United States and Canada signed up for Larry Kane's syndicated reports of his travel with the Beatles. Before he was due to set off on his odyssey with them in the summer of 1964, a journey he said took him to "the outer limits of human behavior," his mother, Mildred, died. Despite that wrenching emotional setback, Kane knew what she had wanted him to do and was determined to honor her wishes. He had already begun honing in on the milieu of racial strife connected with civil rights protests in and around Florida and the drumbeat of military conflict half a world away in Vietnam, a place most of America's youth knew nothing about. During the Beatles' North American tour, Larry Kane opened the door for the Beatles to weigh in on both, giving them a platform to articulate their social consciousness. Given all the turmoil going on in America, near one of their upcoming concert stops in Florida, the time was ripe for the Beatles to step forward and assume a new role beyond that of shaggy-haired, playful pinup boys.

17

Beatings and Bloodshed

None of the protests over racial equality in Northeast Florida diminished young Beatle fanatic Kitty Oliver's enthusiasm. The day she heard on WAPE-AM that they were booked to perform live at the Gator Bowl, she made up her mind to go. Soon to be a high school senior, in the summer of 1964 she recalled, "My world was so small and limited, I was ready to break out in any way." In one of the few existing photos of Kitty during this time period, her smile reflects confidence in what lay ahead: a future outside her cloistered world. To afford to buy a ticket, Kitty cleaned house for a retired schoolteacher and brought home her groceries. Her mother was so busy trying to make ends meet herself, she couldn't afford to help pay for her daughter's five-dollar ticket, but she didn't oppose her plans either. As a person of color attending the Beatles concert, Kitty would have to venture outside her comfort zone. Just to take a seat at such an anticipated event among what was sure to be a sea of white fans would require courage.

Kitty's best friend, who shared her enthusiasm for the Beatles and always danced right along to each anticipated new single they snatched up, was forbidden by her parents to *risk* attending the concert. At that point, no one knew whether members of the Klan might attempt to incite violence or intimidate Blacks trying to integrate such a high-profile event at a venue located in a zone of uncertainty. Kitty and other African American residents were well aware the Klan often organized and recruited new members in Jacksonville, making their presence known by way of terrifying "night rides" through African American neighborhoods. Call it a young girl's enthusiasm or just plain naivete, but not one bit of that dampened Kitty's determination to see the Beatles. Granted, in the 1960s, before round-the-clock cable news, Twitter, and TikTok, the Beatles' demands for integrated seating were not widely known. At this juncture, theirs was an unspoken contractual demand and nothing more. The dangerous street fight over racial equality in Florida would soon change that.

To many locals, St. Augustine, guarded by the ancient Castillo de San Marcos opposite Matanzas Bay, was no more racist than any other southern city. Tourists flocked to the historic district to be transported back in time along charming, narrow, cobblestone thoroughfares with plentiful restaurants and shops. At 56 St. George Street, up-and-coming artists like eighteen-year-old future country-rock pioneer Gram Parsons, a student at the prestigious Bolles School in Jacksonville, played folk music at Dan Holiday's Café Collage. The Spanish-motif Cathedral Basilica, home to the first Catholic parish before there *were* United States of America, offered a spiritual escape from the hustle and bustle of crowds and cars whizzing past.

At the top of the rise leading away from the waterfront, Henry Flagler's architectural jewel of the Gilded Age, the Ponce de Leon Hotel, known today simply as Ponce, became home to students attending Flagler College. Turn back down toward the water, at the bottom of St. Augustine's Plaza de la Constitution, past the eighteenth-century Governor's House, and you come to what looks like a nondescript open-air market. After Flagler's hotels and railroad sparked a tourist boom in the late 1800s, opportunistic photographers sold images to tourist customers of this pavilion labeled the "old slave market." Some locals disputed that term, but historic accounts have confirmed that human beings were sold here, just like any other goods coming into port. The unassuming structure became a symbol of the oppressive antebellum South, a focus of demonstrations and clashes in 1964 widely known as the St. Augustine Struggle.

In early June, Martin Luther King had obliged Dr. Robert Hayling's urgent request to come to St. Augustine and witness injustice. Repeatedly, Hayling had endured drive-by shootings into his home.

Once, while his pregnant wife and children were inside, a round fired through the door killed their family dog. During another episode, when Hayling tried to figure out who his enemies were by observing the goings-on at a Klan rally, he was pulled from his car at gunpoint, beaten with a chain, and nearly burned alive. When four Klansmen were brought to trial, only Hayling *himself* was convicted and fined in state court for assaulting his attackers. Eventually, Hayling lost what had been a thriving dental practice. Within the lawlessness and violence, King saw an opportunity to make another national statement in support of the civil rights bill now bogged down in the United States Senate. The proposed Civil Rights Act faced staunch opposition from southern hard-liners Strom Thurmond of South Carolina and Robert Byrd of West Virginia.

Segregationists wasted little time sending an ominous message to King that his presence in St. Augustine was not wanted. Prior to his arrival, a small beach house at 5480 Atlantic View, where King and his Southern Christian Leadership Conference (SCLC) staff had planned to stay, was strafed with gunfire and vandalized. King posed for what has become an iconic photo, pointing out a bullet hole in a porch window. His close associates had a well-founded concern that this was no idle threat. "My fear was that vigilante Klan types were setting a trap to kill Martin," said the SCLC's executive director and King's close confidant, Andrew Young. "There were just too many fanatics in that town." To make matters more volatile, some local law enforcement were tolerant of these intimidation tactics.

When King arrived on Tuesday, June 9, the audience at St. Paul AME Church, already stoked with anticipation to lay eyes on him, broke into a rousing version of "When the Saints go Marching In." Upon his entry, their words became, "Who is our leader? Martin Luther King!" The singing and clapping picked up to chants of "We shall not be moved." While King greeted and encouraged residents due for a protest march that evening, women and children among them, veteran Florida journalist Mabel Norris Chesley, sized him up. "To his lowliest followers he is virtually a saint. Joy was written on every face there," Chesley observed. Their unquestioned leader, who gave them inspiration to move forward out into a dangerous night, was now there with them, in person and in spirit. Meanwhile, a group of men acted as sentries outside, scrutinizing each car that passed.

Upon King's arrival, Young strongly discouraged him from leading marches in St. Augustine due to the volatility of counterprotesters. To avoid the oppressive daytime heat, some marches were held at night, heightening the already tense atmosphere. "Before I'll be a slave," King told the audience of three hundred from the church pulpit, "I'll be buried in my grave." In his booming pastor's voice, King urged them on: "March tonight like you've never marched before." Voices joined in prayer as those assembled sang and clapped in unison to spirituals that have given comfort and strength to generations, sanctifying the cause upon which they were about to embark. Marchers young and old, male and female, took up signs saying, "My Father Died Defending This Country Too" and "Segregation Must Go." Marchers embarked into the ghostly, foreboding St. Augustine night, led by Rev. Andrew Young, singing softly, "We Love Everybody in Our Hearts."

At various points in their single-file march to the old slave market, forces of opposition were waiting. One carried a sign that read: "Martin Luther Coon and His Little Coons Are Going Down." According to sworn court testimony, individuals using nighttime darkness of the greenspace along the route as cover, threw rocks, bricks, and bottles at marchers. At one street corner, Andrew Young approached a group of them in the hope of starting a dialogue. His move was misinterpreted by some as trying to provoke a confrontation. "They stared at me like I was crazy and, as I was talking to one man looking to my left, another guy slipped up behind me from the right and slugged me in the jaw. Then someone hit me in the head from the rear with a blackjack, and I don't remember anything after that," Young wrote of his initial, harrowing night in the nation's oldest city. "I felt like we were martyrs on the way to the lion's den." Others turned on a white marcher, Rev. William England, a thirty-three-year-old chaplain from Boston University, a divinity school friend of Dr. King's. "They grabbed me and tried to pull me into the bushes," England told a reporter after his ordeal. "But I fell down, and they stood and kicked me for a while."

Police made tacit attempts to shoo away attackers brutalizing marchers, but no one in the mob who attacked Young, England, and others was arrested. In the few cases where attackers were taken to jail, their bonds were low and easy to post. Still in a state of disbelief, Young and his marchers made it to the old slave market, knelt and said a prayer, and then returned to church.

The violence came within close range of the Roman Catholic Basilica of St. Augustine, the nation's oldest parish. One witness, standing in the safety of a darkened doorway on King Street, was Father Michael Gannon. Ironically, the city's four-hundredth birthday celebration, the event he'd told President Kennedy about, and controversy over whether Blacks would be included became a flashpoint to the violence he'd just witnessed. Gannon was haunted by the unwillingness of church leaders, himself included, to condemn it in any forceful way: "There was an opportunity to have, to have tried to do something, and I didn't do it. I didn't do it because I would have lost everything I'd worked for." Eventually, Gannon stood up to injustice again and again, left the priesthood, and became a revered historian at the University of Florida.

This was the Jim Crow reality for protesters on the ground in St. Augustine, making the same call for racial equality as the Beatles were in their 1964 concert contracts. When words eventually required action, for those who took up the cause, there was hell to pay. Had the Beatles not been performing in Hong Kong and been better aware of the growing level of hostility and oppression in the streets of Northeast Florida, it's possible the unrest would have been enough for Brian Epstein to cancel the Jacksonville concert. He'd already given up on his original plan to stage another stadium show in Montgomery. Why take the risk? It's not as if the Fab Four didn't have many offers in other cities, including Miami. In the end, it took the violence playing out in St. Augustine that spring and early summer, and ensuing precedent-setting court rulings, to bring forth a new day of equality across America; the Beatles' Gator Bowl show would serve as one high-profile example. But there was much that had to happen before that was even a remote possibility.

Due to the danger posed by forces marshaled against him, it was never made public where King was staying while in St. Augustine. On Wednesday night, June 10, a local nurse, Mrs. Janie Price, and her husband hosted King and another close SCLC confidant, Rev. Ralph

The St. Augustine home of Mrs. Janie Price, where Rev. Martin Luther King Jr. and his colleague Rev. Ralph Abernathy stayed the before their arrest at the Monson Motor Lodge. Courtesy of the author.

Abernathy, as overnight guests at her home at 156 Central Avenue. Price first met King when he was a sixteen-year-old student at Morehouse College in Atlanta. She only knew him as Martin back then, a quiet, studious, impeccably dressed young man who caught the eye of young ladies. Now here he was, the face of America's civil rights struggle, lying on the floor of her home in Lincolnville. Price said King was well aware he would likely be assassinated at some point during the struggle, but he thought it would happen in Mississippi. "I once asked him, 'Dr. King aren't you afraid?'" she remembered. "He said, 'I'm not afraid because if it's not worth dying for, it's not worth doing.'" Still, it had to distress King to see his marchers the night previous, close associate Andrew Young among them, come back to church after having been attacked. This was the very real risk King had told people about in Tallahassee while conducting workshops on nonviolent protest. That night, to calm himself enough to sleep on the Prices' floor, King sang his favorite spiritual, "Precious Lord, Take My Hand."

In retaliation for Mrs. Price hosting Dr. King, vandals turned her four-door Buick over on its top in the driveway. She called a tow-truck driver to right the car, had a mechanic check it out, and proceeded to drive it all around town to show those trying to intimidate her that she was not afraid. This was one example of the daily acts of strength and fortitude of local residents, including many courageous women, who'd committed themselves to the struggle for equality. Price and her husband started hosting student marchers who would spend the night at their home before taking part in demonstrations and getting arrested. In the front bedroom, the couple kept their shades closed and changed in the dark so their shadows wouldn't make them easier targets for armed hoodlums.

Coverage of the repeated beatings against peaceful, nonviolent protesters was carried in newspapers and television nationwide. In Vermillion, South Dakota, where Reverend England had been a minister at the local Congregational Church before moving on to Boston University, a couple who had known him, Mr. and Mrs. Ernest Dewey, fired off an angry letter to the mayor of St. Augustine and their congressional representatives: "This is the only way we know how to express our shock and horror that an American city can accept and indeed condone such brutality." King's strategy to ignite the nation's outrage against injustice in St. Augustine was working. But there was much more violence to come.

On June 11, 1964, King and an integrated group of protesters including Reverend England stood on the front steps of the Monson Motor Lodge, a popular tourist destination in St. Augustine overlooking Matanzas Bay, intent on being seated and served together. Manager James Brock blocked King's entry. Despite the presence of the press, and despite the local economy's dependence on out-of-town tourists, Brock, president of the Florida Hotel and Motel Association, was calm and defiant: "You are on private property. We reserve the right to refuse service. I ask you on behalf of myself, my wife and my two children to leave."

"We are sorry you have that attitude," King said. "You are doing a disservice to the nation."

"We serve negroes in the service area," Brock told him. "That's where we serve all the tourists' maids and chauffeurs."

Standing his ground, King replied, "Can't you see how this humiliates us?"

Brock said he would acquiesce only under two conditions: a federal court order or if a "responsible group of St. Augustine citizens" asked him to.

"We are glad to know that you would do it under those circumstances," King replied.

As reporters took notes and film cameras rolled, the tense standoff continued.

"Look, we are a small business. We are caught in the middle of something between two armed camps," Brock explained. "If I serve you, my business would be hurt—badly hurt."

Undeterred, King proclaimed, "We will stand here and hope that in the process that our conscious effort will make this a better land."

With that, St. Augustine's police chief, Virgil Stuart, announced, "You're all under arrest," taking King and those with him into custody for violating Florida's unwanted guest law, a legal remedy often used by landlords to evict problem tenants. King, Rev. Ralph Abernathy, Reverend England, and others became the latest of dozens of African Americans and white sympathizers to be taken to jail for wanting to eat lunch in a tourist restaurant, swim in a public pool, or use a gas station restroom. A week later, in a fit of anger, Brock sealed his infamy and stunned the nation by pouring muriatic acid into his motel pool while an integrated group of young people staged a "swim-in."

The local state attorney, Dan Warren, impaneled a grand jury to try to barter an end to the demonstrations. That evening he extended not a subpoena, but a less confrontational invitation, to King to testify. By the time that invitation reached King, he had stripped down to his T-shirt and boxer shorts due to the oppressive heat inside the St. Johns County Jail. The next day, Warren welcomed King as a respected guest and asked the wary young minister to tell the grand jury what his protesters would accept to end the demonstrations. At the very least, King made it known, there would have to be a biracial committee, as Mayor Carr had promised and delivered in Orlando, to begin a discussion about ending segregation in St. Augustine. After the testimony, one unimpressed grand jury member approached Warren and said King was "no different from any other blue gum n----- from South Georgia."

Martin Luther King Jr. in a patrol car next to a police dog, on his way to the Duval County Jail, where he was held in solitary confinement. Also pictured is King's colleague Andrew Young. Photo by AP Images.

Others, with a more moderate view, still resented King for bringing so much negative attention to their city.

That afternoon, under orders from Governor C. Farris Bryant, local authorities transferred King to the Duval County Jail in downtown Jacksonville for "safe keeping." Just before his departure from St. Augustine, news photographers captured King, dressed in a suit and tie, being directed to the back of a patrol car. Then the officer loaded his police dog into the back seat alongside King. Whatever the officer's motive, resulting images of King being forced to endure a forty-mile ride to Jacksonville seated next to a German Shepherd police dog had an indelible impact. "All the work we had put into an attempt to create a picture of fairness and understanding by the citizens of St. Augustine," Warren wrote, "was destroyed in an instant by that single photograph." The dog's countenance however, did not appear at all vicious or intimidating. Thus King, in photographs seated next to the dog, appeared more bemused than nervous.

Since King stood at the foot of the Lincoln Memorial during the March on Washington and delivered one of the most important speeches of the twentieth century, 288 days had elapsed. "I Have a Dream" became his world-famous invocation, echoing Lincoln's Gettysburg Address, which proclaimed that all men, Blacks included, are created equal. Yet, one hundred years later, for people of color, King said, the promise of equality had turned out to be a check written with "insufficient funds. But we refuse to believe that the bank of justice is bankrupt." King, now riding in the back of a patrol car with a police dog companion, would need a sizable check just to make bail for demanding equality in a Florida tourist restaurant and seeing his dream deferred yet again.

Due to concerns about threats made on his life, King was housed in solitary confinement at the Duval County Jail in downtown Jacksonville. The time had come for King to make his case before the most powerful jurist in the region. What resulted was a historic and crucial turning point in the struggle to bury America's Jim Crow shame.

18

The St. Augustine Dilemma

The second week of June 1964, the Beatles landed half a world away for their first Australian tour dates, as far as they could be from the escalating battle against Jim Crow in America. Throngs of fans turned out to welcome them. Brian Epstein took out a five-hundred-thousand-dollar life insurance policy for each Beatle in advance of their upcoming North American tour. Reporter Larry Kane signed on to cover them at every stop. Epstein and the Beatles could only follow in the newspaper and on television the confluence of events happening to facilitate their demand for integrated shows in America. At this uncertain point, the buck stopped with one man with the legal authority to bring justice and order to Northeast Florida—and the backbone to use it—when others failed to do so.

When it appeared that local authorities were more apt to arrest protesters than protect their right to stage nonviolent marches, Andrew Young and the Southern Christian Leadership Conference (SCLC) filed suit against St. Johns County sheriff L. O. Davis in US federal court. This was a common tactic used by civil rights advocates in the South to gain a foothold when local law enforcement became adversarial. That move brought myriad legal issues surrounding the St. Augustine Struggle before Bryan Simpson, chief judge of the United States Court for Florida's Middle District, appointed in 1950 by President Harry S. Truman. Judge Simpson, whose grandfathers fought on opposite sides in the Civil War, had developed a reputation as a fair-minded jurist who paid no attention to the personal or political ramifications of his decisions, which, in this case, were considerable. Gray-haired, bespectacled, and imposing at six foot two inches tall, Simpson had grown up in rural Kissimmee when it was cattle country, decades before it became known as a strip mall suburb to Walt Disney World. By the time Martin Luther King was arrested in June 1964, Judge Simpson had already made multiple rulings that riled the local establishment.

Where other southern judges were hesitant to involve themselves in civil rights lawsuits, Simpson acted more decisively. He ordered Florida governor C. Farris Bryant to call in the Highway Patrol to keep the peace in St. Augustine. When Simpson concluded Bryant was ignoring his orders, he threatened to hold the governor of Florida in contempt of court. In another controversial decision, Simpson barred local authorities from housing arrested protesters in a sweltering outdoor compound nicknamed "the bullpen." Simpson referred to it as a "sweat box" designed with "studied and cynical brutality, deliberately contrived to break men physically and mentally." This outdoor holding area, operated by police in St. Johns County, had been frequented by the Klan to identify protesters they wished to harass upon release.

In a rare Saturday hearing in federal court on June 13, Florida's attorney general, James W. Kynes, tried a new tactic to persuade Judge Simpson to halt nighttime marches in St. Augustine. He argued that the protests presented a "clear and present danger" to public safety. It was up to Simpson to decide if it was the protestors or their opponents creating the danger. This emergency motion to ban after-hours demonstrations set the stage for two icons of America's civil rights era to come face-to-face in a Jacksonville courtroom: Judge Bryan Simpson and Reverend Martin Luther King Jr., the latter still in custody and fresh from a night in solitary confinement at the Duval County Jail.

King was called to the witness stand. "I'm in a lonely, dark and desolate cell here, cut off from everybody. The light is so dim I can barely see," said King. *Time* magazine's "Man of the Year" was now an inmate under questioning in a Florida courtroom. King testified that protests were intended to draw attention to "the problem of segregation and discrimination, that local black citizens faced daily. And we are seeking to do that through engaging in nonviolent direct action . . . to arouse the conscience of the community and the nation over the injustice and indignities that Negroes continue to face in the oldest city in our nation." King said his "nonviolent army" had gone to great lengths to avoid engaging in violent defensive tactics, despite the fact that "several of my staff have been brutally beaten."

Rev. William England, the white clergyman from Boston University who'd been arrested alongside King outside the Monson Motor Lodge, recounted on the witness stand how he and Andrew Young, the plaintiff in the SCLC'S ongoing federal lawsuit versus Sheriff Davis, had been attacked during the peaceful march two nights previous. If any policemen bothered to try to catch them, the young attackers sprinted off into the dark greenspace. "I was hit a couple of times and I fell down and then I was kicked on numerous times, probably ten times," England testified. Judge Simpson asked, "Did you make any effort to defend yourself by striking back?" "No," England responded. "Because I'm part of the nonviolent movement and I don't believe in that."

Under questioning from Judge Simpson, state officers brought in to help maintain order in St. Augustine gave chilling testimony about how guns and ammunition they confiscated from vehicles driven by out-of-town segregationist agitators were returned to them hours later by local authorities. Simpson grilled St. Johns County sheriff L. O. Davis to the point of his admitting that his men had made little or no effort to arrest those assaulting marchers. Davis acknowledged he'd appointed known felons and members of the Ku Klux Klan as auxiliary deputies. Simpson questioned the willingness of Davis to make arrests, especially at night, when tensions were high and when some of the counterprotesters had ready access to firearms and ammunition, which Simpson saw as "a clear and present danger."

At the end of a long weekend day in a Jacksonville courtroom, Simpson was swayed. He ruled that it was not King and his protestors creating the clear and present danger. To the contrary, he found that they were the ones facing extreme danger, exacerbated by the unwillingness of local law enforcement to do more to protect them. Simpson scolded Florida's attorney general for this abject failure of law enforcement to control those who were there for the specific purpose of intimidating and brutalizing peaceful demonstrators. In his ruling, which upheld the right of nonviolent civil rights marches to continue at night, Judge

Simpson made his wishes unequivocal: "I suggest rigid and strict law enforcement and some arrests be placed against these hoodlums that everybody down there seems to be afraid to move against, and I make that with deadly seriousness."

Judge Simpson had put his considerable credibility and the power of the federal government on the side of King, Andrew Young, and protesters of all races. In return, he endured harsh criticism from segregationist hard-liners like South Carolina senator Strom Thurmond, who denounced Simpson's rulings as "Federal Judicial Dictatorship." In one of the numerous protest letters he received, a local woman told Simpson she wished he would just "drop dead." Simpson asked US marshals to keep an eye on his car parked outside the courthouse. He changed his home phone to an unlisted phone number to spare his wife and son from verbal abuse. Friends distanced themselves. Years later, Simpson explained that in his rulings he was just following "binding precedent." The explanation seemed simple and straightforward enough, but the crucial and unprecedented shift of American justice in King's favor was an important step forward.

After the hearing, King was transported back to the Duval County Jail. Supporters helped him post the nine-hundred-dollar bond in time to catch a flight out of Jacksonville. On Monday, June 15, 1964, before ten thousand people at Yale University's 263rd commencement, King accepted an honorary doctor of laws degree as he was praised for his "eloquence that has kindled the nation's sense of outrage" and given a standing ovation. Meanwhile, back at ground zero in St. Augustine, that night Jackie Robinson, already a legend for breaking Major League Baseball's color barrier during a 1946 spring training game in Daytona Beach, urged President Lyndon Johnson to take action in support of their cause.

From a distance, many in the establishment blamed King and his marchers for bringing violence upon themselves and hardening the attitudes of more tolerant whites against them. An editorial in the *Tampa Tribune* put blame for the ongoing strife squarely on King: "The only person who could benefit from the senseless tumult is Martin Luther King, in nationwide publicity which will tie-on his self-sewn mantle of Negro leadership." During this era, when local broadcast stations still showed the courage to take editorial stands, Orlando television station

WFTV took an opposing view, characterizing the beatings of marchers as "gang terrorism" and placing blame on extremists and city leaders' tolerance of their wanton violence: "This is a frighteningly sad case of advance cowardice."

On the floor of the United States Senate, South Dakota senator George McGovern lauded the actions of protesters in Northeast Florida, particularly Reverend England, whom he'd met as a student chaplain in South Dakota: "He has followed the Christian ethic, in the cause of human dignity and human rights. He has suffered torments by the ignorant and the cynical and has not been deterred by unjust treatment. He did not answer force with force but turned the other cheek. His cause—which is the cause of all of us—will triumph." McGovern successfully moved to have coverage of the beatings against nonviolent protesters in St. Augustine entered in to the *Congressional Record*. King and the SCLC's efforts, with scores of everyday people like Robert Hayling, Janie Price, and William England, had finally moved the collective conscience of those in Congress to act. On June 19, the US Senate voted on and passed an amended version of JFK's Civil Rights Act, paving the way for President Johnson to make it law.

On the ground in Florida, the news enraged opponents, who reacted with unprecedented violence. Despite Judge Simpson's recent order for state and local police to crack down on racist thugs, on Thursday, June 25, a crowd of segregationists in St. Augustine broke through a police line and started beating those involved in another protest march near downtown. Before the city's worst night of racial violence was over, forty-five people were injured. This time, counterprotesters had to be clubbed by police and dozens arrested in connection with their hit-and-run rampage.

On June 30, Governor Bryant, under pressure from Judge Simpson and the federal government, announced the formation of a biracial committee to restore communication in St. Augustine, a key step forward in the standoff. Local authorities, still hoping to discourage King, had drummed up new charges. On June 30, he turned himself in to the St. Johns County Jail on four counts of contributing to the delinquency of a minor, for encouraging youth to participate in demonstrations. This time, he was released on his own recognizance.

Memorial statue to residents who fought for equality in St. Augustine. Courtesy of the author.

By then, the old guard's pro–Jim Crow stance had taken a devastating toll in St. Augustine: three hundred arrests in the previous two weeks, a loss of $8–10 million of the city's $22 million annual tourist revenue; restaurants and motels reported business was off by more than 50 percent. In light of the governor's willingness to finally start a dialogue, King declared a truce. Through nonviolent tactics, aided by the courage of those who endured violence used against them, King had impacted city leaders where it hurt most: in their wallets. He exposed apathy and corruption in local law enforcement. Had it not been for Judge's Simpson's rulings affirming the constitutional rights of protesters and ordering state officers in to protect them, retribution against those involved in the St. Augustine Struggle could have been deadly. That no one, King included, was killed in June 1964 in St. Augustine given the emboldened nature of racist agitators, was miraculous. "In retrospect," Andrew Young wrote, "St. Augustine turned out to be the SCLC's most violent and bloody campaign."

On July 2, less than three weeks after he'd been held in solitary confinement in Duval County, King stood behind President Lyndon Johnson in the White House, watched him sign the Civil Rights Act of 1964 into law, and shook his hand. King vowed to members of the media that his supporters would test the new law all across America to ensure it was being observed. Finally, the Civil Rights Act provided a legal foundation to end segregation and ensure equality in public places like the Monson Motor Lodge in St. Augustine, where King had been arrested for demanding to be seated with whites, and at the Gator Bowl, where the Beatles' concert was two months away. Whether it was Brian Epstein responsible for the contractual integration requirement, or John Lennon, or the entire band, the Beatles' call for integration on their 1964 American tour had turned out to be prescient and courageous.

Jim Crow oppression, however, would not leave the hot and humid streets of St. Augustine quietly. When James Brock acquiesced to legally mandated integration at his motor lodge, the motel was firebombed. Pro-segregation forces were embarking on an underground reign of terror as a last-ditch effort to preserve the status quo. Two weeks after the passage of the Civil Rights Act, upon his return to St. Augustine, King bore witness and expressed his dismay. Journalist Mabel Norris Chesley wrote, "Re-segregation had become the order because of threats by segregationists against the owners of businesses."

Chesley herself was on her way to becoming a legend in Florida journalism for repeatedly speaking truth to corrupt power and paying a steep price. Chesley's home had been firebombed, her dog poisoned, and racist Klan graffiti painted on the window of her newspaper in Mount Dora, Florida, for calling out again and again Lake County's criminally corrupt strongman sheriff, Willis McCall. It was the autocratic McCall who played a central role in getting Chesley's newspaper shut down for lack of advertising, forcing her to leave town; she'd had a cross burned in her yard and feared for her own life on many occasions. Now she was working for the Daytona Beach newspaper, covering the St. Augustine Struggle, and as a confidante of Dr. King, contributing pro–civil rights articles and editorials.

To that point, the biracial committee formed by Governor Bryant had neither communicated nor met. Still smarting from his defeat in federal court the month previous, Florida's attorney general went so far as to advise a statewide sheriffs' group how to bypass locally, the new federal law. King was dispirited but resolute. "Now, I can't just walk out of St. Augustine and leave the frustrated Negro community in defeat," King told Chesley in an article she titled "King Discusses His St. Augustine Dilemma": "Can I let violence triumph here and form a pattern that would be adopted in many other places? If anyone can reach the power structure here and persuade it to call off the Klan, we will welcome it." In Northeast Florida, forces still engaged in the bare-knuckle street fight against integration remained emboldened.

The Beatles would soon be in a position to help King further the cause, by speaking out again and again to their legion of impressionable young fans. With the help of newsman Larry Kane, the Beatles used the notoriety of their American tour as a bully pulpit. On the surface, Americans were falling in love with Brian Epstein's carefully crafted image of the Beatles: cheeky, well-dressed albeit shaggy-haired boys still wide-eyed with wonder that their dream was happening, trading jabs with the press and not yet aware that the fame they were craving would become a lifelong crown of thorns.

Upon its American release to five hundred American theaters on August 11, the Beatles' first film, *A Hard Day's Night*, proved to be a sensation. The film took the Beatles to greater heights artistically, due to the surprisingly enthusiastic reception it received from adults and film critics. The soundtrack, all original songs they'd worked on in Paris and Miami, was similarly lauded: "Can't Buy Me Love," "Tell Me Why," and "I Should Have Known Better" proved to be rollicking fun. In America, the Beatles' third album had already shot to the top of the charts before the film came out. The ballads, including Paul's "And I Love Her," accompanied by the soaring harmonies in John's "If I Fell," to this day remain among their most enduring love songs. Despite their workmanlike, assembly-line timetable to come up with new material, Lennon and McCartney were stoking the staggering success of Beatlemania with one home run composition after another. Upon deeper analysis, the film helped open doors for the Beatles in less obvious ways.

A Hard Day's Night featured all four Beatles in their own starring story lines, capturing different aspects of their personalities. Writer Alun Owen didn't try to shoehorn the boys into some ridiculous exploitation story line à la Elvis. Having followed them around for several days touring in Europe, Owen developed a strong sense of each one's character and then, in an inspired move, allowed their natural charisma and comedic abilities to shine. A number of scenes came across as if the Beatles were just clowning around, improvising and thumbing their noses at establishment types. The film, which cost less than $500,000 to make, raked in $11 million at the box office. *A Hard Day's Night* went on to be nominated for two Academy Awards, including Best Score and Best Screenplay.

Within the potboiler that was the summer of 1964 in America, *A Hard Day's Night* also won the Beatles added gravitas to speak out about injustices they witnessed. While cheeky and fun-loving just as the film depicted, the nonfictionalized Beatles made it clear that there was no backing down from their demand that seating be integrated. The four innocents who'd landed in Miami in February wondering if anyone would be there to greet them were evolving, through words if not deeds, into social activists. Jacksonville proved to be the first opportunity to advance their developing worldview as agents of social change.

While the Beatles were busy conquering the world and reveling in their hard-won success, Martin Luther King was back in Northeast Florida, appealing to Mabel Norris Chesley and her readers for a solution to his St. Augustine dilemma. Would his nonviolent army need to take to the resegregated streets of St. Augustine and incur more hostility to make their point? King was still weeks away from the answer. With every Beatles concert ticket sold to fans regardless of race, the Brennan family planned to honor the contract they signed that allowed equal seating for all in Jacksonville. Despite ongoing turmoil, giddy Beatle fans like Kitty Oliver were counting down the days.

19

Outer Limits

During the first story he filed about the Beatles at Miami International Airport, Larry Kane bore witness to the gashes suffered by fans when the terminal windows gave way. The jarring sounds of panes of glass falling and shattering on the tarmac not far from where he was standing was etched in his memory. Compared to what he was about to experience, however, that was nothing. On the upcoming tour, Kane and other traveling journalists would witness Beatlemania Babylon: a police investigation into possible sexual misconduct with minors, death threats, bomb threats, drug and alcohol abuse, extreme weather, property damage, sleep deprivation, racism, mechanical issues, and a well-known psychic's ominous prediction.

Not knowing the magnitude of all that lay ahead and still subdued from his mother's death, Larry Kane boarded a plane in Miami for San Francisco. The Beatles' first tour stop was the Cow Palace on August 19, three weeks before they were due to play Jacksonville. This historic tour gave the Beatles a front-row seat to turmoil and divisiveness as Americans struggled to figure out if the country was evolving or devolving the summer after JFK's assassination. Kane, the Florida newsman still just twenty-one years old, got to know the Beatles during this watershed time as few ever would. His first extended encounter with

John Lennon, however, left him fearful he'd blown the assignment before it even started:

"What's your problem, man?"

Seemingly just as Kane had shambled into the Beatles' San Francisco Hilton suite, he was being confronted. After a draining cross-country trek, there he was; tape recorder slung over his shoulder, microphone in hand. Brian Epstein had just finished welcoming him to the traveling press pool and ushered him back to meet "the Boys," when Kane ran into John Lennon's sledgehammer-blunt sense of humor. "Why are you dressed like a fag ass man?" Lennon asked. "What's with that? How old are you?" Though shocked at Lennon's language, Epstein made no effort to stop or admonish him; it would do no good anyway. To Kane, it didn't appear Lennon was kidding. Pissed-off, all he could think of to say in reply was, "It's better than looking scruffy and messed up like you." He smiled awkwardly; Lennon didn't.

Instinctively, Kane got down to business, moving on to the other three Beatles. After short introductions, he interviewed each one without any similar rough patches. When he learned Kane was from Miami, George asked him to say "hello" to his former roommate Buddy Dresner. Then the only thing left to do was go back to Lennon after the initial meeting, which, in the Miami newsman's eyes, was a disaster. If he had insulted the leader of the group he was supposed to be traveling with for the next month, what chance did he have to get anything of interest to broadcast to *forty* stations now paying for syndicated reports? Kane decided to show Lennon "I was not a deejay; I was a serious guy." With that, he asked Lennon's views on the United States' escalating military presence in Vietnam. Surprised, Lennon gave him an animated, informed, and scathing critique of the US buildup, more militant than his conversations with Buddy Dresner in Miami Beach, where Lennon characterized US actions as "butting in."

Untold numbers of young men who bought Beatle records and attended their early concerts were drafted, fought, and died in Vietnam. Many girls who screamed their heads off for the Fab Four during the early era of innocence added their voices when protests broke out all across a nation fissured by increasing US participation. Kane said the Beatles "were putting down the Vietnam War right from the very beginning." In 1964, the United States suffered two hundred casualties in Vietnam. In 1968, during the worst of a hopeless quagmire, that number mushroomed to more than sixteen thousand. The so-called generation gap soon became a chasm between young people fighting in an unjust war waged by older adults, who remained safe at home. No popular music act prior to the Beatles would dare take such a risky stand as speaking out directly against US government policy.

As he walked down the hallway after that troubling encounter with John Lennon, still unsure about what had just happened, Kane got a tap on the shoulder. He turned around and was face-to-face once more with Lennon, who, to Kane's immense relief, thanked him for the question about Vietnam. "Liked the talk, look forward to more stuff," Lennon said. "Sorry about the clothes bullshit." All Kane could say was, "John, it was great meeting you." Kane's odd, but not atypical, Lennon encounter began a friendly rapport between the two that lasted long after the Beatles broke up.

No one before the Beatles, positively no British act, had the ambition, success, and audacity to attempt the kind of behemoth and unprecedented North American tour Brian Epstein was setting them out on. Thirty-two performances in twenty-four cities across America and Canada, for which the Beatles would rake in an estimated $1–1.4 million depending on final attendance figures. For the Beatles, it was one thing to have played live before a small studio audience and a bank of cameras broadcasting them to tens of millions American fans. It was quite another, night after night, city after city, to have that ear-splitting hysteria hitting them like a concussion grenade, *in person*, courtesy of their supercharged fans. Most were still children and had come nowhere close to experiencing a concert, or an event of any kind, of such magnitude. No wonder so many were overwhelmed. "They would walk onstage, and it would sound like thunder," said Lillian Walker of the Exciters, her voice still punctuated by a sense of wonder. Fresh from similar frenzied fan receptions in Australia and New Zealand, the Fab Four was as ready as they could be for the heightened experience in America.

Before the Beatles embarked on the trip back stateside, they had also attracted the interest of the FBI. Clearly aware of their contractual stand against segregation, the Bureau ordered agents to be on high alert for possible race riots. In a memo entitled "Racial Matters," agents in the Los Angeles and San Francisco offices were warned that Beatle appearances could be "a perfect vehicle for riots if racial elements or organizations, subversive or otherwise, would decide to capitalize." The "emotional pitch of the crowds," the memo warned, could be used by unnamed subversive elements to turn these disturbances into riots. The FBI's concern about Beatle appearances becoming dangerous was well-founded.

Starting in San Francisco and continuing in cities like Jacksonville and New Orleans, fans on the floor, caught up in the moment of seeing the Beatles bound on stage for the first time, surged forward to get as close them as possible; God help anyone or anything in their way. It was a frightening and dangerous stampede Larry Kane bore witness to when he decided to take in the beginning of that first Cow Palace concert among the fans. As soon as the Beatles broke into "Twist and Shout," the first song of the tour, Kane wrote, "I felt a hammer-like strike to the back of my neck and rolled into the middle of an aisle where I was trampled . . . I glanced to the left, where a young woman was screaming, but not for the Beatles. Her leg was twisted and she was writhing in pain, her elbows scraped to the bone. When the guys with the stretchers arrived, they diagnosed a broken leg." Girls who'd fainted were being carried out; a section of seating area resembled a MASH unit for triaging the injured. Now, Kane's first *two* shared experiences with Beatle fans, February in Miami and now August in San Francisco, had devolved into bloody chaos.

For Beatle opening acts like the Bill Black Combo, the cachet of touring with the hottest rock band in the world wore off the second they hit the stage. Soon they were met with waves of boos or persistent chants of "We want the Beatles!" A group of girls did chase Reggie Young and his bandmates around backstage, until they learned the "BBC" embroidered on their blazers stood for "Bill Black Combo" and not "British Broadcasting Corporation." Jackie DeShannon and the others fared no better. Having warm-up acts at all for a crowd already whipped into a titillated frenzy at the thought of finally seeing the Fab Four was pointless.

There were other, less obvious dangers. In a press conference, George had mentioned John was taking his Jelly Babies candy—a smaller, softer version of American jelly beans. In an apparent act of devotion, American fans brought along bags full of the larger, harder kind. Soon, trying to avoid the hail of jelly beans being thrown by kids as projectiles became common practice concert after concert. Even the Beatles were targeted. Show after show, teens pelted opening acts with the candies to punctuate their disapproval. "The girls threw them angrily," said Young, remembering how much it hurt to be struck by them.

British journalist Ivor Davis, also covering the tour for a London newspaper, described the jelly beans raining down "like friendly fire." Witnessing the madness close to the stage, Davis said, "More than a few clattered like hailstones on to Ringo's drums, others fell far short stinging my ears, and hitting my head like sharp pellets. I grabbed a newspaper as a kind of makeshift shield." For those not caught up in the hysteria, the thirty minutes the Beatles actually appeared on-stage became a half hour of hell: screaming, writhing, fainting, flying projectiles, little hope of hearing the Beatles, who rarely deviated from the songs to try to have witty banter with the audience. With the nonstop, jet engine–like torrent of shrieking and the primitive PA systems, why bother? When the dozen songs had been delivered, the Beatles sprinted for whatever vehicle could get them away from the venue without being enveloped and crushed by fans. It's a wonder they put up with this madness through 1966.

In San Francisco, roadie Mal Evans, the bespectacled gentle giant who'd been with the Beatles since meeting them as a doorman at the Cavern Club, and the Beatles' American tour manager Bob Bonis, a no-nonsense New Yorker who had just come off managing the Rolling Stones' first American tour, herded them offstage and into an ambulance, which sped off, sirens blaring. With their ears still ringing, the traveling press party also had to make their way to a waiting car without getting trampled or cut off and left behind. The Beatles' limo had been swamped by fans who attached themselves to the top of the passenger compartment in such numbers that it finally buckled under their weight. The press pool's driver had to navigate around it, being careful not to run anyone over. In all, Davis reported nineteen fans had to be treated for some sort of injury; at least two had been arrested.

And the police, those poor police officers trying to maintain at least some semblance of order, "rugby tackled" some fifty or so fans who had tried to climb onstage. Then it was back to the swank hotel and twelfth-floor suite, their small cocoon of pseudonormalcy. The Beatles never had a chance to set eyes upon the hotel's rooftop pool.

The Beatles' share of the gate in San Francisco came to just under fifty thousand dollars. Then it was on to the next city, Las Vegas, and more of the same. On the short flight from San Francisco to Vegas, Kane staked out a spot not too far away from the Beatles. Still trying to build a rapport with them, he made a calculated decision to wander down the aisle to where they were, without his microphone and recorder. "How did it feel out there?" Kane offered to any of the boys who cared to answer. "Not safe," Lennon replied. "Can't sing when you're scared for your life." Kane wished them all luck in Vegas and returned to his seat. As it turned out, all of them, Larry Kane included, would need it.

20

Broken Silence

In light of the mutual trust developing between Larry Kane and the Beatles, they began to welcome his questions about more controversial subjects and didn't quibble in their responses. Kane would start off by telling nationwide listeners he was having a conversation with them backstage, in a hotel room, or on the airplane. Often, these sessions were far less relaxed and spontaneous than he indicated. Kane was getting access to the Beatles during the paltry free time they had in between frantic tour stops. These intimate sessions were usually miles ahead, content-wise, of the rapid-fire press conferences the boys were obligated to give city to city. Some of the less-informed reporters still didn't know, or perhaps care, which Beatle was which and wasted their time by asking vapid questions about appearance, hair length, or rumors that they were breaking up.

These pro-forma press conferences were so boring and tedious that the Beatles and their tour manager, Bob Bonis, devised a strategy to spice them up. "Someone like myself would scream from the back, a pre-arranged question that would at least make it a little more interesting. And we'd wait for some kind of funny answer. The guys were unaware what our questions were, but they knew they'd get some different questions from us, just to make it more interesting for them. Otherwise they'd be bored to tears. Same questions city after city," Bonis recalled. Quiet, but with a New York tough-guy air about him,

Bonis occupied an extraordinary place in music history, having managed the Rolling Stones' and Beatles' first American tours in 1964. If all was going well, you might see him at a press conference, hanging toward the back, snapping a few pictures, not looking for any attention.

Larry Kane had no one trying to shout over him, and the Beatles were more at ease with a newsman their age who gave them the time and intellectual space to ponder his questions. In Las Vegas, after Kane had done a batch of fresh interviews, he made an awful discovery. Due to technical problems, he had nothing but a hum—and definitely no interviews—on his tape recorder. Dozens of stations were expecting to be fed fresh content in a matter of hours. Desperate, he grabbed a cab and searched well into the night for a replacement. He got lucky and found an appliance store still open and purchased a smaller-sized recorder.

With the morning deadline approaching, Kane had to do the newsman's walk of shame: going back and begging for new interviews with the Beatles. Derek Taylor, the Beatles' urbane and smooth-talking spokesman, took pity on him, and arranged for another session in their room at the Sahara Hotel. In retrospect, it produced some of their most provocative comments of the American tour. Kane asked Paul McCartney to expand on a recent comment he'd made about segregation. In contrast to his image as the band's winking, horny happy guy, wanting to be liked and smoothing over anything controversial, Paul didn't hold back. In a year of defining moments for the Beatles in America, this interview in Las Vegas became one of them.

"We don't like it if there's any segregation or anything like that because we're not used to it," McCartney offered. "It just seems mad to me." Kane pressed him further: "Well, you're going to play Jacksonville, Florida, do you anticipate any kind of difference of that opinion?" With a strong sense of conviction in his voice, McCartney said some of his best friends were "colored people," a characterization of Blacks still accepted in 1964. "Over here there are some people who think they're just animals or something, it's stupid you know. You can't treat other human beings like animals," McCartney concluded. "That's the way we all feel," Ringo added. They made it clear they would not perform before segregated audiences. The silent, contractual stand they'd taken before the tour started was now spoken, amplified, and on the record for everyone in Larry Kane's massive coast-to-coast radio audience to hear. As the hard-fought Civil Rights Act was still being defied in Northeast Florida, the Beatles used their growing gravitas to draw a clear line in the sand in favor of integration and civil rights. African American artists on the tour appreciated that their conviction on the subject was genuine and unshakeable.

Among the acts they'd chosen to open for them, the Beatles were developing a warm kinship with the Exciters, the young trio of African American female singers from Queens, New York. Consisting of Lillian Walker, Carol Johnson, Brenda Reid, and her husband, Herbert Rooney, the group scored a top-five smash in January 1963 with the upbeat single "Tell Him," featuring Reid's confident and bawdy lead vocals. The Beatles also bonded with Reid's gregarious mother, Jernice, along on the tour as a chaperone. Hearing the Beatles lament eating late-night, same-old, same-old, room-service fish-and-chips everywhere they'd been, Jernice promised them a home-cooked meal the first chance she had.

Eighteen-year-old Walker never went anywhere without a portable record player and a stack of 45s. During flights, the two groups cracked jokes and indulged their shared passion for music, the singular calling that had brought them together. About the Beatles in 1964, Walker said, "They ate, slept, drank, sat, and stood music. Everything was music, music was their world." At that time, it was all new. Neither fame, nor politics, nor pop culture, nor controversy, had taken over—though it was all on the horizon. The Beatles were still young pranksters who indulged in on-board pillow fights, food fights, epic games of cards and Monopoly; they were always up for a laugh, unconcerned about the pigmentation of their new friends' skin. For the young lads from Liverpool who'd embarked on chasing an impossible dream just like the girls from Queens, it was still hard to fathom that they were blowing up this way in the United States, where other British acts had failed.

The Bill Black Combo's tall, hotshot lead guitarist, Reggie Young, often punctuated his cool image by resting a cigarette in the neck of his guitar. George Harrison was especially impressed, intimidated even. To the youngest Beatle, it didn't matter that their audiences paid

First North American tour, 1964: the Beatles with Brian Epstein to the far right, the Exciters, the Bill Black Combo, and members of the touring party. Courtesy of the author.

little attention to Reggie and his bandmates or pelted them with jelly beans. Young was already an in-demand session guitarist in the southern music meccas Memphis, Tennessee, and Muscle Shoals, Alabama. The combo, named after Elvis's original bassist Bill Black, had numerous instrumental hits, including "White Silver Sands," which made the top ten in 1960. In 1964, however, Black was ill with a brain tumor and could not tour. After America, Brian Epstein had contracted with Young and the band to go on to Europe and open for another up-and-coming artist Epstein managed, Billy J. Kramer. Two fresh-faced rock-and-roll acts, the Kinks and the Yardbirds, were signed as opening acts for the European leg. Initially, Young was far more interested in meeting the Yardbirds' innovative guitarists, Jimmy Page and Eric Clapton. "I had no idea who the Beatles were," Young confessed. That was prior to the thundering hysteria he was experiencing at every Beatles' tour stop.

Between cities, Harrison sat with Young on the plane asking all kinds of questions: how he bent guitar strings when he played, where he'd gotten the amp that sounded far superior to anything the Beatles had. Onstage George was the star guitarist and Reggie the minor character. On the airplane, you might think it was the opposite. It's as if George had an intuitive sense of the career Young had ahead of him. From 1965 well into the 1970s, as one of "Memphis Boys," Young contributed riffs on dozens of classics: Elvis Presley's "Suspicious Minds," Dusty Springfield's "Son of a Preacher Man," and "Sweet Caroline" by Neil Diamond among them.

At 5:00 a.m. in Vegas, Kane completed the interviews on his replacement tape recorder and collapsed into bed for a few hours of fitful sleep. In the middle of it, a loud knocking on the door rattled him awake. It was Beatle roadie Mal Evans with an urgent request. "I will never forget his words," Kane recounted: "We need you. Can you put on a tie and jacket?" With questions swirling in his sleep-deprived mind, Kane took a few minutes to splash water in his face and get dressed. Outside in the hallway, Evans was joined by Derek Taylor and the band's trusted road manager, Neil Aspinall. Taylor explained that fifteen-year-old twin sisters had gotten past security and ended up in John Lennon's room. Their mother, who'd been gambling and not paying attention to where her daughters had gone, found out they were upstairs and was demanding access. After being turned away, she was threatening to take the matter to local law enforcement.

A public police investigation involving the Beatles and accusations of late-night hotel room improprieties with minor children would be a public relations disaster. No doubt they all remembered 1957, when rocker Jerry Lee Lewis admitted during a tour of England that he'd married his thirteen-year-old cousin. That revelation ruined his career, making Lewis a pariah in the music business for years. Given Epstein's careful cultivation of the Beatles' image as clean-cut, fun-loving jokers, this kind of allegation could bring down the whole tour. Realizing the gravity of the situation, Kane was wary and refused to lie. "It's okay," Taylor assured him. "Not a damn thing happened in there." Regardless, the optics of it were terrible; fifteen-year-old twin sisters were now asleep in a bed next to John Lennon, who was married and had a child of his own. The Beatle brain trust wanted Kane to go down, smooth things over with the girls' mother, and assure her nothing improper had gone on. "You're a reporter," Taylor said. "You look trustworthy."

Before he would do anything for them, Kane ordered the Beatles' road men to get the girls out of Lennon's room and send them downstairs immediately. Sure, the Beatles had done Kane a favor by giving him those late-night interviews after his tape recorder busted. Now, their staff was asking him to cross the line of professional detachment, get involved in something potentially illegal, and risk his job if it all went awry. There was a hell of a lot at stake for everyone. In November 1960 Paul McCartney and the Beatles' original drummer, Pete Best, set fire to a condom they'd pinned to the wall of a squalid nightclub storeroom they were moving out of for a new, better-paying gig. The two tried to explain away the prank; they had just needed more light. Besides, the fire left no damage to the wall. Nevertheless, the nightclub owner got pissed off and called the police. The two were arrested for arson. Before Paul McCartney could grasp what was happening, at the tender age of eighteen, he and Best were deported from Germany. Now, in August 1964, the Beatles were superstars, and God knows what kind of consequences this brush with police in America might have.

In the lobby, Kane identified himself to the mother and assured her the girls had only gotten photos and autographs from Lennon. A few moments later, the siblings arrived downstairs happy, recounting John's kindness to them. Still, their mother wasn't convinced. In the Sahara Hotel, authorities launched an investigation into whether any improprieties had occurred between the girls and a member of the Beatles' touring party. To everyone's considerable relief, nothing came of it, and the boys narrowly escaped their first major US scandal. Whatever happened in Vegas that morning in John Lennon's room stayed in Vegas—but not, as it turned out, without a price. Months after the tour ended, Derek Taylor admitted to journalist Ivor Davis that they had arranged a ten-thousand-dollar hush-money payoff to the siblings' mother, who had threatened to press for a more thorough investigation. Had she planned the whole thing as an extortion ploy? Taylor said blackmail payoffs were becoming more common as the Beatles' popularity increased, especially with young women claiming Paul had impregnated them. As for Las Vegas, Kane confessed, "To this day, I don't know what happened in that hotel room."

In less than seventy-two hours of covering the Beatles tour, Miami newsman Larry Kane pushed Lennon and McCartney further to the forefront of American culture by getting them to publicly denounce two of the most controversial issues: military escalation in Vietnam and racial segregation. Kane had been trampled by fans in San Francisco and in Las Vegas, and, at significant risk personally and professionally, had helped the Beatles quash a potential public relations disaster. What could possibly come next?

21

New Songs and Snapshots

Amid the madness of the Beatles' first American tour, everywhere they went, either Paul or Mal Evans made sure a certain scruffy brown briefcase went with them. The case contained a trove of Beatle song lyrics and scraps of ideas. That they somehow managed to find quiet corners to create and keep up with Brian Epstein's pressing contractual commitments for new material while trying to function in their traveling circus all around North America is a testament to Lennon and McCartney's furtive creativity. That notion stuck with their road manager Bob Bonis.

"I didn't realize just how talented they were at first. The electricity was there, but I didn't understand the extent of their talents," Bonis recalled. "John and Paul were unbelievable. Songs just dropped out of them. They might be playing Monopoly and a song would just come to them."

During the tour, inside the one place that remained a relative safe haven, the Beatles' Lockheed L-188 Electra, at least two new Beatle songs were born. "I remember the song John was writing," said Jackie DeShannon, the golden-haired songstress known for her two biggest hits: "Put a Little Love in Your Heart" and "What the World Needs Now." "I'd sit across from him and he'd play it over and over on his guitar. 'I'm a loooser, and I'm not what I appear to be.'" This introspective Lennon composition, which ended up on the *Beatles for Sale* album later that year, reflected Bob Dylan's influence and foreshadowed the electrified folk-rock blend pioneered by Dylan's American disciples the Byrds. DeShannon bore witness to the Beatles' interest in all things musical, John Lennon and George Harrison's penchant for Monopoly, and the band's sense of humor, despite the intensity of the situation around them.

On flights, they often took time to sit with other artists and ask how they were doing. The boys heard the chorus of boos or chants of "we want the Beatles" that usually greeted DeShannon and others opening up for the hottest band in the world. "They were fabulous to me as a fellow artist," DeShannon said. Just to be with one of the Beatles, she recalled, never mind trying to open for them in front of a raucous crowd, could be overwhelming. When George Harrison approached her on the plane, guitar in hand, and asked if she could teach him the opening chords to her song "When You Walk into the Room," DeShannon was so flustered, she could not immediately remember how.

Ringo, often miscast as the quiet or sad Beatle, showed his intellectual curiosity by asking people, reporters included, about their jobs and families. It was Ringo to whom Larry Kane opened up about his mother's death. Ringo shared Kane's personal news with Lennon and McCartney, both of whom had lost their mothers during their teens. To be sure, the two front men always shared a creative rivalry over whose songs would be bigger, better hits. Their true brotherhood, however, came in a shared, intense childhood pain that only those who've experienced it can fathom. "Both of them made a point of coming over and talking to me about it," Kane remembered. "I was sort of hiding my emotions during that time." In a period when the Beatles could be forgiven if they'd become self-absorbed with their growing stardom, pursuit of sexual conquest, and mushrooming wealth, they'd taken time to show empathy to a reporter they still barely knew. To be sure, "they talked," said Kane. "But they also listened."

So did Kane—during the only extended peaceful hours the Beatles could enjoy within the protective lair of their airplane. On the Lockheed, "somewhere over Kansas," Kane recalled watching all of the Fab Four huddled, working together on another new song. It was a tune born of one of those famous Ringo sayings, this one about how hard they'd been working. "Eight days a week . . . he said it as if he were an

Twenty-one-year-old Miami newsman Larry Kane, covering the Beatles' first North American tour, 1964. Courtesy of Larry Kane.

overworked chauffeur," Paul remembered. "When we heard it we said, 'Really. Bing! Got it.'" Not only did Kane watch them working up the song; he also participated. "I did tell them to speed it up a little bit and they laughed," Kane said. "But they did."

Only with the unimaginable access Kane knew he'd be getting could he have witnessed, and participated in, the Beatles working up one of their early hits. During this window of time in which everything Lennon and McCartney wrote seemed to be sprinkled with stardust, Larry Kane was a part of a moment so rare and extraordinary that any reporter or Beatle fan would have died to be there, with all four Beatles breathing life into a new song, somewhere over the wide-open spaces of Kansas. In 1965, "Eight Days a Week" became another worldwide number one for the Beatles, selling more than a million copies in the United States.

The two songs "I'm a Loser" and "Eight Days a Week" represent the yin and yang of Lennon and McCartney's historic partnership. In this touring era, with the exception of his classic "Yesterday," Paul tended to stick with more upbeat, money-in-the-bank love songs whereas John started to explore his downbeat, introspective side. Paul later commented about how much courage it took for John to come out and declare himself a loser. But that was John: never one to sugarcoat things, always willing to share what was on his mind and in his soul, and at times tortured with self-doubt and far more insecure than he usually let on. As the creative train continued to chug along, all of their output went into the old brown case. "It was our filing cabinet," Paul told Ivor Davis, "a kind of good luck charm. Most of the stuff we wrote we simply stuck into the bag, and we took it with us wherever we went." No wonder they treated it as if it contained nothing less than the Crown Jewels. And that's an apt comparison: in recent years, the Beatles' song catalogue, much of its contents initially jammed into that old briefcase, has been valued at $1 *billion*.

Even their reclusive American road manager, Bob Bonis, was documenting history himself that spring and summer of 1964. After Bonis had worked as road manager for the Rolling Stones, it had gone so well that soon after, he received a phone call from Brian Epstein asking him to serve the Beatles in the same capacity. Bonis ended up by their side for each of the Beatles' 1964–66 American tours. It wasn't until more than fifteen years after his death, in 2008, when Bonis's son Alex was going through some of his father's souvenirs stashed away in a duffel bag, that he made a breathtaking discovery; Bonis had kept thousands of candid snapshots. Like unguarded vacation photos of both groups, still so young. The resulting collection, the Bob Bonis Archive, documenting those archetypical American tours, became the subject of books and exhibits.

Tested by fire within the Beatles inner circle, Larry Kane developed a genuine rapport with the band. All of them got a kick out of greeting Kane with, "Hello, Larry." In his interviews, they expressed frustration over family members being thrust into gossip coverage, not knowing whether to talk to reporters. Ringo defended his single band mates wanting to meet and date local girls. If they didn't, he said, it was likely some critic would call them "queer." John said he could tell the difference between genuine fan letters and others trying to manipulate them out of autographs to turn around and sell. Lennon wasn't one to ignore fan requests. As recently as 1963, he wrote back to two die-hard female fans, giving them all four of the Beatles' *home* addresses.

The trust Kane earned on tour manifested itself in a different way with Brian Epstein, who was often reserved with the press. Epstein invited Kane to his room and unexpectedly offered him a glass of wine, something he'd never done before. The Beatles manager then offered a toast: "Here's to you and me," Epstein said, with an air of expectation. Only then did Kane realize the personal nature of Epstein's intentions: Brian was hitting on him. "Honestly, in 1964 the word 'gay' did not exist in my language. 'Homosexual' or 'queer' were used, and it was against the law in 1964 to be homosexual," Kane said. Yet here was Epstein, putting his reputation at risk by coming on to a reporter on assignment. "When he did come on to me, it was very courteous," Kane remembered. "It wasn't anything with any great emotion or assertiveness. I thought, 'I gotta get outta here.'"

After he had excused himself from Epstein's room and the shock began to wear off, Kane felt as though he'd left too much unsaid. Epstein's come-on was exceedingly low-key, but it could also be seen as unprofessional and, to many heterosexual men, highly offensive. Like his initial encounter with John Lennon, the intuitive young reporter worried there could be tension in future interactions with the man who controlled access to the Beatles. If Brian no longer wanted him on the tour, that's all it would take; Kane was as good as gone. He approached Epstein the next day and explained to him he wasn't uptight about him being gay; he just didn't share the same orientation. "I understand, I understand," Epstein replied, and that was that.

Kane had witnessed the Beatles writing one of their million-selling singles, and he'd been hit on by the gay impresario who'd discovered them. He was becoming a national correspondent whose career was being transformed by his experience with the Beatles. He filed it all away in his memory bank, like Bonis's snapshots, among the extraordinary events becoming commonplace within the realm that was Beatlemania. Soon, the tour was due to wind its way back toward the Sunshine State, where trouble was boiling up on multiple fronts.

The tour schedule, mercifully, had two open dates before their September 11 outdoor concert at the Gator Bowl—two precious days of downtime in the midst of all the madness. Weeks previous to the tour getting back to Florida, promoter Norman Weiss sent Brian Epstein a letter notifying him he had made arrangements to reserve a charter boat in Jacksonville, the *Fostoria*, for the Beatles to use during their two days off. "This way the boys will be able to get complete privacy and two days of rest," Weiss assured Epstein. Judging from a picture on the pamphlet Weiss included, the diminutive *Fostoria* looked more like a charter fishing boat with little room to accommodate four road-weary men for two days. That didn't account for the rest of traveling party. Epstein declined the offer, citing security concerns. Given the historic events about to unfold, an undersized boat anywhere near Jacksonville is the last place the Beatles would have wanted to be.

22

Dora and a Dilemma Solved

On Friday, August 28, 1964 a low-pressure system took flight off the coast of Dakar, Senegal, a hotspot off the coast of Africa known as the birthplace of many tropical cyclones. At that early stage, a storm spinning to life more than four thousand miles from Florida's east coast drew little notice. On August 31, the Trios VIII weather satellite captured the first images of a robust convective system with strong outflow and banding features. The following day, ship captains noted tropical storm conditions in the central Atlantic. A Hurricane Hunter aircraft dispatched to investigate measured winds at 60 miles per hour with barometric pressure at 998 millibars and dropping, proof that this was an intensifying system. On September 2, the initial advisory was issued out of San Juan, Puerto Rico; the storm was now strong enough to be given a name: Hurricane Dora.

A tropical system spinning far out to sea still wasn't enough to raise significant alarm in and around Jacksonville. Dora had been tracking along a latitude far to the south. And besides, longtime residents knew they could bank on the Gulf Stream, a warm, swift current flowing from the Gulf of Mexico, south to north off of Florida's east coast. While Dora was still gaining strength far away in the central Atlantic in late August, the Gulf Stream took hold of another hurricane, this one named Cleo, and like a conveyer belt, transported it up the coast, with minimal impact to Jacksonville. Residents had seen this Gulf

Stream effect time and time again. They had good reason to assume the same thing would happen if Dora threatened.

Thirty-year-old Jacksonville meteorologist George Winterling, however, was growing more concerned. After feasting on warm Atlantic waters, Dora had blown up into a Category 3 hurricane. Within a few more days, another ominous sign: Dora turned from the northwestern trajectory to due west, on a path right into Jacksonville. By Sunday, September 6, Dora's central pressure was measured at 942 millibars with winds of 135 miles per hour; a major hurricane capable of catastrophic destruction. Winterling, who was inspired to pursue meteorology after watching Hurricane Donna claim more than 350 lives in 1960, made a dire prediction. Given his scientific analysis, he forecast Dora would be the outlier storm First Coast residents had always dreaded. "I didn't see how it could miss us," he recalled. "I drew a 100 on the map right over the St. Johns River and said winds would be up to 100 miles an hour, and that got their attention." Still, in the pre-internet era, long before twenty-four-hour weather hype, Dora was still an abstraction.

The Brennan family shared Winterling's feeling of dread. From a financial perspective, they had stuck their necks out to bring the Beatles to Jacksonville. Ticket sales were brisk. Their plan to stage the first Beatles' stadium concert before a crowd of forty thousand would be, by far, the group's largest live US audience to date. Their concert venue, the Gator Bowl, was located right on the St. Johns River, close to the coast. It stood to take a wallop should Winterling's forecast hold. The Brennans were prepared to deal with any issues surrounding the Beatles' contractual demands for integrated seating. The power outages, wind damage, and flooding a major hurricane was sure to bring with it, however, were far beyond their control. The concert, scheduled for Friday, September 11, at the very peak of the Atlantic hurricane season, was less than a week away; no one had a clue what the city might look like by then.

For the Beatles and their management, the possibility of a nightmare storm hitting their only Florida tour stop became the latest in a series of unplanned dramas that kept cropping up everywhere they went. In Denver, the promoter of the Beatles' concert at famed Red Rocks Amphitheater, received a letter warning him to cancel the show, or else: "I'll be in the audience and I'm going to throw a hand grenade instead of jelly beans." The author fashioned the message with letters cut out of a magazine and signed it, "Beatle Hater." After an FBI investigation, the show went on. George Martin recounted how he and Brian Epstein ascended a lighting gantry giving them a vista from above the spectacular mountain venue. "We looked down at the boys below during the performance and the amphitheater is such that you could have a sniper on the hill who could pick off any of the fellows at any time," Martin recounted. "I was very aware of this and so was Brian and so were the boys."

By this time, the opening acts had grown accustomed to rejection. For the Exciters, the vitriol reached a new low in Denver. As they took the stage, they were greeted with boos and shouts of "N-----, go home!" Devastated, Lillian Walker and her costars retreated; Herb Rooney stayed put and encouraged them to come back out and go on with the show. Even in the face of such humiliation, Walker and the Exciters sang their hearts out and won the crowd over. Still, they thought, if the reception was this bad in Denver, what would it be like on their three southern stops? The group was not accustomed to any sort of discrimination. Only once before, during a tour stop in the Carolinas, had they been refused service in a whites-only restaurant, Walker recounted. Pissed off, Rooney was willing to stay and make an issue out of it, but the rest of the group convinced him it wasn't worth it.

At a press conference in Detroit came another key vote of confidence from the Beatles. George Harrison declared the Exciters, and an array of Motown acts including Marvin Gaye and Mary Wells, "our favorites." When asked about their demand for an integrated audience during their Jacksonville date, Paul and John stood firm. "We understand they let them [African Americans] sit in the balcony but not on the main floor. That is part of our contract—we will not appear unless they are allowed to sit anywhere," Paul declared. John, as always, was more defiant, "We never play to segregated audiences and we're not going to start now."

To the Exciters, knowing that the Beatles had their backs publicly meant everything. Said Lillian Walker, "They were really cool guys. We respected them a great deal and were glad they respected us." In press coverage from this time period, there's no indication anyone in Jacksonville was pushing back against the integration mandate. By this time, it would have been fruitless, even risky, to do so. Integration's most formidable ally on the ground in Florida had thrown down the gauntlet against anyone looking to roll back equal rights guaranteed within the new Civil Rights Act. More than a month after the historic bill's passage, Martin Luther King and activists who'd fought so hard and suffered could finally celebrate a solution to their St. Augustine dilemma.

In August, Judge Bryan Simpson issued an injunction against St. Augustine business owners who continued to defy the Civil Rights Act. Some argued that they had no choice due to ongoing threats and intimidation tactics by segregationists. In an ironic turn, one of those business owners appealing to Judge Simpson for help was James Brock, the former Jim Crow darling who'd refused Martin Luther King the right to sit with white friends. The standoff lead to King's historic arrest. But that was two months and, from a legal standpoint, light-years from where they were now. Brock and his business had become the target of pro-segregation forces, angry that he had given in to the new integration mandate. They firebombed the lodge and threatened Brock to the point he was afraid to identify the perpetrators during federal court testimony.

Simpson levied fines against the most defiant offenders and warned them not to test him further. His injunction, backed by the threat of jail time, provided the solution to King's St. Augustine dilemma. Dan Warren, the local state attorney who'd worked long hours to mediate some sort of truce, lauded Simpson's precedent-setting ruling as "a dramatic breakthrough. This ruling and others like it would be the main tool for breaking the back of segregation throughout the country." Martin Luther King made a brief trip back to St. Augustine in August to applaud Judge Simpson's actions and declare victory for his nonviolent movement. "King tipped his hat to the Jacksonville-based judge and well he might," wrote journalist Mabel Norris Chesley, calling Simpson's ruling a "double-barreled order."

A powerful judge from a court located right in the heart of downtown Jacksonville had made it clear to local power brokers and everyday citizens that anyone looking to defy his orders enforcing desegregation in public places would have to answer to him. The Beatles did their part, continuing to make public, pro-integration statements as another example of how social mores were changing, and a new day of equality had arrived for people of color.

After Detroit, the Beatles' meandering schedule called for two shows in Montreal on Tuesday, September 8. Canadian authorities warned Ringo of a death threat they received from a fringe political group who said they would shoot him because they didn't like his big nose and Jewish heritage. "The one major fault is, I'm not Jewish," Ringo responded. But he admitted the threat was something neither he nor the Beatles could just let roll off their backs. "This was one of the few times I was really worried," he said. Up on his drum riser, Ringo tilted the cymbals toward the audience to give himself a little bit of protection. Throughout the performance, a plainclothes policeman sat close by. But what could he do if some deranged person made good on the threat? That realization made Ringo "start to get hysterical." The Beatles made it through the last of two performances, all of them shaken by the added worry. George Harrison described how they settled on moving up their itinerary and flying out that night: "We decided, fuck this. Let's get out of town." The Beatles were due those couple days of downtime before their next gig, 1,100 miles away, right in Dora's crosshairs: Jacksonville, Florida.

The tour had already been in the eye of a figurative hurricane, now all thoughts turned to where they could go to avoid a genuine disaster for Northeast Florida. They considered Miami. Larry Kane, now a veteran of three weeks inside the eye of Beatlemania, weighed in: "I told them Miami's no good. Probably the best place would be Key West." Even after fans on the South Florida mainland found out the Beatles were back, Kane reasoned, it would take four or five hours to drive down the island chain to get to that remote location. He even agreed to embargo his daily Beatle reportage several hours so fans wouldn't know right away the Beatles were back in Florida. To Epstein the logic was solid; after all the drama in Canada and elsewhere, for the morning of Wednesday, September 9, at the very least, the Beatles and the rest of their touring party could find some peace. Tour staff called ahead and arranged for rooms in Key West.

Like a necklace opened out into the sea where the Atlantic Ocean and Gulf of Mexico meet, each Florida Key is an island strung together by US 1, the Overseas Highway. At the southwesternmost link in the chain sits the largest island, Key West, a tropical paradise, a feast for the senses beloved broadcast journalist Charles Kuralt once described as "the greatest of all end-of-the-road towns." Known as a fishing paradise to presidents and former home to America's celebrated author Ernest Hemingway, Key West was about to have new chapters added to its lore, thanks to four Brits in the midst of their own odyssey. For the Beatles and their exhausted entourage, just getting there proved to be an ordeal. Compared to the Beatles' initial, February frolic discovering Florida paradise in Miami Beach, their return to the Sunshine State in September 1964 was fraught with peril.

Dora's path toward a Florida landfall had started to wobble. Still, by the time the Beatles' plane entered Florida airspace the morning of September 9, the outlier storm was doing exactly as George Winterling predicted. There was nothing they all could do now but take shelter in an exotic, island paradise far to the south, and wait to see the devastation Dora would leave in its wake. No one could answer the question on young fans' minds up and down the Florida peninsula: Will the show go on?

23

Key West

On the flight through towering storm clouds, British journalist Ivor Davis wrote, "Our plane was bucking and bouncing so badly that our stomachs were in our throats the whole way." To compound the anxiety, psychic Jean Dixon, whom the Beatles would normally dismiss as a peddler of psychobabble rubbish, predicted their plane would crash and three of the four Beatles would perish. During the awful turbulence, Davis described George's face as "gray green." Of Dixon's prediction, Harrison told Larry Kane, "It's not a nice thing to say, especially when you're flying every day." The doom would materialize a year and a half later.

On April 22, 1966, Reed Pigman, the pilot who flew the Beatles all across the continent in his Lockheed L-188 Electra, overshot a runway in Ardmore, Oklahoma, and crashed into a hill. The plane burst into flames, killing Pigman and eighty-three of the ninety-eight people on board, most of them young soldiers. The investigation blamed Pigman for failing to disclose he was diabetic, had a history of heart disease, and was suffering from arteriosclerosis. In 1964, the Beatles' tour pilot was keeping a high-stress, breakneck schedule just as they were; Pigman was not nearly as healthy as he'd claimed, and he was now flying them overnight into Florida's southernmost reaches, over long stretches of open water, through severe turbulence.

Not long after the Beatles flew out of Montreal, an anonymous tip came in to staff at the *Key West Citizen* that a large block of rooms had been reserved for the Beatles and their traveling party at the Key Wester resort, right next to the airport. Smelling a major scoop, the small but enterprising newspaper team wasted no time. Tapping a source at air traffic control, reporters learned that the plane's flight plan still called for Montreal-to-Jacksonville. Once the plane was an hour out of its intended destination, the pilot confirmed his diversion to Key West. A local radio station was also tipped off and alerted young people on the island of the Beatles' imminent arrival. In newspaper photographs, a crowd of seven hundred young people who had managed to convince their bleary-eyed parents to drive them to Key West International, waited for the 3:30 a.m. arrival. Deputies chased off a small group of teens standing on the edge of the roof. One guard grumbled, "I wouldn't put it past them to jump right off the roof as soon as they get sight of the Beatles."

The airport had a smaller runway, and landing there in the middle of the night would be challenging. "The giant Electra turboprop appeared in the sky," Bud Jacobson of the *Key West Citizen* reported. "Screaming and crying at the top of their lungs, the mob chanted for their 'loves.' The plane touched down and for one frightening moment, the crowd watched it hurtling towards the end of a relatively short runway at 150 mph." Pigman threw the engines into full reverse thrust to bring the Electra turboprop to a safe and, out of necessity, abrupt stop. Frazzled passengers burst into applause. "Where are we?" Ringo asked Davis. "I haven't a clue," the journalist muttered. As he deplaned in a coat and tie, Ringo still managed a wave to the crowd. In the middle of the night, John still kept a last modicum of privacy by wearing sunglasses. Bright-eyed as ever upon seeing lovestruck fans, Paul gave them a friendly smile. The immigration agent who was supposed to check the Beatles and their party through customs had failed to show up. It took an hour to find out that their papers had been filed and approved before they ever left Canada.

Key West police lieutenant Nilo Albury showed the Beatles to his cruiser. His head spinning, Larry Kane had to be helped from the airplane. It wasn't fear or exhaustion that had left Kane weak in the knees, so weak that Mal Evans feared he might fall down the steps. Despite the nail-biting trip, cheeky George Harrison had the flight attendant spike Kane's Coke with small amounts of rum. Kane, known as a teetotaler, was finally back on the ground in Florida, but, thanks to George, he'd unknowingly gotten "lost in the sauce." A crowd of girls thrust themselves on to Albury's cruiser, momentarily preventing it from leaving. To the Beatles, this kind of behavior had become quite commonplace. For their two days off, September 9 and 10, the Beatles checked into the oceanfront Key Wester motel, an expansive resort on Roosevelt Boulevard tucked away on the windward side of the island, adjacent to the airport.

The turboprop on approach had rattled walls and windows at the naval air station. The source of that big, loud buzz that jarred John Trusty and other sailors awake in the middle of the night became hot gossip in the chow line. "Did you hear the Beatles are here?" one of them asked. "Ya, right," Trusty shot back. The more he heard, though, the more he realized it was true; the guys whose music caused him to do donuts in his brother-in-law's car on that snowy interstate outside Chicago were within walking distance of the base. Just as interesting to Trusty was knowing that blond singer-songwriter Jackie DeShannon was with them.

After their arrival, the Beatles managed to get some decent sleep in their cabana near the Key Wester's main entrance. What a relief it must have been to wake up to relative peace and quiet in an island paradise, hearing nothing but rain hitting the roof. At noon, Ivor Davis got a call from Derek Taylor, informing him they were all hanging out with John. Davis got there just as Mal Evans was pulling up a breakfast cart of toast, eggs, tea, juice, and whiskey. For a journalist, this was a rare opportunity to spend time with the leader of the Beatles just being himself, still willing to put on show.

Davis found John sitting in front of the television, watching the dramatic mannerisms and oratory of Cuban dictator Fidel Castro, droning on and on in Spanish. During the Cuban Missile Crisis, military weaponry pointed south along the oceanfront became an unsettling part of life in Key West. Finally, tired of the blather, Lennon turned down the sound and started holding court himself, giving a pretty fair Castro imitation. Davis witnessed John popping Preludin, often referred to by the boys as "Prellies," which John called his "belly warmers." It's well documented that the band started using speed during their marathon gigs in Hamburg. Given the crazy schedule they were on now, Davis said the Beatles kept the pills in "plentiful supply," along with blue, heart-shaped Drinamyl, made famous by the Rolling Stones' song "Mother's Little Helper."

According to Davis, their assistant Neil Aspinall kept watch over the pharmaceuticals. "In the event that they were discovered," he wrote, "the Beatles could claim ignorance, and Neil would have to fall on his sword." It was the ultimate test of employee loyalty. Elvis used a similar strategy in 1960 upon his return to America from military service in Germany. A female assistant was entrusted to smuggle a jug of amphetamine pills in her luggage so neither Elvis nor one of his Memphis Mafia yes-men would have to assume the risk. By early afternoon in Key West, the sun had come out, and John and his cabana mates were now into the whiskey.

Larry Kane planned to rent a car and head up the Keys to home in Miami to visit and retrieve clean clothes. He invited Lennon to come along for the scenic, three-hour drive up the Keys, with no crush of screaming fans. Due to security concerns, John declined. Kane had agreed to a six-hour embargo on his daily syndicated radio report to assure the Beatles some downtime before fans on the mainland got word they were in South Florida—as far south as one could be. In his rented car, Kane made his way across miles of turquoise-blue water, traversing the Seven Mile Bridge into Marathon and the Middle Keys. Soon the traffic jam of kids driving in the opposite lane toward Key West was proof his report had aired in Miami and word of the Beatles' return to Florida was out.

Once John Trusty was convinced it really was the Beatles on the island, he suspected many excited young women would be part of that scene. He and another sailor headed in that direction. Trusty had been to the Key Wester nightclub, regarded it as a good-time hangout where the Budweiser was cheap and, most importantly, the prevalence of young, female tourists made it a target-rich environment. As the sailors were finishing the three-quarters-of-a-mile walk from the base hospital, around a bend in Roosevelt Boulevard to the Key Wester, a throng of young fans appeared, many of them girls clad only in bikinis.

The Beatles' villa was in view from the main drag along the ocean. A perimeter had already been set up by police, but the wide-open nature of the complex made for a lot of cat-and-mouse with fans looking to sneak in. Said John Trusty, "It was like trying to keep a colony of ants from getting to a sugar cube." Fortunately for Trusty and his acquaintance from the base who'd come along, a woman on the security team knew them as regular paying customers at the lounge. They were thoroughly frisked and allowed in with one serious admonition from the guards: no pictures of any kind.

Happy to have some R&R and intent on jamming, a number of tour musicians had already gotten to the lounge and plugged in. The newspaper took note that Clarence Henry, "fine Negro pianist, made a big hit with guests in the Key Wester Carousel lounge." Trusty headed for the bar, focused on the sprinkling of more bikini-clad women. Beers in hand, primed and ready to party, Trusty almost plowed down a young man directly in his path. "Excuse me," he said to the stranger and nodding toward the women who'd occupied his attention, "I was, uh, distracted." In that instant, Trusty recognized that the shorter stranger who almost wore his beers was Paul McCartney, who responded with a trademark wink and understanding grin. All was forgiven, seeing as both were there for the same reason. In fact, Paul's prowess with women in the club gave Trusty another reason to admire him. "I'm gonna tell you, this guy could work a room," he marveled. "He really was a ladies' man."

Up on the small stage, members of the Bill Black Combo had begun what would be an hours-long jam session featuring a variety of musicians, some on the tour, some local. Trusty caught sight of George Harrison sitting on a one-step riser at the foot of the stage, continually observing Reggie Young. "All I want to be is as good as him," George said. Executives at Hi Records, the Memphis Soul label, had other plans for Young. When they became aware he was off for a couple days, they made arrangements to fly him back home for an afternoon session the following day with Willie Mitchell at Royal Studios. The resulting instrumental, an infectious toe-tapper, "Percolatin'," features Reggie Young riffs recorded in a matter of hours before he flew right back to Florida to rejoin the tour.

Near the back bar, Trusty was standing next to a guy in blue jeans, flip-flops, and a white dress shirt. Sporting a Ron Jon shirt and a military buzz cut, Trusty towered over the man next to him. "My God," he said to himself. "That's John Lennon." Something else caught his eye: the way Lennon was holding his cigarette, with the fire pointed at, not away from, his hand. Lennon noticed Trusty looking and turned to him: "Would you like a fag?" In Europe, "fag" was common vernacular for a cigarette. In Key West, among sailors certainly, it was derisive slang for a homosexual. "No thanks, man," said Trusty, wondering if he might have given Lennon the wrong signal. "I'm just here to pick up chicks." Lennon smiled, "Well good luck to you, man," and walked out. Ever since that moment he had with John Lennon, Trusty has regretted turning down that cigarette: "I kick myself in the ass all the time for getting the wrong message and not getting a chance to meet a musical genius." He learned later that Lennon was drinking an enormous glass of Scotch and Coke. Trusty, never a fan of Scotch, learned to drink and tolerate it as a tribute to his Lennon encounter.

Lillian Walker and the Exciters were enjoying the balmy September evening poolside. Just outside the lounge, the trio was laughing at Ringo, who was waddling down the diving board à la Charlie Chaplin and jumping into the water. As Trusty was enjoying cold beer at forty-five cents a draft, still hoping to find his female quarry for the night, Jackie DeShannon walked out the triple-glass sliding door to the pool area where Ringo was putting on a show. "He looked like a drowned rat with all the hair hanging down," said Trusty. "The Exciters were sitting there by the edge of the pool, and they were all in one-piece bathing suits, just pretty women, giggling, watching the show . . . I stood there drinking my beer watching this whole thing go on. Ringo thoroughly enjoyed being a goofball." But there was something else that left the young sailor taken aback.

Regardless of who the Beatles and Exciters were, never mind that Ringo and the fetching young women were just splashing around and having a little innocent fun; collectively, they were crossing a line that had potential to bring them serious blowback. He was white, and they were Black. It was still the American South, and, in the eyes of many, the recently passed Civil Rights Act was nothing more than a piece of paper. "Nobody crossed that line," said Trusty. "It was shocking to me to see those girls there. I'm seeing something that's really out of the norm. I can guarantee you Florida had some really die-hard feelings about race relations." So, too, did the Beatles. Despite their fun-loving nature, Walker said the band refused to compromise on civil rights and any other issue they felt strongly about: "They didn't play when it came to something serious."

Trusty shared the Beatles' progressive attitude. He'd befriended a number of Bahamian kitchen employees back at the base hospital chow hall. One of them, Kermit "Shine" Forbes, who gained local renown as a professional fighter with ultrafast hands, participated in exhibitions in the 1930s with literary icon Ernest Hemingway outside the writer's home. During a chow line dispute with a racist newbie intent on making trouble for Shine, Trusty stood up for his friend and told the commander Shine wasn't the one causing all the trouble. "That guy was just an asshole plain and simple," Trusty declared. From that point, he and Shine remained friendly, but never friends. It was Shine who ended up telling him that it might not be good for Trusty to be seen around town hanging out with a Black man. In September 1964, two months after LBJ signed the Civil Rights Act into law, the color line remained firmly in place. Key West was still a long way in time, attitude, and custom from the freewheeling, live-and-let-live, color-blind island it is today.

After hours of drinking and partying, the navy men encountered Paul McCartney and struck up a conversation. Now drunk, Trusty's acquaintance seized the moment to pull a Kodak instamatic from his sock and snap a picture of Paul. As soon as the flash went off, the two sailors were set upon by security and bounced from the compound. To further the humiliation, a large security guard took the camera and smashed it. "We told you, no cameras," he scolded. Just that quickly, Trusty and his dim-witted navy comrade were kicked out and deflated, now on the outside looking in. Their Beatles adventure, and a lifetime of memories the evening provided, came to a halt as abruptly as the Beatles' plane had stopped at the Key West airport. On the walk back to base, the guy exacerbated Trusty's frustration by failing to realize what his boneheaded decision had cost them; they'd been in the presence of greatness. They could have returned the next night for more adventures; all sorts of potential had been squandered by his selfish decision. "The lyrics to Nowhere Man seem to sum up my lost opportunity," Trusty joked.

Nonetheless, his transformative experience of hearing the Beatles on the radio for the first time, having such an exuberant and unforgettable reaction, and then actually meeting them is the stuff of dreams. Right away, Trusty said he was convinced, "These guys were not going to be a flash in the pan." How could they be? By September 1964 they'd been dominating the American music scene like no group before them. But there was more: seeing Ringo swimming with the Exciters, showed Trusty the change in American culture these young Brits were helping usher in, even in this far-flung southernmost outpost. John Trusty's memories of meeting the Beatles on a balmy summer night became indelible moments in his life. The next night, Lennon and McCartney had a defining experience with one another.

24

An Emotional Landmark

Contrary to local newspaper reports that the Beatles were prisoners in their rooms, members of the group slipped out Thursday to explore the Florida Keys. John attracted a swarm of autograph-seekers shopping at Leeds clothing store on Duval Street in Key West. When Lennon made it inside, store management locked the door to allow him time to shop in peace. He picked out three striped polo shirts, a polka dot men's sport shirt, socks, and underwear. Cecilia May, the star-struck sales clerk who waited on Lennon, also recounted what a thrill it was to measure his neck size, fifteen-and-a-half. The motivation for Lennon's shopping trip marked another significant milepost in his career.

Later that day, John posed solo for LA hotshot photographer Ron Joy, for images to accompany an interview in the December 1964 issue of *Cosmopolitan* magazine, often referred to as *Cosmo*. The magazine's editors published one of the first in-depth American articles to take the Beatles seriously as artists, singling out John as the one with most potential staying power. The notion sounds preposterous now. But then it was a natural assumption, given that John was the leader of the group and the first Beatle to step out on his own with a significant solo project: a book of witty musings entitled *John Lennon: In His Own Write*, published in March 1964. In her accompanying article entitled "Beatle with a Future," writer and future feminist icon Gloria Steinem caught Lennon guarded and exhausted near the end of the tour. "I'll tell you this," Lennon confided, "I know this thing can't last. I'm saving the money. And I've got a lot of things I want to do."

After the shoot in Key West, Lennon, Derek Taylor, and Neil Aspinall loaded in to a convertible for some sightseeing farther up the Keys. Photographer Curt Gunther, who took some of the most memorable images of the tour, went along to document what appeared to be a relaxing trip where John dressed more like a Floridian than a Beatle. Riding in the backseat, Lennon had a chance to get some sun as the wind whipped through his hair along the Overseas Highway. Taylor later told reporters John went all the way up to Key Largo, was able to do more shopping, and dine—unrecognized—before returning early that evening.

Paul and George accepted an invitation from the family of longtime state representative Bernie Papy to enjoy their estate on Sugarloaf Key, fifteen miles north of Key West. The secluded paradise known as Punta Roquena sits on a peninsula at the end of a long, winding driveway surrounded by palm trees and lush, tropical greenery. Papy, a larger-than-life politician and real estate wheeler-dealer for many years, had died the month previous. According to Papy's grandson, his mother and aunt played cards at the house, allowing Paul and George to enjoy the swimming pool, guest house, and expansive, oceanfront grounds with a stunning view out into the limitless expanse of Atlantic Ocean. The family didn't ask for pictures or autographs. After the visit, though, they did sell small vials of Beatle pool water as a fundraiser for their local women's club.

Only Ringo chose not to venture out. After all the trauma he suffered in Montreal and the exhausting, nail-biting travel to get to the Keys, his desire for solitude was understandable. The local newspaper noted that he did cause a stir among the Key Wester kitchen staff when he called room service requesting "porridge." At a loss, staff finally sent the Beatle drummer a steaming bowl of oatmeal, which apparently suited him. The real news of that day didn't get out until later; two Beatles had already been victims of a crime.

From the Beatles' cabana, thieves had helped themselves to a number of items of clothing. The Beatles told police escorts, who had to have felt some pangs of embarrassment this had happened on their watch, that they didn't want to press charges but did want the clothes

The Key Wester resort, Key West, Florida. Courtesy of State Archives of Florida, Florida Memory.

back. Detectives put out word across the island that the culprits would not face prosecution if they would just come forward with the clothing. Not coincidentally, a girl had shown up at Key West High that day selling squares of John Lennon's shirt. Another student, an aspiring musician, was walking around in Paul McCartney's collarless jacket. The police swooped in, reclaimed what they could, and solved the missing clothes case. Beatle spokesman Derek Taylor was resigned about the burglary. "It happens everywhere we go," he said.

Once the Fab Four reassembled, Brenda Reid's mom, Jernice, who finally had enough downtime to go shopping, made good on her promise to feed the Beatles a home-cooked, fried-chicken dinner she made in a kitchenette at the Key Wester. The Beatles came to love her warm, outgoing nature and started calling her "Mama." The Exciters playfully chided the boys for liking her better than them. The Beatles sat down to a meal with their African American friends, still a small act of defiance when you consider Martin Luther King had tried to do the same with a group of white friends three months previous and was arrested and jailed. Once the Beatles' home-cooked meal was over, trouble arrived. Jernice answered a knock on the door, and a group of fans, convinced the Beatles were still there, barged in. "They just bum-rushed her," Lillian Walker recounted. "We're in our pajamas, I was in the bathroom. I mean, who does that?" Now annoyed, Brenda's mom assured them the Beatles were no longer there and pushed all the room invaders back outside. The security detail, so adept at smashing the camera of a young sailor who dared to snap a late-night barroom photo of Paul, failed again and again to keep strangers out of the artists' rooms.

Once Larry Kane completed his Miami visit and was driving back down the Keys, he had time to reflect. This had been the young journalist's first trip back home since his mother Mildred's death. Her loss weighed on him. Kane was living a reporter's dream assignment thanks to her sage advice, and he regretted not being able to share with her tales of all his adventures during a month like no other with the Beatles. "The experiences of the tour would have really amused her," Kane reflected. "I guess that inability to talk to her brought home the reality of her death." When he arrived back in Key West, Kane noticed the crowds outside the Key Wester complex had grown. Their short window of tranquility in America's southernmost outpost had closed. Fans hanging around the police line on the outskirts of the Key Wester, hoping for an encounter, a glimpse, anything really, had taken to calling the practice "Beatling."

That night, the Beatles joined the Exciters poolside, and inevitably the conversation turned to music, always music, and then to singing. Herb Rooney, the lone male member of the Exciters, spotted a keyboard just off the pool deck and started playing. Then John Lennon took a turn, informing the group that he'd been trained on classical music. To everyone's surprise, he played a selection for them. As the warm night pulsed and the singing got more spirited, one of the Beatles shouted, "Let's get our axes!" From that point, Walker and the Exciters basked in the wide-ranging repertoire the boys honed, out of necessity, in the early days, when they made their bones cranking out drunken, speed-addled marathon sets in the sleazy dive bars along Hamburg's Reeperbahn. Those were long—miserably long—nights of paying dues, trying to avoid being knocked out by flying bottles or groggy street toughs. Anyone in America who thought the Beatles were an overnight sensation had no clue of the many hardships they'd endured to get there; that they were now a great live band was no accident. The Beatles wrote killer songs, and there was no substitute for the hundreds of hours they had already played together live. "We sang rock and roll, R&B, they knew so many blues songs—oh God, could they play the blues," Walker gushed. "That was my favorite night of the entire tour."

Islanders knew the Beatles' short but eventful stay would become another significant chapter in Key West history. That sense was especially keen among those in Key West's thriving live music scene. Word got around that the Beatles, now rested and refreshed, had plugged in and were jamming. What musician would pass on a chance to play with the hottest music act in the world? A local promoter named Howard Rosenberg called the Key Wester to inform them he was on his way out and bringing "a Black Beatle" with him.

Pianist Lofton "Coffee" Butler was a baritone, blues-singing fixture on the island who'd performed for President Harry Truman, a frequent visitor to Key West during and after his presidency. A one-time Negro Leagues baseball player with the Kansas City Monarchs, Butler had hoped to follow in the footsteps of Jackie Robinson. By 1964, he had settled on music, the blues in particular. That night he had finished his regular gig at the Bamboo Room downtown and made the scene at the Key Wester for a late-night jam. At 4:00 a.m. a swarm of people crowded around the bandstand while Butler, accompanied by George on guitar and Ringo on drums, played a rousing version of Fats Domino's "Blueberry Hill." The flustered bar manager failed to get their attention and approached McCartney. "It's after four," the manager told him. "I'm trying to tell them they can't play here after 4 o'clock in the morning." Feigning empathy, McCartney acknowledged, "It's the Florida law, I heard that," then picked up his Scotch and Coke and turned his attention to a conversation with an attractive flight attendant. Lennon was the only Beatle who'd already had enough and headed back to the cabana.

The manager appealed to a trio of Key West policemen standing outside the bar to come in and break it up. Butler ad-libbed the last line of the song, "Yes, you were my thrill on Blueberry Hill," stopped playing, and announced, "Time to split, fellas, these cats mean it." With a sullen look on his face, Harrison put down the guitar. Ringo scowled and said from behind the cramped drum set, "Let the man play!" The trio of Beatles headed back to their rooms after a long night of fun. McCartney rejoined Lennon for a little more Scotch to top off a memorable night.

Initially, the ensuing conversation held by one of the greatest songwriting teams the world has ever known was written off as little more than drunken ramblings between friends who'd endured a lifetime of stress and pent-up emotion that year. McCartney described it as "one of those talking-to-the-toilet-bowl evenings." But with the passage of time, the encounter took on much greater meaning. It was only in their drunken state, McCartney reasoned, that he and Lennon, who'd created a string of timeless hits despite intense pressure to tour, "got so pissed that we ended up crying about, you know, how wonderful we were, and how much we loved each other. You never say anything like that, especially if you're a Northern man." To fans of the Beatles and their eponymous success story, this admission should surprise no one. The emotion of that night bubbled back to the surface many years later, after Lennon's 1980 murder, via a poem McCartney wrote called "Here Today": *"What about the night we cried, because there wasn't any reason left to keep it all inside?"*

McCartney explained to NPR's Terry Gross how that cathartic night in Key West brought emotions to the surface the two songwriting partners had not expressed to each other in such an intense way. Sixteen years later, after John had been shot and killed, that drunken night between friends was part of the reservoir of grief McCartney felt in the wake of Lennon's loss. "I always remembered it as a sort of important emotional landmark," said McCartney, who reflected on what brought it on. "Probably our mothers dying because John and I shared that experience. My mother died when I was about 14, and his died shortly after, about a year or so after I think. So this was a great bond John and I always had. We both knew the pain of it."

At this juncture, the two who were once so inseparable were starting to go in their own artistic directions. In their most recent 1964 album, *A Hard Day's Night*, Lennon and McCartney showed peak songwriting form, producing, for the first time, all original songs on one of their albums. In previous Beatle hits, the boys' voices were always blended: "She Loves You," "I Want to Hold Your Hand," and "Please Please Me" are among the best examples. Now Lennon and McCartney were starting to sing solo, Paul on his smash hit "Can't Buy Me Love" and the enduring ballad "And I Love Her." He'd also written songs that became hits for other artists, most notably, "A World Without Love," for his girlfriend Jane Asher's brother Peter Asher and his duet act: Peter and Gordon. Meanwhile, Bob Dylan's introspection was proving revelatory to Lennon, whose enduring classic "In My Life" is evidence of his willingness to show more vulnerability.

That eventful night before the Gator Bowl concert, word reached Key West that the Hotel George Washington's management in Jacksonville had canceled the Beatles' reservations for the next night due to their insistence that Black performers be given equal accommodations. Like numerous businesses in the South, hotel management was continuing discriminatory practices that the Civil Rights Act, finally passed after so much suffering, courage, and sacrifice, was intended to outlaw. In an audacious move, hotel management was still expecting to host the Beatles' press conference before the show.

Key West had been such an important respite for the Beatles, Larry Kane, and the rest of the touring party. Now their fun was over. Numerous issues hanging over the next concert in Jacksonville cast a pall from that point forward. Uncertainty over whether the Beatles' demand for integrated seating might force them to refuse to play the gig left the Exciters, still just teenagers themselves, feeling downcast. Walker and her Exciter sisters assumed, "They really don't even want us there." And what about that ferocious storm they'd traveled so far to avoid?

With all the dark clouds on the horizon, no one was in a hurry to leave warm, seductive, paradise in Key West for hurricane-ravaged Jacksonville, far to the north. Once the calendar clicked over to September 11, the plan was to arrive, do the perfunctory press conference, perform, then depart straightaway for the next show in Boston. The Beatles spent the morning drinking, playing cards, and waiting for word on whether the Gator Bowl had survived Dora.

25

Landfall, Destruction, Relief

Five hundred miles up the Florida peninsula from Key West, where the Beatles and their entourage had taken refuge, at 12:25 a.m. on Thursday, September 10, Hurricane Dora roared ashore just north of St. Augustine. Areas to the north and east, like Jacksonville and Fernandina Beach, endured the worst of it. Dora's eyewall made landfall packing sustained winds of 125 miles per hour, gusting to 135. A slow mover, Dora dumped biblical amounts of rain, as much as twenty-three inches in the worst-hit areas. Beachside suffered the battering-ram effect of relentless storm surge, the likes of which even local elders had never witnessed. Like a marauding bully, Dora proved to be the outlier storm locals feared one day would steamroll right over the Gulf Stream and into Greater Jacksonville.

Kitty Oliver and her mother weathered Dora on the second floor of a creaking old boardinghouse on Jacksonville's west side. There's nothing worse for frayed nerves than a hurricane making landfall at night, when the howling, freight-train winds are loudest and most frightening; it's hard not to imagine the worst. With Dora, every stronger gust brought concern, especially among children, that the next one could overcome their home and blow away everything. Beachside, the relentless storm surge was devastating, pouring into homes and businesses, dealing a final, knockout blow to what the destructive winds had already started. Stressed-out and frightened, Northeast Florida residents held their breath and wondered what daylight would reveal.

"Mama rented from a man I only knew as Bubba, a thin, prickly bachelor with rose-tinted skin who rarely tended to our apartment," Oliver remembered. "When it rained, water would seep through the corners of a window or leave a stain in the ceiling."

This time was different. She sat on the window sill at the top of the stairs while unrelenting wind and rain hammered it; making an X on the window with two strips of masking tape was their meager attempt to prevent it from being blown in. Kitty's fear rose every time she could feel the wind pierce the window frame and exhale through the house. Trying to provide some reassurance, her mother said it was good the wind could blow through the aged structure without taking it away or toppling it. Unconvinced, Kitty busied her mind with a more pressing concern.

What about the Beatles? How in the world could they still play the Gator Bowl the very next night, with Mother Nature laying waste to everything? Before the power went out, Kitty watched the news, "more concerned," she remembered, "that they would announce the Beatles concert was canceled than that our house would be blown away." She'd already vowed to see the show alone. Would her taxi driver manage to get through all the floodwater if, by some act of divine providence, the show could still go on? Up and down the peninsula, thousands of young Beatle fans who already had tickets shared Kitty's concern. Even in places the storm had spared, would damage left behind by Dora make it impossible to get to Jacksonville? Parents feared allowing their children to travel, knowing conditions would still be dangerous after the storm passed.

By daylight, residents along the coast saw the worst of Dora's wrath. Forty-five homes along the Jacksonville Beaches were destroyed, twenty of them washed out to sea. The surge tore away six miles of seawall, leaving jagged, ugly beach erosion. Floodwater from the St. Johns River inundated stately homes along Yacht Club Road and Pirates Cove. One man in the midst of a medical emergency had to be taken to an ambulance by boat. High water swallowed downtown parking lots, making them look like part of the river. Power outages

Beachfront destruction left behind by Hurricane Dora. Courtesy of State Archives of Florida, Florida Memory.

everywhere would take days to restore. Damage attributed to Dora totaled $280 million.

The first survey of the Gator Bowl, however, brought good news for Beatle fans. Floodwaters did not reach underground lines to the stadium, meaning—hallelujah—it still had power. Wind damage was not extensive there. It was after these early reports, and knowing this was now or never, that the Brennans decided the Beatles concert the next night would go on. To keep the band safe, they undertook last-minute construction to lift the stage ten feet in the air, behind a chain-link fence. There were other urgent challenges; Dora had knocked WAPE off the air. One of their competitor stations announced the Beatles' concert had been canceled. If fans stayed away and demanded refunds, the family stood to lose a fortune. "We quickly decided to buy on-air ads elsewhere," Dan Brennan's daughter Debbie Brennan-Bartoletti said, "just to announce it was still going on."

Dora tracked as far west as Apalachicola, stalled, then started moving back east, above the Florida-Georgia state line. Though the storm was weakened as it trekked west-to-east, conditions were too dangerous for many to drive to Jacksonville. In Gainesville, thirteen-year-old Tommy Petty had his ticket to see the band whose music he'd spent endless hours devouring since that electrifying *Sullivan Show* performance and the release of *A Hard Day's Night*. He had planned to catch a ride with older friends. His parents, however, were aware of dangerous conditions along the seventy-mile drive to Jacksonville. To his profound disappointment, Petty's mother, Kitty, nixed the idea. "It was pissing with rain and my Mom said, 'There's no way you're driving to Jacksonville.' So I didn't get to see the Beatles," Petty recalled. Due to all of the downed trees, washed-out roads, and power outages, kids all over Florida and Georgia were getting the same bad news from their parents. Concert no-shows numbered more than ten thousand.

In Miami, staunch Beatle fans were undaunted and ready to go. Radio station WQAM, led by disc jockey Charlie Murdock, boarded a chartered airplane alongside 125 teens, mostly contest winners, chaperones, two policemen, and a doctor and a nurse in case anyone was overcome with excitement. The DC-8 dubbed "The National Beatle Jet" had a rival on the tarmac. WFUN's "Super Constellation" aircraft was loaded with more than one hundred fans, some wearing specially designed Beatle blouses. That morning, Burdines sold 125 tickets to young people planning to get to the Gator Bowl, four hours away, on their own. One of the stations falsely reported that celebrity Beatle bodyguard Sgt. Buddy Dresner would also be on board. Dresner was on duty, unable to greet them again as Paul McCartney had proposed in his thank-you letter.

In Key West, the Beatles passed the time Friday morning playing poker, waiting for word on whether conditions would improve enough for them to fly to Jacksonville. Lillian Walker and the Exciters had sent out their concert clothes for dry cleaning and couldn't get them back before three that afternoon. Laundry and weather were mere distractions from their greater concerns: What kind of reception they would receive that night? Would they even be allowed to perform? Would there be severe pushback because of the requirement for integrated seating? The Beatles' advocacy for equal treatment, however, gave the Exciters the will to move forward. In the end, they had no choice.

After a momentous two days off spent jamming, sightseeing, and, for John and Paul, connecting on a deeper level than perhaps they ever had, the group and their entourage packed and prepared for the short taxi ride to the airport. Outside the Key Wester, twelve-year-old Karen Wade and her mom, who'd seen the Beatles on *Ed Sullivan*, were taken aback by the Fab Four they saw in person. Wade said, "Everybody in Key West was pretty tan, and they were pale, like, green pale. They were looking pretty rough." At the airport, Karen joined a large group of screaming girls standing up against the airport fence to bid the Beatles farewell.

It was a different world up north on Jacksonville Beach—blustery, ragged, and chaotic. Ten-year-old Mary Ann Joca went to the coast with her family to see the destruction Dora had left in its wake. Up and down the shore, everywhere, shocking and surreal images hit them; homes and beloved family businesses like Le Chateau Restaurant and the Sea Turtle Inn were demolished. It was a horrible thing to behold. The cherished beach where Mary Ann spent carefree summer days was swept out to sea, leaving large, slippery rocks exposed, and the ugly and jagged shoreline was dangerous just to walk on. As she stood in a pretty dress, with neatly combed hair with a white headband, a tall, grandfatherly man she didn't know, dressed in a dark suit and tie, suddenly took her hand.

As if the scene wasn't already surreal enough, surrounded by serious-looking men on the devastated beach she loved so much, Mary Ann was now holding hands with the president of the United States, Lyndon Baines Johnson (LBJ). While the Beatles' pilot had been instructed to stay in a holding pattern over Jacksonville airspace, Johnson arrived ahead of them on Air Force One to survey the damage. The man who had tried his best to soothe the nation after the Kennedy assassination just ten months earlier, and in July made integration in public places like the Gator Bowl the new law of the land, was now trying to provide reassurance once more while navigating what looked like a war-torn beachhead. Film footage shows a Cadillac limousine whisking LBJ, Senator George Smathers, and Governor C. Farris Bryant through the flooded streets and out to the hardest-hit areas. Johnson declared the damage far worse than had been described and immediately pledged federal aid.

In their own way, the Beatles brought more immediate relief to Jacksonville, a welcome distraction from all of the drama beleaguered

President Lyndon Baines Johnson takes the hand of Mary Ann Joca during his inspection of damage caused by Hurricane Dora. Courtesy of State Archives of Florida, Florida Memory.

residents had experienced and would continue to endure. After months of protest, clashes over racial equality, the slow death of segregation, and Hurricanes Cleo and Dora, a new day was at hand, a historic day residents of Jacksonville would never forget. As dark as the days and weeks had been, finally music fans had something to celebrate. On Friday night September 11, 1964, the Beatles' concert at the Gator Bowl, the show that seemed to have everything working against it; the first integrated stadium concert in the southeastern United States, was set to go on as scheduled.

26

Windblown History

Long before the Beatles' plane descended into Jacksonville the afternoon of September 11, 1964, the Gator Bowl and surrounding sports
complex had already been the scene of considerable music history. On
May 13, 1955, twenty-year-old unknown Elvis Presley played a scaled-
down stadium show at Jacksonville Baseball Park. After his short set,
he announced to overheated fans who'd stormed barricades to get a
better view, "Girls, I'll see you backstage." Soon, a flood of titillated
young women intent on taking him up on the offer invaded his dressing room. They stripped the shirt off Presley's back, forcing his retreat
to remote area under the stands. Legend has it, that's when his bom-
bastic, cigar-chomping manager-to-be Tom Parker saw Presley's revenue potential and set his sights on gaining control of his career. The
shows Elvis played during his Florida tours in 1955–56 were segregated.
At Tampa's Homer Hesterly Armory, Blacks were only allowed to sit in
the roped-off "Negro" section.

The evening of September 11, 1964, Kitty Oliver was poised to bring
about social change in her own quiet but determined way. Her taxi
pulled up outside the stadium. Just the imposing sight of it, given Kitty's sheltered life, was awe-inspiring. A more timid girl might have
turned around and gone home. Not knowing how she would be received, or whether she might be jeered, left Kitty anxious. The act of
crossing over from her Westside segregated neighborhood into this

zone of uncertainty took courage. "It was almost like, well, I've got nothing to lose," Oliver reflected. "I've got this spirit to know there's more than just where I am right now, and that's the way I felt." She walked up to a ticket booth out front and, with the money she earned cleaning house and delivering groceries, bought a ticket to sit on the field. She got in and was shown her seat with no difficulty.

All of this historic import was lost on white fans like eighteen-year-old Margaret Shepherd, who'd taken the train from Tampa with her older sister to see the show. Attending Memorial Junior High, going to high school in the Northeast, through all of that, Shepherd lived a polarized existence. "Race never came into my awareness because there was no other race," she said. At the Gator Bowl, Shepherd recalled, "It was just a sea of white faces around me. I don't think it was mixed at all." Hearing that Kitty Oliver was among a very small number of Blacks wading in to test the waters of integration, Shepherd marveled, "Oh, my God, kudos to her."

From the air, the Beatles picked up on the foreboding nature of Dora's aftermath. "It was windy as hell, and it was dark with heavy black clouds everywhere," George Harrison recalled. "As we were approaching, we could see the devastation—palm trees fallen over and a mess laying everywhere." When they finally landed, the Beatles made their way through a crush of fans to get to their press conference in downtown Jacksonville. Management at the Hotel George Washington refused to budge on their segregated protocol. Without rooms, the Beatles were forced to grab a bite to eat in the midst of their press conference. "Hey, Ringo," someone shouted, "did you hear President Johnson was in town today?" Alluding to the slight, Ringo piped up, "Well I hope he had better luck getting a room than we did." John Lennon was uncharacteristically vague when referring to the hotel's discriminatory policies: "We don't do the booking or the cancelling. Must be some reason why we're going on. We're trying to catch the hurricane."

Just a few steps down Julia Street from the Hotel George Washington stood the federal courthouse where Martin Luther King had testified before Judge Simpson. That testimony led Simpson to make historic rulings on behalf of King and his nonviolent army and, eventually, to sanction those defying the new Civil Rights Act. Had the Beatles opted to make an issue of equal accommodations being denied to Black artists, hotel management could have faced public repudiation in court. The Beatles didn't know that through this small act of defiance—their refusal to stay at the segregated hotel—they were walking a parallel path with Martin Luther King Jr., who'd been advocating for civil rights in court on that very same street weeks earlier. King had spent time in two county jails, endured threats on his life, had a beach house where he'd intended to stay strafed with bullets as an intimidation tactic, but he finally prevailed in federal court versus those intent on preserving Jim Crow oppression.

Many in Jacksonville's establishment shared the hotel's derision for the Beatles and their demands. An editorial in the *Jacksonville Times-Union* labeled the Beatles "Scourges of Liverpool . . . a passing fad, perfectly timed and fitted to the mores, morals and ideals of a fast-paced, troubled time." Given the lies and distortions upon which the Johnson administration was basing its escalation of US involvement in Vietnam, which the Beatles also publicly opposed, far more troubled times lay ahead. The night previous to his arrival in Jacksonville, LBJ's Republican opponent in the upcoming 1964 election, Arizona senator Barry Goldwater assailed the administration for "a lack of leadership that has turned our streets into jungles." Goldwater blamed Johnson's propagation of the Civil Rights Act for leading the nation "down the road of lawlessness." Goldwater's thinly veiled rhetoric showed that racism and prejudice were not just a southern problem. LBJ clobbered him in the November election, winning the presidency outright for the first, and only, time.

After yet another pro-forma press conference, the Beatles had to fight their way through a crush of fans who'd massed in the hotel garage. With the help of beleaguered policemen, they got out of the service elevator and into a Ford sedan driven by Jim Atkins, general manager of WAPE. Atkins had struggled to get his station back on the air and to be sure conditions were safe enough at the Gator Bowl to stage the show. Thanks to the throng of screaming fans outside the hotel, his progress to get out on to Monroe Street and head east toward the concert venue was maddeningly slow. At the stadium, it was warm and winds were brisk, but the rain everyone anticipated held off. As show-time approached, the audience grew to a respectable twenty-three thousand fans. To pass the time, they feasted on pizza and Cokes and were encouraged to buy small, plastic binoculars for a better view of the concert.

Starting at 8:30 p.m., the Bill Black Combo, Clarence "Frogman" Henry, the Exciters, and Jackie DeShannon took turns performing before the disinterested crowd. By that time they were used to trying play and sing over persistent chants of "We want the Beatles!" As much as they dreaded what might be waiting for them, the racial slurs and hostility the likes of which Lillian Walker and the Exciters had experienced elsewhere never materialized in Jacksonville. To say they all were relieved is an understatement. "It was kind of scary until we got there," said Walker. "We were treated with nothing but respect. It was completely enjoyable." The wind was still blowing near tropical-storm force as time approached for the Beatles to go on. When Ringo saw the height of the stage, and his drum riser on top of that, he demanded a banister be installed around it and the drums be nailed down to prevent the possibility of being blown off. At the last minute, the Brennans had carpenters erect a railing to give Ringo added peace of mind. This was also his first gig since the anxiety-ridden shows amid death threats in Montreal.

Just before 10:00 p.m., the group took refuge in their aluminum trailer dressing area near Gate G. As they greeted members of their fan club and ate hamburgers, a new controversy erupted. Derek Taylor spied a group of cameramen set up near the stage. In Australia, one of them managed to film an entire concert and sold the footage for a small fortune. "I can't allow you to shoot movies of the Beatles," he screamed at one of them. "Between here and the stage yes, but onstage, no!" How could they be assured one or more of them wasn't going to reap more pirated profits off their footage? The men with their cameras refused to budge. Pissed off, his long hair blowing in the wind, Taylor approached the microphones, announced that the Beatles were only twenty feet away but would not play if the cameramen stayed.

Hearing the ultimatum, WAPE radio man Jim Atkins jumped into the fray. He and his staff had endured far too much to make this concert happen to see it fall apart now. "You can't cancel my show!" he yelled at Taylor. As the cameramen filmed the showdown, Taylor turned to a police captain to resolve the matter, and Atkins joined him. "This show is for the kids, not the cameramen!" Atkins implored. The crowd grew angry and impatient. One of the cameramen was punched in the jaw. Then and only then did they decide to withdraw in the face of increasing hostility. With that, Dan "The Music Man" Brennan ascended the stage. Beaming with pride, his daughter Debbie, who was only seven, her mom, and other young siblings sat in the front row for the moment they thought might never come.

Wasting no time, Brennan kept it short: "Let me say right now that you've been a swell crowd here tonight. And it gives me a great deal of pleasure to present . . . THE BEATLES!" Brennan's introduction unleashed a jet-engine-like roar from pent-up fans who had suffered through days of anxiety over whether the Beatles would—or could— play. For a few moments, once the boys bounded up the staircase, Debbie Brennan-Bartoletti could see her dad standing there with John, Paul, George, and Ringo. They had gone through so much just to get to that point. "I was never more proud of my family than I was that night," she reflected. The Beatles tore into "Twist and Shout," and more ear-splitting screams erupted. Ian Glass, the Miami newsman who'd had fans ask if they could pretend to be his daughter to get in to the Beatles' press conference at the Deauville Hotel, also covered the Gator Bowl show: "The frenetic welcome the British singers received in Miami last February," he wrote, "was but a whisper to this."

In the front row, a rumble from behind jarred Debbie and her family. A stampede of fans looking to get closer to the band, similar to one that mowed down Larry Kane in San Francisco, was headed straight for them. In seconds, all the folding chairs on the field were down as fans trampled forward. "It was such a massive rush, it was scary," said Brennan-Bartoletti. The entire seated section from behind seemed to wash over them like a tsunami, a Beatle storm surge. Girls lost their shoes and didn't care; some screamed, others stared, still others clawed at the ten-foot-high chain-link fence separating the band from the hysterical masses. For the Fab Four, Jacksonville presented the most uncomfortable conditions in which to play. John Lennon told Larry Kane they felt like "four Elvis Presleys" with their hair whipping around in all the wind.

Halfway back, on the field, Margaret Shepherd had a good view of the band but heard only momentary chirps of sound thanks to the din of screams from the audience. "It was so overwhelming just to be in their presence," she marveled. "I was never any place where there was an event that big." John Lennon did a little dance onstage, and while waving his hand accidentally smacked George Harrison. While bashing his drum kit, Ringo dropped one of his rings, forcing him to skip a beat, as if anyone would notice.

Tom Petty's classmate and neighbor Kathy Harben Arce and two of her friends were there on the field also: 53rd row, Section A, seats 7–9. After suffering through the opening acts, listening to some kid in the row in front of them claim he was a Beatle fifth cousin, then joining the chant of "We want the Beatles!" Kathy and her friends finally were getting what they came all that way for. "Susan, Mary and I said we weren't gonna scream," Kathy wrote in her diary. "But we were so excited we couldn't help acting a little bit silly." Kathy made sure to take a long, in-depth look at each of them. George: "He had a real pretty red electric guitar"; Paul: "the pretty one"; John: "the married one"; and finally Ringo: "My favorite one . . . he had long sideburns and shook his head-a-hair."

Somewhere in that sea of throbbing, screaming, pulsating humanity, Kitty Oliver sat, trying to make herself small. Now, being unapologetically among so many white people for the first time in any public place, anywhere at all, was nerve-wracking. Prior to the Beatles taking the stage, no one looked at her, no one smiled or acknowledged she was even there. For all intents and purposes, Kitty remained invisible and ignored. "I just remember being very, very nervous sitting there," she recalled. "The guy next to me had a buzz cut. I just tried to keep my elbows in and not make contact."

Then Kitty was caught up in the joy of seeing her favorite band and started screaming her head off, just like everyone else. On this night, along a bend where the brackish St. Johns River makes its way toward the Atlantic Ocean, a teenaged girl from have-not, Westside Jacksonville rode a cab out of Jim Crow Apartheid America, sat down among the haves and fulfilled her dream of watching the Beatles perform. It was just what John, Paul, George, Ringo, and Brian Epstein wanted. A new, hard-fought era of equality was at hand that night in storm-ravaged Jacksonville.

The Beatles, September 11, 1964, performing at the Gator Bowl in Jacksonville amid tropical-storm-force winds. Photo by Charles Trainor.

The Beatles played a dozen songs comprising the standard thirty-minute concert. After "Twist and Shout," John took the lead again on the song he wrote in Miami Beach, "You Can't Do That." George took a solo turn performing "Roll over Beethoven," Ringo had his moment to sing lead on "Boys" and then got up and gave a proper bow. Paul and John alternated on lead vocals with multiple songs from the new *Hard Day's Night* soundtrack. "If I Fell," one of their greatest-ever love songs, was sung by John. Paul took over lead for "Can't Buy Me Love." Their finale, Little Richard's "Long Tall Sally," had also been performed by Elvis during his 1956 Florida tour, serving as a reminder of how Black music helped integrate America. Before the evening of screaming, shouting, stampeding, and other wind-whipped histrionics was over, a mother escorted her daughter out of the stadium and was heard to say: "Darling, believe me, you just CAN'T marry Paul."

As the Beatles hurriedly retreated from the stage, a group of policemen formed a ring in front of the fence as protection against a last surge from fans. They loaded into a limousine and sped off toward the airport, intent on flying to the next gig in Boston that very night. The last of their momentous 1964 visits to Florida was over. Unlike their extended stay in Miami Beach and two-day respite in Key West, they wanted to spend no more time in Jacksonville than was contractually required. Their limo driver dodged downed trees and other storm debris on the way back to the airport.

With indelible memories of her favorite band and Ringo, her favorite Beatle, still fresh in mind, Kitty Oliver strode by herself outside the stadium. For the first time, she came upon other African Americans, a brother and sister, who'd also been at the concert. After a brief greeting, one of them exclaimed, "You came *alone?*" Only then, Oliver said, did the gravity of what she'd done that night become more apparent. There were no angry segregationists to protest her attendance, no police to sanction her for sitting somewhere out of bounds. Kitty Oliver appreciated those who had fought hard and sacrificed to win her that right: "A lot of folks fought and died to kick the door open for people like me," she reflected. "And I was one of those who walked on in." The following year, Kitty took advantage of newly opened doors at the University of Florida, eventually earning a doctorate. Starting with the Beatles' concert, Kitty Oliver would no longer be marginalized.

Larry Kane confirmed that Jim Crow's segregated last stand at the Gator Bowl never materialized. "The Gator Bowl concert, which people had long assumed would become a simmering controversy over racial injustice, ended quietly by Beatles standards," Kane wrote. "Blacks and whites sat side-by-side, sharing an experience. The Beatles had prevailed." So had all of those who'd gone through far more than the Fab Four to pave the way for integration in Northeast Florida.

More than fifty years after he was arrested alongside Dr. King at the Monson Motor Lodge and attacked as he accompanied Andrew Young and nonviolent marchers to St. Augustine's old slave market, by proclamation September 25, 2016, became "Rev. William L. England Day" in Maine. The eighty-five-year-old former Boston University chaplain had made Maine his home and lived there quietly. England never sought out fame or notoriety and left it to family members to collect the proclamation in his honor. Reverend England now, by official proclamation, has his own day in Maine.

His short stay in solitary confinement in Jacksonville marked the last time Martin Luther King spent time in jail prior to passage of the

Civil Rights Act. On October 14, 1964, at thirty-five years of age, King became the youngest person ever awarded the Nobel Peace Prize for his nonviolent resistance to racial prejudice in America. In December, King accepted the award in Oslo, Norway, donating the fifty-five-thousand-dollar cash prize to the ongoing civil rights struggle. Today, the Monson Motor Lodge is gone, and another motel has taken its place. Along a nearby walkway stands a small monument to the efforts of those who fought for civil rights. The very steps where King made his fruitless case to gain entry to the Monson restaurant have been preserved and landmarked. Janie Price's former home, where King sang himself to sleep on the floor hours before his arrest, is a stop on the Freedom Trail, a series of markers and monuments throughout the city dedicated to retelling the St. Augustine Struggle. So is the beach house, once strafed with gunfire, out on Atlantic View Street.

On September 22, 2003, a new federal courthouse opened across the street from the ornate 1933 structure; the $84 million, fourteen-floor modern courthouse is named in honor of Judge John Milton Bryan Simpson. The grandson of a Confederate soldier preserved the rights of nonviolent demonstrators in St. Augustine and, in the face of public scorn and death threats, proved to be a beacon of righteousness. "Judge Simpson symbolized the true strength of justice in our nation," Andrew Young wrote. In a rare interview, Simpson characterized it all as a question of having the backbone to determine who was right and who was wrong, regardless of their status. "Another judge might have said, well, this is, this is all a mess and swept it under the rug," Judge Simpson reflected. "My conscience wouldn't let me do that."

The Beatles' 1965–66 American tour contracts continued to require integrated venues. To now know how closely they followed Martin Luther King's Florida footsteps that stormy summer adds more historic import to the stand they took on behalf of racial equality. Said music scholar Anthony DeCurtis, "The connection between the Beatles and MLK deepens and enhances our notions of their cultural significance." Ringo Starr later confirmed that the Beatles would have made good on their threat not to play and endure the blowback, if their demand for integration was not met: "We didn't think we were breaking any real big taboos. We play to people . . . we didn't understand segregation. We were just lads and we weren't going to do it."

That breakthrough, as proponents of equality and social justice in America, became one of the Beatles' most significant and enduring accomplishments, among many, in 1964. At the core of all their immeasurable success, to this day, remains the music: forever young, imbued with joy, harmony, and the power to spark change. The Beatles' timing could not have been better, weeks after the Kennedy assassination, when a rudderless, wounded, and grieving America, needed them most.

27

Markers

Each of us remembers songs so remarkable, so visceral, that they become emblazoned in our minds the first time we hear them, as markers in our lives. How many of these markers are the Beatles responsible for? It might be easier to count how many steps there are between the earth to the sun and back. How many times, hopeless or joyous times, have people all over the planet found comfort and escape in their music? From a random sampling of YouTube comments for the song "If I Fell:" "John and Paul's harmonies take me to a place of beauty, truth and hope." For "In My Life:" "Played and sang this song on guitar for my mother during her last five minutes of life." These small time capsules form the soundtrack of our lives; these markers represent the eternal gift left behind by John, Paul, George, and Ringo. What they accomplished was far greater than just composing, recording, and performing all that timeless music. They create for eternity an ocean of markers, of moments frozen, places remembered. And it's not over; as long as this relationship endures, many more markers lie ahead.

From a small hamlet on Long Island, where he and his loved ones took refuge as the COVID-19 pandemic swept through New York City, Robert Lipsyte reflected on being in that dank South Florida locker room when Cassius Clay met the Beatles. To Lipsyte at least, that momentous day, this first meeting of cultural icons, marked the beginning of the 1960s and popular culture. It's hard for him to get his head around the significance of it, of a time so distant culturally when the Beatles were a little-known band from England, and Cassius Clay a brash but minimally educated dilettante whom many assumed Sonny Liston would dispatch to intensive care. Given the gravity of that meeting, now as a marker in his own life, Lipsyte struggles to believe he was the solitary witness in that locker room. "You know, sometimes I think I made up this shit," Lipsyte chuckled. "That I dreamed it. That I went around peddling absolute bullshit. That never could have possibly happened."

In my own life, as the youngest of six siblings, the markers started as soon as I inherited my older sister's collection of Beatle albums, original pressings, precious vinyl. While my peers were listening to more age-appropriate bubble gum acts, I was watching and listening to *A Hard Day's Night* and *Help*. To listen to and then watch the Beatles from such a close vantage point, long before smart phones and streaming, to see the give-and-take between them and their frenzied fans, increased their songs' appeal. The first album I ever got for Christmas was *The Beatles Live at the Hollywood Bowl*. I remember riding in my cousin's olive-green Plymouth Duster the first time I heard Ringo's solo hit "It Don't Come Easy." We were all in Pennsylvania for a family wedding—my mom and dad, brothers and sisters, aunts and uncles, all kinds of cousins.

A vivid new marker came along almost fifty years later, when Ringo took the stage to sing that same song live. I was sitting in a pew among the faithful at the Ryman Auditorium in Nashville, known, of course, as the Mother Church of Country Music. After so many decades had passed, Kitty Oliver's favorite Beatle was still on the road performing; his eightieth birthday has now come and gone. As I sat watching him from a good vantage point, the elder of the two still-living Beatles at that time reminisced: "When I was young in Liverpool, I listened to country music stars like Ernest Tubb and Willie Nelson . . . when Willie still wore suits. And now I'm on this same stage. It's amazing. I'm so blessed."

It was on my mind that warm, August night standing in the alleyway behind the Ryman, taking in the considerable ambiance of the one and only, original Grand Ole Opry. A group of women all dressed up for a bachelorette party stopped to pose for a photo at the back door of Tootsie's Orchid Lounge, the legendary watering hole where Willie Nelson first played on the jukebox the demo of a song he'd just written. He was drinking a beer with Patsy Cline's husband, who liked what he heard and insisted on taking the song to her that very night. It was 1961, and the song Nelson originally wanted to title "Stupid" he had wisely renamed "Crazy."

As I stood there in the alley next to a gleaming black Cadillac Escalade, a policeman came and gazed down at the sewer grate, apparently to make sure there was nothing harmful down there. Shortly after, the back door of the Ryman opened to my left, and out walked Ringo Starr, flanked by security guards. A white jacket accented his short, dark hair and beard, and he still looked remarkably thin and youthful. He paused for a few moments to take in the atmosphere, extended both arms, flashed peace signs to a few fans who called to him from the street, and got inside the Escalade. As his flashy ride started to roll out past where I was standing, his tinted window came down. Not three feet from me, Ringo flashed a peace sign and said, "Peace and love, God bless." Then he disappeared into the Nashville night, having brought things full circle for the little kid riding in his cousin's Duster a half century previous. Still pondering my good fortune, I walked down past the Nashville Opera House to catch an Uber, and there in the marquee was a poster promoting the upcoming appearance of "1964," a renowned Beatles tribute band.

On May 28, 2022, I experienced similar good fortune outside Camping World Stadium in Orlando. Hours before Paul McCartney was due to take the stage, a convoy slowed to enter the final security checkpoint. From a distance you could see a hand extended from an open window of the second SUV. Moments later, the small group waiting in the searing heat for just this moment got their payoff. As his SUV drove by, there was Sir Paul, riding in the back seat. In dark sunglasses, he pointed and waved at everyone. Women shrieked. As I recorded images of the historic moments, I managed to ask, "Sir Paul, how are you?" He looked at me with a smile and gave a thumbs-up. I responded, "Good Day Sunshine!" After all, what exactly do you say to a Beatle in just a few fleeting seconds?

With that the convoy disappeared inside, leaving the fans still standing behind a barricade, thunderstruck. A woman in a black Beatles tank top was overwhelmed, red-faced and crying. Her mission accomplished, a younger woman from Mexico, still holding her sign, "*I Missed My Senior Prom to See You*," had tears streaming down her face. As the father of a daughter about her age, her obvious joy put a lump in my throat. Six decades after the Fab Four stormed American shores, triggering the British Invasion, the spirit of Beatlemania remained alive and well, at a time when many of the Beatles' earliest fans are now grandparents. They're still leaving markers in our lives.

In 1964, from their perch as avatars of popular music and culture, the Beatles made known their collective conscience—about Vietnam, racial equality, about the American underbelly they witnessed for the first time: racism, violence, the drumbeat of an unjust war. They embraced their role at the forefront of American youth culture, willing to call out the status quo when they felt it was wrong. John Lennon's unabashed certainty of purpose as leader of the band, his willingness to say something, anything that was on his mind, emboldened the others. In 1974, when it was time for John and his former band mate brothers to gather at a posh New York hotel, to sign their names one more time as Beatles on legal documents to dissolve the greatest band that ever was, John didn't show. Could he not bring himself to do it?

Lawyers finally caught up with Lennon to get that last signature in the most unlikely of places: Walt Disney World. There, in his modest room at the Polynesian Village Resort, John gazed at the blank space requiring one more Beatle signature. This enormous marker in his own life gave John great pause. His loving companion at the time, May Pang, had succeeded in helping bring John back to his music and reunited him with his eleven-year-old son, Julian. His fling with another woman prompted Yoko Ono to ask him to leave their home. Incredibly, Yoko Ono was the one responsible for bringing him together with May. Up to that point, May had been their devoted assistant and nothing more. Their move to Los Angeles brought newly single Lennon into the West Coast life-in-the-fast-lane party lifestyle. His drinking binges were epic and self-destructive. In 1974, his move back to New York was born out of necessity for self-preservation.

Ten years and ten months after the Beatles first touched down in Miami, their leader was back in Florida, poised to make his band's dissolution final. "Take out your camera, Linda," Lennon joked, alluding to Paul McCartney's photographer-wife. In the darkened hotel room, May Pang did as he asked, focusing her lens on Lennon, preparing to capture history. "He looked wistfully out the window," Pang recalled. "I could almost see him replaying the entire Beatle experience in his mind." And then, with a single stroke of his pen, at Walt Disney World in Orlando, John Lennon signed one last time as a Beatle.

Lennon, his paramour, and his eleven-year-old son had also started to frequent West Palm Beach to get away from the New York winters. A local photographer, Ken Davidoff, was incredulous when his father informed him that they all would be hanging out with John Lennon at a friend's condo the next day. As promised, the starstruck young photographer encountered Lennon relaxing poolside, still wearing a Mickey Mouse T-shirt from Disney World. Stunned but able to initiate a conversation with the former Beatle, something Lennon told Davidoff has stuck with him: "I can't stand the fame," Lennon told him. "I don't want to be famous. Fame attracts too much attention."

On December 8, 1980, Lennon saw his worst fears about fame and gun violence realized: a deranged fan shot and killed him outside his apartment in New York City. At the time, Larry Kane was a television news anchor in Philadelphia. While trying to deliver the shattering news, he broke down. "It was just so unprofessional," he said, his voice still reflecting the impact of Lennon's loss. Once, while promoting his 1974 solo album *Walls and Bridges*, Lennon paid Kane a visit at the station in Philly and stuck around to do the weather forecast, on-air. Sixteen years after those crashing panes of glass startled him out on the tarmac of Miami International Airport, and all the adventures they shared, this tragic marker ended Larry Kane's personal association with John Lennon.

The worldwide outpouring of emotion over Lennon's murder, included a gathering of fans outside a West Palm Beach mansion John and Yoko purchased earlier that year. Ken Davidoff had encountered them at a health food store he frequented, and at Lennon's request, he brought to their expansive new home some photos he'd taken of John, May, and Julian during their 1974 poolside encounter. John stood at the front door of his West Palm Beach property, signed one of the photos, and drew a little caricature as a thank-you. That was the last time Davidoff saw him. The young photographer was now back in the same courtyard, trying to make sense of madness. Mourners were allowed onto the property, held hands around the swimming pool, and wept. "Nobody in their wildest imagination thought that John Lennon would be murdered," said Davidoff. "Just insanity." Lennon had big plans for 1981: a new album and world tour to include his first concerts in England since the Beatles' filmed rooftop performance at Apple Records, January 30, 1969.

For all their remarkable experiences in Florida, there are no *historic* markers, none of any kind, to commemorate them, nothing to mark the first integrated stadium concert in the southeastern United States, nothing to mark where they fell in love with America during their Deauville Hotel residency. In 2017, that landmark property closed after an electrical fire stemming from unpermitted work. For years, the hotel sat empty and fell into disrepair. Transients took advantage of lax security and got in. The owners filed lawsuits, made myriad excuses, and racked up $2 million in fines levied by the city. In October 2021 Judge Michael Hanzman of the Eleventh Judicial Circuit Court ordered them to get moving on a demolition application. A front-page article in the *New York Times* decried the loss of a Beatle landmark. None of the outrage, it appeared, could save it.

In early 2022, a Miami Beach city building official, citing safety concerns, ordered the hotel be demolished. That included the lower-slung part of the Deauville campus containing its historic heart: the Napoleon Ballroom and the very stage where the Beatles made history. The demise of one of the most important Beatle landmarks in North America is the definition of Demolition via Neglect. "I'm not having another Surfside case," said Hanzman, "because the Beatles played the Deauville in 1964." He was referring to the June 2021 collapse of an occupied condominium, the Champlain Towers, in the Miami suburb of Surfside, which claimed ninety-eight lives.

To some, these were two different situations—apples and oranges. Hanzman's zeal to see the unoccupied Deauville Hotel demolished—and his equating it to the devastating loss of life in an occupied condominium tower in Surfside—compounded one tragedy with another. Rob Precht, Ed Sullivan's grandson, who once stood on the Napoleon Ballroom stage transfixed by the Beatles, called it "an abomination." Precht said, "It's a neglect of culture and heritage. Miami Beach lost part of its soul." Besides the Beatles' historic Deauville residency, what about JFK delivering a speech from that same stage during the height of Camelot? The shuttered hotel's new owner, Stephen Ross, known best for his ownership of the Miami Dolphins, grew up on Miami Beach and vowed to honor the Deauville's history.

The only place where the Beatles' historic time in Florida is commemorated, albeit informally, is their former cabana suite at the Key Wester motel; the only building preserved when the complex was torn down in 1999 to make way for an upscale timeshare. The small, stand-alone building where the Beatles stayed has been renovated and recast as the Abbey Road Snack Shack, a place to buy sodas and ice cream, get out of the rain, or stop and play a game of pool outside on the checkered tile porch. There's a small plaque providing a minimal retelling of its historic ties to the Fab Four. It's hard to get into the private compound just to look at it, and, it appears, that's the way management wants it.

A living, and far more tangible connection to the Beatles, the next marker, is waiting for me to arrive. I pull up to a single-story block home, not far from where John Trusty was stationed generations ago. An older man seated in a metal chair was having his blood pressure taken by a male nurse in blue scrubs. By the time I parked on the street and sidestepped a big puddle from the afternoon rain, the nurse had finished and headed to his car. There, in a white tank-top undershirt and dark shorts, was ninety-one-year-old Lofton "Coffee" Butler. With the world still in the throes of the COVID-19 pandemic, I put on a surgical mask and greeted the aging entertainer and Key West treasure. He smiled and offered me a seat on the front porch. Just then, from the long grass in the corner of his fenced yard, a small rooster gave a full-throated crow. Butler responded as if addressing a friend, "I hear you over there!"

We moved into his cozy front room with scattered ephemera of Butler's seventy years as a performer: an upright piano, above it a framed publicity shot, a ball cap commemorating service in the Korean War. From a table next to his recliner, he pulled out an eight-by-ten color photo and proudly showed me the newly named "Coffee Butler Amphitheater at Truman Waterfront Park." When I asked him about that 1964 Beatles jam session at the Key Wester, he beamed: "My manager

Key West musician Lofton "Coffee" Butler in June 2020, recalling his jam session with the Beatles in Key West. Courtesy of the author.

Herb Rosenberg called out there and said, 'I got a black Beatle I want you to meet.'"

The consensus is that Butler managed to get in two songs with Ringo and George backing him before the police shut it down. The only one he recalls playing was the Fats Domino standard they all loved, "Blueberry Hill." Once again, a smile lit up his face when Butler quoted Ringo Starr, "Let the man play!" Dressed in a festive shirt, Coffee Butler flashed that smile once more, allowing me to take a few photos of him.

In 1964, it was perfectly acceptable for two of the most famous white musicians in the world to back a Black man on a Key West bandstand, but scandalous for a group of young Black women to swim alongside one of them in a motel swimming pool. Such was the incongruity of the American South at that time. The echoes of all the turbulence that finally spelled an end to segregation came rushing back as soon as Butler's niece Beverly turned on the television. Late in the spring of 2020, coverage of the deadly pandemic was supplanted by Black Lives Matter protests in the wake of the killing of George Floyd, an unarmed Black man, by a Minneapolis policeman. A man of few words, Butler just watched.

To mark his eightieth birthday on July 7, 2020, Starr held an epic, virtual birthday party fundraiser concert that included an appearance

The Honorable Judge Debra Nelson, now retired, with the card the Beatles signed for her at Buddy Dresner's home in 1964. Courtesy of Debra Nelson.

by McCartney, for beneficiaries including the Black Lives Matter (BLM) movement. BLM started in Florida from a hashtag used to protest the killing of an unarmed South Florida teen, Trayvon Martin, by a security guard named George Zimmerman. A worldwide audience watched the televised murder trial and Zimmerman's acquittal. In an odd bit of synchronicity even Paul McCartney and Ringo Starr are unaware of, the judge who presided over Zimmerman's trial, Debra Nelson, now retired, is the same precocious neighbor girl, Debbie Nelson, who lived next door to the Dresners. Debbie Nelson, the fangirl who figured out it was the Beatles—not Uncle Harold—coming to dinner that night in 1964.

She treasures the card the Beatles signed for her, as a souvenir of meeting and having dessert with them at the Dresner home. "I smile every time I see it," Judge Nelson recalled. "I wish I was older because I would have been able to do something other than just gawk. It just seemed so surreal at the time. Here are the Beatles everyone screams about, and I'm sitting in a room with them." Nelson retains warm memories of her childhood on 160th Street, of the Dresners, Dottie especially. In their working-class families, Nelson said, there was no distinction between races. When she saw "white and colored" water fountains and bathrooms at places Jefferson Department Store, "I was so shocked . . . What is colored?" she wondered. About the Trayvon Martin case and more recent polarizing incidents, Nelson said, "I guess we haven't come that far, have we?"

Coffee Butler, the entertainer some called, "The Louis Armstrong of the Florida Keys," died on February 1, 2022, at age ninety-three. His legacy of mentoring generations of musicians, his bluesy baritone voice, and his connection to the Beatles' Florida travels of long ago will be cherished. All of it is part of the soul of Key West, the southernmost island outpost where royal poinciana trees blaze bright orange, crowds admire sunsets at Mallory Square, and hidden beneath flower baskets, strutting through the city cemetery, and maybe just to keep people company, roosters crow loud and proud, even on rainy afternoons. Cultures mix easily now, and characters of all kinds find peace and acceptance in an end-of-the-road paradise. That was not always the case in 1964, the year John, Paul, George, and Ringo took refuge here from Hurricane Dora.

All that's left to do now is take flight one last time. From that imaginary drone's-eye view, we're high above the chain of islands strung together by forty-two bridges. Below us is that translucent, turquoise water and, if you look more closely, rows of little green signs on either side of the Overseas Highway to use as reference points. They commence at famed Mile Marker Zero in bustling Key West and stretch all the way up the Keys to a final marker, at mile 127, on the mainland in Florida City. Near Mile Marker Seventeen, we spy Bernie Papy's former estate, visited by Paul and George, tucked away under swaying palm trees.

For many of us who feel the pull to return to the Keys and their enduring magic, those little green mileposts evoke a sense of familiarity, a feeling of home. It's an apt parallel to the Beatles' legacy. Each marker along the highway awakens a cherished memory rooted in their music, fading into the misty expanse, and disappearing into a restless ocean of tomorrows.

Acknowledgments

Every book begins as a dream. I owe a special word of thanks to Mr. Barry Dresner, who has lovingly recorded the extraordinary life and career of his father, Buddy Dresner, at buddyandthebeatles.com. Thank you to the Honorable Judge John Antoon, whose staff helped me locate the transcript of a little-known, June 1964 federal court hearing in Florida presided over by Judge Bryan Simpson, with testimony from Dr. Martin Luther King Jr. Thank you to Retired Judge Debra Nelson for sharing her story of meeting the Beatles. Thank you to Dr. James "Mike" Denham at Florida Southern College for his scholarship and support. Special thanks to Professor William McKeen at Boston University for his early encouragement.

Thanks to Larry Kane for the hours spent with me, detailing his extraordinary travels with the Beatles and enduring friendship with John Lennon. Thank you to Lillian Walker-Moss for a wonderful interview that made me feel like I was right along with the Beatles and her vocal group, the Exciters. Thanks to John Trusty and Dr. Kitty Oliver for sharing their lives. Thanks to dozens of interviewees, who took time to provide their first-person experiences with the greatest band that ever was.

The Flagler College Civil Rights Collection is a remarkable repository of stories of many courageous individuals, men and women, who risked everything during the St. Augustine Struggle. Thank you to Jeff Nolan and Hard Rock for access to the "Hard Rock Vault" to research their Beatles collection of primary source documents and one-of-a-kind photographs and artwork. Thank you to friends at the Key West Public Library. Thanks to Ralph De Palma in Key West for connecting me with the iconic Lofton "Coffee" Butler. De Palma's book *The Soul of*

Key West is a definitive primer on the island's array of notable artists past and present.

Thank you so much to everyone connected to Tom Petty's legacy in Gainesville. Thanks to Mudcrutch guitarists Danny Roberts and Tom Leadon. Also Rock and Roll Hall-of-Famer Bernie Leadon and the introduction to him from Bob "Hig" Higginbotham. Thanks to Keith Harben and his sister Kathy Harben Arce. Thanks to Marty Jourard, whose book *Music Everywhere* spotlights the area's remarkable contributions to rock and roll. Thanks to Mike Boulware, Greg Young, Dan Speiss, Dave Melosh, and Heartwood Studios. Thanks to my generous friend Jim Carlton.

I'm especially proud to have interviewed the entire team from *Life* magazine, who covered the Beatles' Miami Beach residency: Gail Cameron Wescott, Michael and Martha Durham, and legendary photographers Bob Gomel and the late John Loengard. A very special thank-you goes to Charles Trainor Jr.

Thank you to my friends Gary McKechnie, Amy Hughes, Margot Winick, and her Beatles in Florida Facebook page, Tanya Bhatt, Miami Beach Commissioner Steven Meiner, Tim Reid and all of those who fought the good fight to save the one-of-a-kind landmark to the Beatles' 1964 Florida residency, the Deauville Hotel. That it could not be saved and restored is a tragedy, and a call to action not to let property owners avoid responsibility via endless litigation. At least one remarkable chapter in the hotel's history will live on through this book. Thank you to Sara Schmidt and meetthebeatlesforreal.com. Thanks to Jude Southerland Kessler for your scholarship.

Thanks to everyone at University Press of Florida. Thanks to Seminole County Sheriff Dennis Lemma, Chief Bryan Beyer, and Kim Cannaday.

Thanks, as always, to my family: KK, Kristen, and Will.

Notes

Chapter 1. Sparks amid the Darkness

"As he left": Historian Michael Gannon, interview by David Colburn, Civil Rights Library of St. Augustine, undated, civilrights.flagler.edu.

"I actually started doing donuts": John Trusty, interview by author, December 16, 2018.

"'White' radio station": Kitty Oliver, interview by author, December 6, 2018.

"I describe it": Ibid.

"WAPE The Big Ape": Ibid.

"It made me think": Ibid.

"They're gonna play a new record": Keith Harben, interview by author, April 13, 2020.

"Eppy": Brian Epstein, *A Cellarful of Noise* (New York: Little, Brown, 1964), 104.

"They, like me": Ibid., 41.

"You must be out of your mind": Ibid., 97.

"I found out that apparently my wife Sylvia": Ed Sullivan quoted in *The Guardian*, February 1, 2004.

Chapter 2. Toppermost of the Poppermost

"God Damnit, this better be good!": Louis "Buddy" Dresner, interview by his son, Barry Dresner, buddyandthebeatles.com.

"Captain Stewart": Ibid.

"We just assigned you": Ibid.

"What the hell": Ibid.

"The phones exploded": "Rick Shaw, Miami Radio Legend," September 24, 2017, StephenKPeeples.com.

"It was just explosive": Anthony DeCurtis, interview by author, September 17, 2021.

"I was in love with them": Carol Lee Gallagher, in "Beatles 20th Anniversary," special issue, *Rolling Stone*, February 16, 1984, 45.

"Oh my God": Ibid.

"The 1950s saw": DeCurtis interview.

"Hey, look": Brian Epstein, www.beatlesbible.com, Thursday, January 16, 1964.

"There can be nothing": Brian Epstein, *A Cellarful of Noise* (New York: Little, Brown, 1964), 66.

"We didn't come down for a week": www.beatlesbible.com, January 16, 1964.

"We all started": Ibid.

"I'd say": Lennon, September 20, 2019, amontheradio.com.

"I took myself": Harry Benson, "The Most Influential Images of All Time," *Time* magazine, November 23, 2018.

"Cuban exiles": Larry Kane, interview by author, December 19, 2018.

"Unpredictable": Ibid.

"Both said": Ibid.

Chapter 3. On to Miami

"Literally lifted me up": Gail Cameron, interview by author, April 3, 2020.

"Get out of here": Ibid.

"The contagious joy": Ibid.

"It's like everyone": Ibid.

"Listen you all": Susan Lilley, February 9, 2014, thegloriasirens.com.

"I'm not going to miss it": Ibid.

"I had unconsciously": Ibid.

"It wasn't just": Ibid.

"World-shaking": Cameron interview.

"Get on the plane." Ibid.

"Mop-headed": Joe Monteleone, interview by author, April 3, 2018.

"Being a Brooklyn guy": Ibid.

"In case this bubble bursts": Ibid.

"Can we go with you?": Ibid.

"I was just stunned": Carol Lee Gallagher, in "Beatles 20th Anniversary," special issue, *Rolling Stone*, February 16, 1984.

"I noticed the pilot . . . waving": Monteleone interview.

"On the plane": Cameron interview.

"Do you think": Gallagher, in "Beatles 20th Anniversary."

"Public statements have been made": Miami Beach Police memo, February 13, 1964.

"How many men": Louis "Buddy" Dresner, interview by his son, Barry Dresner, buddyandthebeatles.com.Buddy.

"Hundreds": Ibid.

"The same one": Miami Beach Police memo.

"Ringo insisted": Gallagher, in "Beatles 20th Anniversary."

"Glass started falling": Larry Kane, interview by author, December 19, 2018.

"The door opened": Becky Pierce, special teen correspondent, *Miami News,* February 14, 1964.

"We want the Beatles!": Ibid.

"Then it happened": Ibid.

"It took me about three days": Gallagher, in "Beatles 20th Anniversary."

"Smashing": *Miami News,* February 14, 1964.

"This wouldn't have happened": Ibid.

"Beatlemania": Ibid.

Chapter 4. The Deauville Hotel

"Looking back it seems funny": Dezo Hoffman, *The Beatles Conquer America: The Photographic Record of Their First American Tour* (New York: Avon, 1985), 102.

"We're in the middle": Gail Cameron, interview by author, April 3, 2020.

"The hotel lobby": Louis "Buddy" Dresner, interview by his son, Barry Dresner, buddyandthebeatles.com.

"I've often wondered how Murray": George Harrison, quoted in The Beatles, *The Beatles Anthology* (San Francisco, CA: Chronicle, 2002), 119.

"I don't want anything to happen to you": Buddy Dresner interview.

"Miami was like paradise": Paul McCartney, quoted in The Beatles, *The Beatles Anthology*, 120.

"They also wanted": Mardy Durham, interview by author, July 15, 2021.

"He told me": Michael Durham, interview by author, August 17, 2021.

"They were yelling": Ian Glass, "The Beatles: Golden Geese of Public Relations," *Miami News,* February 14, 1964.

"What do you boys plan to do?": Sheila Moran, "I Was Alone with the Beatles for 45 Minutes," *Fort Lauderdale Times,* February 14, 1964.

"What else": Ibid.

"Setback": Ibid.

"Can Beatlemania": Ibid.

"Do you date much?": Ibid.

"What are you doing?": Ibid.

"Still serious": Ibid.

"We can't have it": Ibid.

"Well, then": Ibid.

"Sure": Ibid.

"I'm here": Ibid.

"Well, we were thinking": Ibid.

"The three other": Ibid.

"Pretty": Thomas Hauser, "Clay, 'I'm a Little Special,'" *Sports Illustrated*, February 24, 1964.

"No one produced a cent": Moran, "I Was Alone with the Beatles for 45 Minutes."

"More composing": Ibid.

"We wear it this way": Ibid.

"You know": Ibid.

Chapter 5. In the Water, on the Town

"No, no, no, I can": Louis "Buddy" Dresner, interview by his son, Barry Dresner, buddyandthebeatles.com.

"You gotta be cool": Ibid.

"They were sweet about it": Howard Cohen, "Miami Meets the Beatles," *Miami Herald*, February 13, 2004.

"They said, 'let's try it'": Buddy Dresner interview.

"I thought John": Gail Cameron, interview by author, April 3, 2020.

"Okay love": Ibid.

"It was a thrill": Ringo Starr, Beatlesbible.com.

"Rock and roll gods": *The Beatles Anthology* (San Francisco, CA: Chronicle, 2002), 123.

"Imposing figure": BuddyandtheBeatles.com.

"I like them": Ibid.

"We used to play": AP, "Beatles Called Fine Group of Young Men," *Troy (NY) Record*, February 18, 1964.

"We tried to keep": Ibid.

"Followed by a statuesque blond": buddyandthebeatles.com

"I got home": Buddy Dresner interview.

Chapter 6. Grace Kelly and a Third-Rate Photograph

"I'm going to start": Louis "Buddy" Dresner, interview by his son, Barry Dresner, buddyandthebeatles.com.

"'Boody' or 'Bood'": Ibid.

"The Beatles are coming over tomorrow": Linda Pollak, "In 1964, the Beatles Came to My House," *Chicago Tribune*, February 9, 1989.

"What? You've gotta be kidding!": Ibid.

"My impression": Michael Durham, interview by author, August 17, 2021.

"I had in mind": John Loengard, interview by author, May 25, 2019.

"They look really scruffy": Gail Cameron, interview by author, April 3, 2020.

"Every photographer on this planet": Ibid.

"Then, in came the Beatles": Pollak, "In 1964, the Beatles Came to My House."

"Get in . . . *Life* is supporting you": Loengard interview.

"I remember Paul screaming": Bob Gomel, photographer, interview by author, April 20, 2020.

"These were four": Ibid.

"We've heard about this": Cameron interview.

"Ow, me 'ead": Pollak, "In 1964, the Beatles Came to My House."

"Don't let it": Ibid.

"We had a wonderful day": Ibid.

"It's like another piece": "The Beatles House in Miami Beach about to End Its Run," *Forbes*, April 29, 2014.

"All sorts of reasons why": Loengard interview.

"Understandably": Cameron interview.

"The the most important thing": Michael Durham interview.

"Maybe it had some quality": Loengard interview.

Chapter 7. Fatherly Advice

"They were white": Diane Levine, "Do You Want to Know a Secret?," in "Beatles 20th Anniversary," special issue, *Rolling Stone*, February 16, 1984, 57.

"I backed up": Ibid.

"I don't want": Ibid.

"I really felt": Ibid.

"Come see the show": Ibid.

"The sweetest, nicest lady": Louis "Buddy" Dresner, interview by his son, Barry Dresner, buddyandthebeatles.com.

"Everything went well": Ian Glass, "Twenty Years Ago, Moptops Wanted to Hold Our Hands," *Miami News*, February 4, 1984.

"Americans are funny": Buddy Dresner interview.

"You're right": Ibid.

"cool room": Dezo Hoffman, *The Beatles Conquer America: The Photographic Record of Their First American Tour* (New York: Avon, 1985), 103.

"Every night my sister": Barbara Glass, interview by author, May 19, 2020.

"He asked us": Ibid.

"I'd rather be in Omaha": Buddy Dresner interview.

"Here, here's another one of your group": Ibid.

"Why don't you get a job": Ibid.

"Got myself a proper job": *The Beatles: Let It Be,* dir. Peter Jackson (Apple Corps Ltd., Wingnut Films, 2021).

"Bloody 'bout time": Ibid.

"We were not amused": Matthew Wilkening, "When Don Rickles Insulted the Beatles," Ultimateclassicrock.com.

"George, you're getting a roommate": Buddy Dresner interview.

Chapter 8. The Day Before

"Miami": "Remembering John Lennon's Guitars on the Anniversary of His Passing," uniqueguitar.blogspot.com, December 2, 2018.

"Fifteen or twenty": Louis "Buddy" Dresner, interview by his son, Barry Dresner, buddyandthebeatles.com.

"Hey, don't be mad at him!": Ibid.

"Can you account": George Harrison, interview by Charlie Murdock, WQAM Radio, February 21, 1964.

"I don't know": Ibid.

"Very good": Ibid.

"I'd be like": Buddy Dresner interview.

"It was ideal for them": Dezo Hoffman, *The Beatles Conquer America: The Photographic Record of Their First American Tour* (New York: Avon, 1985), 120.

"For the past year": Harvey Pack, "Gaynor Heats up Rehearsals," AP, February 16, 1964.

"The family store": Robert Precht, interview by author, May 21, 2021.

"Overwhelming": Forster quoted in "Beatles 50th Anniversary Count Down," eyesofageneration.com.

"When they started": Precht interview.

"Service to youth": "Local Man Helps Make the Beatles, 'Sigma Chis,'" *Muncie (IN) Evening Press,* March 14, 1964.

"The Beatles kept telling us": Ibid.

Chapter 9. Ed, the Abstract, and a Second First

"He didn't have a particular plan": Peggy Spence, interview by author, August 10, 2019.

"We printed": Doug Spence, "The Beatles in Abstract," *Binghamton (NY) Press and Sun,* February 28, 1964.

"We showed our art": Doug Spence, "Locals Had Their Moments with the Fab Four," *Daytona Beach News-Journal,* February 14, 1994.

"They wore": Ibid.

"We just couldn't believe": Doug Spence, interview by author, August 10, 2019.

"Don and I stayed around": Doug Spence interview.

"Too nerve-wracking." Robert Precht, interview by author, May 21, 2021.

"Dress rehearsal tired them out": Buddy Dresner interview.

"Freeze it": Ibid.

"Get the hell out of the way!": Ibid.

"Ladies and gentleman": Ed Sullivan, *The Ed Sullivan Show,* live from Miami Beach, CBS Network, February 16, 1964.

"I saw a girl": Milt Salamon, "Ed's Miami Man Played Beatle Show," *Florida Today*, February 11, 1994.

"Truthfully, the screaming": James Pomerance, interview by author, June 17, 2020.

"Suddenly the stereotype": Larry Kane, interview by author, December 19, 2018.

"We told some folks": Doug Spence interview.

"It was inexcusable": Tucker, "Beatle Fans Lose in Ticket Mix-up."

"Who's this Paul McCartney": Diane Levine quoted in "Beatles 20th Anniversary," special issue, *Rolling Stone*, February 16, 1984, 57.

"Oh my God": Pomerance interview.

"In many ways": Precht interview.

"Thank God": Louis "Buddy" Dresner, interview by his son, Barry Dresner, buddyandthebeatles.com.

"I've got some news": Ibid.

"Oh ya": Ibid.

"Does the hotel know?": Ibid.

"Well": Ibid.

Chapter 10. Fast Times, Mob Ties, and a Surprise Visit

"They still sound like": Cary Schneider, "What the Critics Wrote about the Beatles," *LA Times*, February 17, 1984.

"Musically": Ibid.

"The Beatles are not": Ibid.

"Rock, we've got a problem": Louis "Buddy" Dresner, interview by his son, Barry Dresner, buddyandthebeatles.com.

"What are they gonna do?" Ibid.

"Beats the hell out of me": Ibid.

"Just keep doin' what you're doing": Ibid.

"The boys want to stay": Ibid.

"I'm sleeping here": Ibid.

"Well, . . . they appreciate": Ibid.

"When Ruth got home": Bob Gomel, interview by author, April 20, 2020.

"Lost": Ibid.

"I don't think the Beatles": Terry Tomalin, "Racing Boat That Roughed up the Beatles Is Restored," *Tampa Bay Times*, February 21, 2014.

"White as ghosts": Ibid.

"One magazine": Dezo Hoffman, *The Beatles Conquer America: The Photographic Record of Their First American Tour* (New York: Avon, 1985), 103.

"You want we should take care of them?": Kenneth Womack, *Maximum Volume: The Life of Beatles Producer George Martin, the Early Years, 1928–1965* (Chicago: Chicago Review Press, 2017), 78.

"Sinister moment": Ibid.

"They said, 'let's go.'" Barry Dresner, interview by author, February 19, 2019.

"It all seems": Ibid.

"They sneak down": Ibid.

Chapter 11. Molding Clay

"Sissies": Tony Violante, "The Beatles and Muhammad Ali," *Villages-News,* June 10, 2016.

"A bum": SI Staff, "C Marcellus Clay Esq.," *Sports Illustrated*, June 10, 1963.

"Den of thieves": Linda Robertson, "Flashback Miami, Muhammad Ali," *Miami Herald*, June 4, 2016.

"The cops would call": Ibid.

"Those were the best": Ibid.

"This man won": Ibid.

"So I could follow": Robert Lipsyte, interview by author, March 27, 2020.

"It was our four": Ibid.

"Where's that big mouth": Ibid.

"Hi, I'm Robert Lipsyte": Ibid.

"Hi, I'm Ringo": Ibid.

"Oh Sonny's": Ibid.

"We all kind of gasped": Ibid.

"Hey Beatles": Ibid.

"You aint as dumb as you look!": Ibid.

"No, but you are!": Ibid.

"When Liston": Ibid.

"He whispers": Ibid.

"I shook up the world!": Dan Gelston, "14 of Muhammad Ali's Greatest Quotes," *Boston Globe*, June 4, 2016.

"Fellas": Barry Dresner, interview by author, February 19, 2019.

"I don't have to be": Robert Lipsyte, "Clay Discusses His Future, Liston, Black Muslims," *New York Times*, February 27, 1964.

"A card-carrying": Ibid.

"We didn't appreciate": Bob Gomel, interview by author, April 20, 2020.

"Slave name": Alexandra Sims, "Ali, "Why Did Boxing Legend Change His Name from Cassius Clay?," *Independent UK*, June 4, 2016.

"When Cassius Clay": AP, "Negro Leader Battles Clay," *Orlando Sentinel*, March 27, 1964.

"Why is the United States butting in?": Barry Dresner, interview by author, February 19, 2019.

"John, why": Ibid.

"Cassius Clay was born": Flashback Miami, *Miami Herald*, flashbackmiami. com.

Chapter 12. Dinner with Uncle Harold

"Who is this?": Circuit Judge Debra Nelson, interview by author, February 5, 2021.

"Who is coming to dinner?": Ibid.

"She wasn't fazed": Buddy Dresner, "The Beatles in Miami," *Miami News*, February 4, 1984.

"kiddies": Barry Dresner, interview by author, February 19, 2019

"They're here!": Ibid.

"Wait a minute": Ibid.

"Kind of the biggest betrayal": Ibid.

"It was a simple": Dezo Hoffman, *The Beatles Conquer America: The Photographic Record of Their First American Tour* (New York: Avon, 1985), 102.

"Don't say anything stupid": Jeri (Dresner) Greenberg, interview by author, February 5, 2021.

"Paul was always": Hoffman, *The Beatles Conquer America*, 104.

"I dropped it": Greenberg interview.

"Are those real?": Barry Dresner interview.

"I wish I was older": Nelson interview.

"It was just a very relaxing": Greenberg interview.

"They kissed": Barry Dresner interview.

"Both Neil and I": Brian Somerville letter to Buddy Dresner, Hard Rock Collection.

"Have any of you boys": Louis "Buddy" Dresner, interview by his son, Barry Dresner, buddyandthebeatles.com.

"Elvis was bigger than religion": Ivor Davis, *The Beatles and Me on Tour* (Los Angeles, CA: Cockney Kid, 2014), 217.

"When I heard": Ibid.

"You started to see them": Buddy Dresner interview.

"Sometimes my adventures": Hoffman, *The Beatles Conquer America*, 4.

Chapter 13. You Can't Do That

"Paul and I": @JohnLennon, Twitter, January 24, 2021.

"We managed": Ibid.

"Determined pursuit": Cynthia Lennon, *John* (London: Hodder and Stoughton, 2005), 376.

"Bloody slow": Cynthia Lennon, Beatlesbible.com.

"Nasty moment": *Beatles Book Monthly*, no. 9, April 1964.

"I thought she was going": Ibid.

"Semi-autobiographical": Callum Crumlish, "The Beatles: John Lennon Had a 'Long Lost' Semi-Autobiographical Love Song," www.express.co.uk.

"So I hope you see": "If I Fell," Lennon-McCartney, *Hard Day's Night* film soundtrack, 1964.

"I wasn't going to miss": Ivor Davis, *The Beatles and Me on Tour: The Beatles' 1964 North American Tour* (Los Angeles, CA: Cockney Kid, 2014), 127.

"We felt like trawlers": Barry Miles, *Paul McCartney: Many Years from Now* (New York: Holt, 1997), 142.

"The town bull": "Paul McCartney Coming to Chicago: Lock up the Wives and Daughters," Chicagolampoon.com, July 5, 2011.

"You kidding": Rob Smith, "How 'Can't Buy Me Love' Changed Everything for Paul McCartney," www.ultimateclassicrock.com.

"I called downstairs": Louis "Buddy" Dresner, interview by his son, Barry Dresner, buddyandthebeatles.com.

"Personal insecticide": Ibid.

"It was a hell of a car": Ibid.

"Here's what you do": Ibid.

"Oh ya, thanks Bud": Ibid.

"I'm in big trouble": Ibid.

"Let me explain": Ibid.

"Look you've got to help me": Ibid.

"Aren't they just too awful?": Cynthia Lennon, Beatlesbible.com.

"Yeah honey": Ibid.

"He loved the Beatles": Ian Glass, "Remembering the Beatles Twenty Years Later," *Miami News*, February 4, 1984.

Chapter 14. Stars on Star Island

"I need your truck": Louis "Buddy" Dresner, interview by his son, Barry
    Dresner, buddyandthebeatles.com.

"You say something bad": Ibid.

"What the hell": Ibid.

"Hugo": "Twenty Years Ago, They Invaded America, the Beatles," *Life* maga-
    zine, February 1984, 66.

"The best place": "Ringo Starr Comes in as a Mystery Guest," Howard Stern,
    On Demand TV, www.youtube.com

"I'd like to thank": The Beatles, interview by Jack Milman, WQAM radio,
    February 21, 1964.

"Making us a member": Ibid.

"Thank you so much": Buddy Dresner interview.

"Get a job cop": Spence autographed artwork, Hard Rock Collection.

"The married one": Ibid.

"Uncle Boody": Ibid.

"Best Wishes": Ibid.

"Beatleful Abstract": *Binghamton (NY) Press and Sun-Bulletin*, February 28,
    1964.

"Isn't that your Beatle art?": Doug Spence and Peggy Spence, interview by
    author, August 10, 2019

"Talk about the thrill": Ibid.

"We were just beside ourselves": Ibid.

"I hope you": Paul McCartney letter to Buddy Dresner, Hard Rock
    Collection.

"We cannot speak too highly": Brian Somerville letter to Chief Pomerance,
    Hard Rock Collection.

"My dad had a fan club": Barry Dresner, interview by author, February 19,
    2019.

"I saw some of your movies": Buddy Dresner interview.

"Mr. Wallace": Ibid.

"I took care of the Beatles": Ibid.

"He was a lovely man," Paul McCartney hand-signed note to Andrea
    Dresner and family, January 30, 2003.

"In America": Brian Epstein, *A Cellarful of Noise* (New York: Little, Brown,
    1964), 12.

Chapter 15. Dreams within Reach

"The Beatles were God's gift": Author's correspondence with Marty Jourard.

"These barbershop refugees": Jean Carver, "This Is . . . Our Town," *Gainesville Sun*, February 16, 1964.

"Cauldron of creativity": Bernie Leadon, interview by author, May 29, 2019.

"I think the whole world was watching": Tom Petty, "What the Beatles Mean to Me," musicradar.com.

"It changed him": Harben interview.

"I saw them and I wanted a guitar": Mike Campbell interview, Australian-musician.com, September 22, 2019.

"They were pretty good": Petty, "What the Beatles Mean to Me."

"I learned to play because I had to": Marty Jourard, *How to Start Your Own Band* (New York: Hyperion, 1997), 3.

"It was unbelievable": Matthew Wilkening, "Styx, Foreigner and Don Felder Share Awesome Beatles Stories," Ultimateclassicrock.com.

"I decided": Bernie Leadon interview.

"Then they were on": Ibid.

"We almost considered": Tom Leadon, interview by author, May 27, 2020.

"You either had a copy": Petty, "What the Beatles Mean to Me."

"One day Tommy": Kathy Harben Arce, interview by author, October 20, 2020.

"When Chris went to number one": Bernie Leadon interview.

"I remember how nervous I was": Tom Leadon interview.

"Petty kept saying": Ibid.

"He just seemed": Ibid.

"He was the closest friend": Ibid.

"Bitten very hard": Petty, in Jourard, *How to Start Your Own Band*, 3.

"Bands were forming": Ibid.

"After we heard the Beatles": Gary Rossington, "This Legendary Band Made Gary Rossington Say Goodbye to Baseball and Hello to Skynyrd," societyofrock.com.

"He looked terrible": Harben Arce interview.

"Mr. Petty threatened and chased him out of the house": Author correspondence with Tom Leadon.

"You could just see": Warren Zanes, *Petty: The Biography* (New York: Holt, 2015), 62.

"I swear, I'm not kidding": Tom Leadon interview.

"They were the first people": Petty, "What the Beatles Mean to Me."

Chapter 16. Seeds of Change

"The Music Man": Mary Colurso, "For Alabama Radio Pioneer Dan Brennan, Life Was a Shower of Stars," AL.COM, May 6, 2019.

"Artists will not be required": Chuck Gunderson, *Some Fun Tonight! The Backstage Story of How the Beatles Rocked America: The Historic Tours of 1964–66*, vol. 1 (Milwaukee, WI: Backbeat, 2016), 222.

"They knew": Ibid.

"That was taking a big risk": Anthony DeCurtis, interview by author, September 17, 2021.

"Shower of Stars": Colurso, "For Alabama Radio Pioneer Dan Brennan, Life Was a Shower of Stars."

"Man of the Year": *Time* magazine, January 3, 1964.

"Segregation is on its deathbed": David Porter, "Living in Two Different Worlds," *Orlando Sentinel*, August 10, 2003.

"Law cannot make a man love me": Martin Luther King Jr., collected quotes, *Orlando Sentinel*, January 25, 2017.

"You can expect scars": Douglas Starr, "1,000 Hear King at Negro Meet," *Tallahassee Democrat*, April 20, 1964.

"Freedom is never given freely": Ibid.

"I thought it was great": Reggie Young, Bill Black Combo band member, interview by author, October 1, 2018.

"There are many whites": AP, Flagler College Civil Rights Collection.

"The Beatles would be pleased": Larry Kane, interview by author, December 19, 2018.

"I had asked for one interview." Ibid.

"We argued": Ibid.

"You can't just say": Ibid.

"I said, 'I just can't go'": Ibid.

"Larry, you should go": Ibid.

"Took him to 'the outer limits of human behavior'": Larry Kane, *Ticket to Ride: Inside the Beatles' 1964 and 1965 Tours That Changed the World* (New York: Penguin, 2004), 9.

Chapter 17. Beatings and Bloodshed

"My world was so small": Kitty Oliver, interview by author, December 6, 2018.

"Night rides": Common vernacular for Klan intimidation tactic.

"My fear was that": Andrew Young, *An Easy Burden: The Civil Rights Move-*

ment and the Transformation of America (New York: HarperCollins, 1996), 295.

"Who is our leader?": Mabel Chesley, "What Manner of Man Is Leading America's Negro Revolution?," *Daytona Beach Sunday News-Journal*, June 7, 1964.

"To his lowliest followers": Ibid.

"Before I'll be a slave": "Dr. King Describes Threats on Return to Florida City," UPI, June 5, 1964.

"March tonight": John Herbers, *Deep South Dispatch: Memoir of a Civil Rights Journalist* (Jackson: University Press of Mississippi, 2018), 150.

"My Father Died Defending This Country": Ibid.

"Segregation Must Go": Ibid.

"We Love Everybody": Ibid.

"Martin Luther Coon": Ibid.

"They stared at me": Young, *An Easy Burden,*292.

"They grabbed me": Herbers, *Deep South Dispatch*, 151.

"There was an opportunity": Historian Michael Gannon, interview by David Colburn, Civil Rights Library of St. Augustine, undated, civilrights.flagler.edu.

"I once asked him": Ms. Janie Price, undated video interview, Flagler College Civil Rights Collection.

"Precious Lord": Ibid.

"This is the only way we know how to express": Letter in the Flagler College Civil Rights Collection.

"You are on private property": John Herbers, "MLK 17 Others Jailed Trying to Integrate St. Augustine Restaurant, *New York Times*, June 12, 1964.

"Swim-in": "Remembering a Civil Rights Swim-In," NPR, June 13, 2014.

"No different": Dan Warren, *If It Takes All Summer: Martin Luther King, the KKK and States' Rights in St. Augustine, 1964* (Tuscaloosa: University of Alabama Press, 2015), 99.

"Safe keeping": Ibid.

"All the work": Ibid.

"I Have a Dream": King speech during the March on Washington, August 1963.

"Insufficient funds": Ibid.

Chapter 18. The St. Augustine Dilemma

"The bullpen": Simpson Ruling, Young vs Kynes, US District Court, June 1964.

"Clear and present danger": Ibid.

"I'm in a lonely": "Before and After: The Old US Post Office and Courthouse," TheJaxsonMag.com, September 4, 2019.

"Nonviolent army": Ibid.

"I suggest rigid and strict law enforcement": Simpson Simpson Ruling,
Young vs Kynes.

"Federal Judicial Dictatorship": Dr. James Denham, "The Battle for Justice:
Judge Bryan Simpson and the St. Augustine Uprising, 1963–1964," Florida
Conference of Historians, St. Augustine, February 1, 2014.

"Drop dead": Ibid.

"Binding precedent": Judge Simpson interview, undated, Flagler College
Civil Rights Collection.

"Eloquence": Yale University commencement speech, June 15, 1964.

"The only person": "King, the Firewalker," editorial, *Tampa Tribune*, June 22,
1964.

"Gang terrorism": Editorial on WFTV, June 22, 1964.

"This is a frighteningly sad case": Ibid.

"He has followed": Sen. George McGovern, *Congressional Record*, June 1964.

"In retrospect": Andrew Young, *An Easy Burden: The Civil Rights Movement
and the Transformation of America* (New York: HarperCollins, 1996), 296.

"Re-segregation": Mabel Chesley, "King Describes His St. Augustine Dilemma," *Daytona Beach News-Journal*, July 18, 1964.

"Now I can't just walk out": Ibid.

Chapter 19. Outer Limits

"What's your problem, man?" Larry Kane, *Ticket to Ride: Inside the Beatles'
1964 and 1965 Tours That Changed the World* (New York: Penguin, 2004),
14.

"The Boys": Ibid., 13

"Why are you dressed": Ibid., 14.

"It's better than looking scruffy": Ibid.

"I was not a deejay": Larry Kane, interview by the author, December 19,
2018.

"Butting in": Louis "Buddy" Dresner, interview by his son, Barry Dresner,
buddyandthebeatles.com.

"We're putting down the Vietnam War": Kane interview.

"Liked the talk": Kane, *Ticket to Ride*, 15.

"John, it was great": Ibid.

"They would walk onstage": Lillian Walker-Moss, interview by author, November 16, 2018.

"Racial Matters": FBI memo August 19, 1964.

"A perfect vehicle for riots": Ibid.

"Emotional pitch of the crowds": Ibid.

"I felt a hammer-like strike": Kane, *Ticket to Ride*, 18.

"We want the Beatles!": Ibid.

"BBC": Reggie Young, Bill Black Combo band member, interview by author, October 1, 2018.

"Bill Black Combo": Ibid.

"The girls threw them angrily": Ibid.

"Like friendly fire": Ivor Davis, *The Beatles and Me on Tour: The Beatles' 1964 North American Tour* (Los Angeles, CA: Cockney Kid, 2014), 28.

"More than a few clattered": Ibid.

"Rugby tackled": Kane interview.

"How did it feel out there?": Kane, *Ticket to Ride*, 21.

"Not safe": Ibid.

Chapter 20. Broken Silence

"Someone like myself": Rob Patterson, "Ex Road Manager Recalls the Beatles," *Scrantonian Tribune*, July 15, 1984.

"We don't like it if there's any segregation": Paul McCartney, radio interview by Larry Kane, Las Vegas, August 20, 1964.

"That's the way we all feel": Ringo Starr, radio interview by Larry Kane, Las Vegas, August 20, 1964.

"They ate, slept": Lillian Moss, Exciters band member, interview by author, November 16, 2018.

"I had no idea": Reggie Young, Bill Black Combo band member, interview by author, October 1, 2018.

"I will never forget his words": Larry Kane, *Ticket to Ride: Inside the Beatles' 1964 and 1965 Tours That Changed the World* (New York: Penguin, 2004), 21.

"It's okay": Ibid., 22.

"You're a reporter": Ibid.

"To this day": Ibid., 23.

Chapter 21. New Songs and Snapshots

"I didn't realize just how talented": Rob Patterson, "Ex Road Manager Recalls the Beatles," *Scrantonian Tribune*, July 15, 1984.

"I remember the song": Jackie DeShannon, interview by Gary James, undated, classicbands.com.

"We want the Beatles": Reggie Young, interview by author, October 1, 2018.

"They were fabulous to me": DeShannon interview.

"When You Walk into the Room": Ibid.

"Both of them made a point": Larry Kane, interview by the author, December 19, 2018.

"They talked": Ibid.

"Somewhere over Kansas": Kane interview.

"Eight days a week": Paul and Linda McCartney, interview by Joan Goodman, *Playboy*, 1984.

"It was our filing cabinet": Ivor Davis, *The Beatles and Me on Tour: The Beatles' 1964 North American Tour*, 106.

"Hello, Larry": Kane interview.

"Queer": Ringo Starr, radio interview by Larry Kane, Las Vegas, August 20, 1964.

"Here's to you and me": Kane interview.

"Honestly": Ibid.

"When he did come on to me": Ibid.

"I understand, I understand": Ibid.

"*Fostoria*": Chuck Gunderson, *Some Fun Tonight! The Backstage Story of How the Beatles Rocked America: The Historic Tours of 1964–66*, vol. 1 (London: Backbeat, 2016).

"This way": Ibid.

Chapter 22. Dora and a Dilemma Solved

"I didn't see": George Winterling, "Forecasting Dora's Landfall," NewsJax4.com, September 9, 2014.

"I'll be in the audience": Anonymous letter received by the FBI, August 1964, "The FBI Vault," www.fbi.gov

"We looked down at the boys": George Martin, Beatlesbible.com.

"N-----, go home!": Lillian Walker-Moss Exciters band member, interview by author, November 16, 2018.

"Our favorites": "Admit All or No Show, Beatles Say," Herald Wire Services, September 6, 1964.

"We understand they let them": Ibid.

"They were really cool guys": Lillian Walker-Moss interview.

"A dramatic breakthrough": Dan Warren, *If It Takes All Summer: Martin Luther King, the KKK and States' Rights in St. Augustine, 1964* (Tuscaloosa: University of Alabama Press, 2015), 168.

"King tipped his hat": Mabel Norris Chesley, "King Claims Victory for Civil Rights in Old City," *Daytona Beach News-Journal*, August 6, 1964.

"The one major fault": Seth Rogovoy, "On His 80th Birthday, Ringo Starr's Secret Jewish History," Forward.com.

"Start to get hysterical": Ringo Starr, quoted in The Beatles, *The Beatles Anthology* (San Francisco, CA: Chronicle, 2002), 153.

"We decided": George Harrison quoted ibid.

"I told them Miami's no good": Larry Kane, interview by author, December 19, 2018.

"The greatest of all end-of-the-road towns": Charles Kuralt, *Charles Kuralt's America* (New York: Anchor, 1996), 28.

Chapter 23. Key West

"Our plane was bucking": Ivor Davis, *The Beatles and Me on Tour: The Beatles' 1964 North American Tour* (Los Angeles, CA: Cockney Kid, 2014), 91.

"Gray green": Ibid.

"It's not a nice thing to say": Ibid.

"I wouldn't put it past them": Bud Jacobsen, "Duval Gets Dora—We Get Beatles," *Key West Citizen*, September 9, 1964.

"The giant Electra turboprop": Ibid.

"Screaming and crying": Ibid.

"Where are we?": Davis, *The Beatles and Me on Tour*, 91.

"Lost in the sauce": Larry Kane, *Ticket to Ride: Inside the Beatles' 1964 and 1965 Tours That Changed the World* (New York: Penguin, 2004), 133.

"Did you hear": John Trusty, interview by author, December 16, 2018.

"Ya, right": Trusty interview.

"Prellies": Davis, *The Beatles and Me on Tour*, 93.

"Belly warmers": Ibid.

"Plentiful supply": Ibid.

"In the event": Ibid.

"It was like": Trusty interview.

"Fine Negro pianist": "Beatle Watching," *Key West Citizen*, September 10, 1964.

"Excuse me": Trusty interview.

"I'm gonna tell you": Ibid.

"All I want to be": Ibid.

"My God": Ibid.

"Would you like a fag?": Ibid.

"I kick myself": Ibid.

"He looked like a drowned rat": Ibid.

"Nobody crossed that line": Ibid.

"They didn't play": Lillian Walker-Moss, interview by author, November 16, 2018.

"That guy was just an asshole": Trusty interview.

"We told you no cameras": Ibid.

"The lyrics": Ibid.

"These guys were not going to be a flash in the pan": Ibid.

Chapter 24. An Emotional Landmark

"I'll tell you this": Gloria Steinem, "Beatle with a Future," *Cosmopolitan*, December 1964.

"Porridge": *Key West Citizen*, September 9, 1964.

"It happens everywhere we go": June Keith, *Postcards from Paradise: Romancing Key West* (Palm Island Press, 2006).

"Mama": Lillian Walker-Moss, interview by author, November 16, 2018.

"They just bum-rushed her": Ibid.

"The experiences of the tour": Larry Kane, interview by author, December 19, 2018.

"Beatling": *Key West Citizen*, September 9, 1964.

"Let's get our axes!": Walker-Moss interview.

"We sang rock and roll": Ibid.

"A Black Beatle": Lofton "Coffee" Butler, interview by author, June 23, 2020.

"It's after four": "The Beatles, an Intimate Portrait," *New York Post*, September 14–20, 1964, Paulsann.com

"It's the Florida law": Ibid.

"Yes, you were my thrill": Ibid.

"Time to split": Ibid.

"Let the man play!": Ibid.

"One of those talking-to-the-toilet-bowl evenings": McCartney, Guardian Unlimited, 2004, quoted in Beatlesbible.com

"Got so pissed": Ibid.

"I always remembered it": Paul McCartney, interview by Terry Gross, *Fresh Air*, 2001, NPR.com.

"They really don't even want": Walker-Moss interview.

Chapter 25. Landfall, Destruction, Relief

"Mama rented": Kitty Oliver, interview by author, December 6, 2018.

"More concerned": Ibid.

"It was pissing with rain": Andrea Rotondo, *Tom Petty, Rock and Roll Guardian* (New York: Overlook, 2014), 61.

"National Beatle Jet": Glass, "Beatle Fans Flock to Jax," *Miami News*, September 11, 1964.

"Super Constellation": Ibid.

"Everybody in Key West": Karen Wade, interview by author, October 5, 2018.

Chapter 26. Windblown History

"Girls, I'll see you backstage": Kim Adelman, *The Girls' Guide to Elvis* (New York: Three Rivers), 39.

"'Negro' section": Paul Wilder and Harry Roberts, "Shouting, Pushing, Mass of Youngsters Stampedes Presley Show Here," *Tampa Tribune*, August 6, 1956.

"It was almost like": Kitty Oliver, interview by author, December 6, 2018.

"Race never came in to my awareness": Margaret Shepherd, interview by author, October 17, 2019.

"Oh, my God": Ibid.

"It was windy as hell": George Harrison, quoted in The Beatlesbible.com.

"Hey, Ringo": Glass, "Beatle Fans Flock to Jax," *Miami News*, September 11, 1964.

"Scourges of Liverpool": Bill Demain, "All Together Now: Civil Rights and the Beatles' First American Tour," mentalfloss.com.

"A lack of leadership": AP, "Goldwater Says Civil Rights Law Incites Violence," *Tampa Tribune*, September 11, 1964.

"Down the road": Ibid.

"We want the Beatles!": Kathy Harben diary. Harben was a close childhood friend and neighbor of Tom Petty in Gainesville.

"It was kind of scary": Lillian Walker-Moss, Exciters band member, interview by author, November 16, 2018.

"I can't allow": Glass, "Beatle Fans Flock to Jax," *Miami News*, September 11, 1964.

"This show is for the kids": Ibid.

"Let me say right now": Newsreel footage taken September 9–11, 1964, youtube.com.

"I was never more proud": Debbie Brennan-Bartoletti, interview by author, January 8, 2019.

"The frenetic welcome": Glass, "Beatle Fans Flock to Jax."

"It was such a massive rush": Brennan-Bartoletti interview.

"Four Elvis Presleys": Lennon to Larry Kane, September 13, 1964, www.beatleinterviews.org.

"It was so overwhelming": Margaret Shepherd, interview by author, October 17, 2019.

"Susan, Mary and I": Kathy Harben Arce, interview by the author, October 20, 2019.

"He had a real pretty red electric guitar": Ibid.

"I just remember": Oliver interview.

"Darling, believe me": Glass, "Beatle Fans Flock to Jax."

"You came *alone?*": Oliver interview.

"A lot of folks": Ibid.

"The Gator Bowl concert": Larry Kane, *Ticket to Ride: Inside the Beatles' 1964 Tours That Changed the World* (New York: Penguin, 2004), 98.

"Rev. William L. England Day": Frances Perkins, "Film about 60s Civil Rights Clash Has Ties—and Parallels—to Maine," www.mainetoday.com

"Judge Simpson symbolized": Andrew Young, *An Easy Burden: The Civil Rights Movement and the Transformation of America* (New York: Harper-Collins, 1996), 299.

"Another judge might have said": Bryan Simpson, interview, Flagler College Civil Rights Collection.

"The connection between the Beatles and MLK": Anthony DeCurtis, interview by author, September 17, 2021.

"We didn't think": Ringo Starr to Dan Rather, *The Big Interview*, AXS-TV, October 2, 2018.

Chapter 27. Markers

"John and Paul's harmonies": Youtube.com.

"Played and sang": Ibid.

"You know, sometimes I think": Robert Lipsyte, interview by author, March 27, 2020.

"When I was young in Liverpool": Starr, during Ryman concert, August 8, 2019.

"Peace and love, God bless." Ringo Starr to the author, August 9, 2019.

"I Missed My Senior Prom to See You," unnamed female fan's sign, written on a pillow case, Camping World Stadium, Orlando, May 28, 2022.

"Take out your camera, Linda": May Pang, *Instamatic Karma: Photographs of John Lennon* (New York: St. Martin's, 2008), 98.

"He looked wistfully": Ibid.

"I can't stand the fame": Ken Davidoff, interview by the author, October 7, 2018.

"It was just so unprofessional": Larry Kane, interview by author, December 19, 2018.

"Nobody in their wildest imagination": Davidoff interview.

"I'm not having another Surfside case": Miamiherald.com, March 3, 2022.

"An abomination": Robert Precht, interview by author, May 21, 2021.

"It's a neglect of culture and heritage": Ibid.

"I hear you over there!": Author's visit with Key West musician Landon "Coffee" Butler.

"My manager": Ibid

"Let the man play!": Ibid.

"I smile every time I see it." Circuit Judge Debra Nelson, interview by author, February 5, 2021.

"'White and colored' water fountains": Ibid.

"I guess we haven't come that far": Ibid.

"The Louis Armstrong of the Florida Keys": Coffee Butler and Friends, Facebook.com.

Selected Bibliography

The Beatles. *The Beatles Anthology*. San Francisco, CA: Chronicle, 2002.

Benson, Harry. *The Beatles: On the Road 1964–66*. Cologne, Germany: Taschen, 2017.

Davis, Ivor. *The Beatles and Me on Tour: The Beatles' 1964 North American Tour*. Los Angeles, CA: Cockney Kid, 2014.

De Palma, Ralph. *The Soul of Key West*. Vol. 2. Self-published, 2015.

Epstein, Brian. *A Cellarful of Noise*. New York: Little, Brown, 1964.

Freeman, Robert. *The Beatles: A Private View*. New York: Big Tent Entertainment, 2003.

Gunderson, Chuck. *Some Fun Tonight! The Backstage Story of How the Beatles Rocked America: The Historic Tours of 1964–66*. Vol. 1. London: Backbeat, 2016.

Hoffman, Dezo, *The Beatles Conquer America: The Photographic Record of Their First American Tour*. New York: Avon, 1985.

———. *With the Beatles: The Historic Photographs of Dezo Hoffman*. Baltimore, MD: Omnibus, 1982.

Jourard, Marty. *Music Everywhere: The Rock and Roll Roots of a Southern Town*. Gainesville: University Press of Florida, 2016.

Kane, Larry. *Lennon Revealed*. Philadelphia, PA: Running Press, 2005.

———. *Ticket to Ride: Inside the Beatles' 1964 and 1965 Tours That Changed the World*. New York: Penguin, 2004.

Kessler, Jude Southerland. *Should Have Known Better*. Vol. 4 of *The John Lennon Series, 1964*. Monroe, LA: Penin, 2018.

Lennon, Cynthia. *John*. New York: Crown, 2005.

Lewisohn, Mark. *The Complete Beatles Chronicle*. New York: Pyramid, 1992.

———. *Tune In: The Beatles: All These Years*. Vol. 1. New York: Crown, 2016.

Norman, Phillip. *Paul McCartney: The Life*. New York: Little, Brown, 2016.

Pang, May. *Instamatic Karma: Photographs of John Lennon*. New York: St. Martin's, 2008.

Rayl, A. J. S. *Beatles '64: A Hard Day's Night in America.* New York: Doubleday, 1989.

Turner, Steve. *A Hard Day's Write: The Stories behind Every Beatles Song.* London: Carlton, 1994.

Warren, Dan. *If It Takes All Summer: Martin Luther King, the KKK and States' Rights in St. Augustine, 1964.* Tuscaloosa: University of Alabama Press, 2015.

Womack, Kenneth. *Maximum Volume: The Life of Beatles Producer George Martin, the Early Years, 1928–1965.* Chicago: Chicago Review Press, 2017.

Young, Andrew. *An Easy Burden: The Civil Rights Movement and the Transformation of America.* New York: HarperCollins, 1996.

Index

Durham, Mardy, 30, 36, 43, 45
Durham, Michael, 30, 36, 41, 43, 46
Duval County Jail, 6, 139, 142
Dylan, Bob, 105, 113, 116, 184; influence of, on Beatles, 158–59

Eagles, the, 115
Ed Sullivan Show, 8, 10, 18, 21–22, 38, 45, 52, 110–11; at Deauville Hotel, 58, 60, 65; Leadon on Beatles performance on, 109; performance on, *67*, 68–69; Petty, T., on Beatles performance on, 109; rehearsals for, 57–58
"Eight Days a Week," 160
England, William, 129, 132, 140, 198
the Epics, 109, 113, 114
Epstein, Brian, 7–9, 13, 21, 30, 32–36, 56–57, 70, 98, 104–5, 118, 142; Dresner, L, and, 72; insurance policy taken out by, 136; Kane, L., and, 123–24, 161–62; marketing plans of, 64–65, 104–5; in Miami, 74–75; North American tour organized by, 147; on southern tour, 124; on success of Beatles, 106–7
Essex, the, 113
Estefan, Gloria, 100
Eubanks, Goldie, 121
Evans, Mal, 88, 149, 172
Everly Brothers, 113–14
Evers, Medgar, 4–5, 42
Exciters, the, 122, 147, 175, 188, 194; Beatles friendship with, 153, 181; negative crowd responses to, 166

Faithful, Marianne, 13
fans, 72–73
The Fantastic Expedition of Dillard and Clark, 115
Fats Domino, 122, 182
Federal Bureau of Investigation (FBI): Beatles monitored by, 147–48
Felder, Don, 110, 111, 117
Fenway Park, 124
56 St. George Street, 127
Flagler, Henry, 127

Floyd, George, 208
Follow That Dream, 50
Fontainebleau Hotel, 65, 91
Forbes, Kermit, 176
Forster, Barbara, 59
Fostoria, 162–63
Freeman, Robert, 49
"From Me to You," 12, 29, 79
Fun in Acapulco, 91

Gainesville, 109–10, 113–14
Gallagher, Carol Lee, 11–12, 21
Gannon, Michael, 1–2, 121–22, 130
Garland, Judy, 15
Garvey, Betty, 100
Garvey, Malachi, 99–100
Gator Bowl, 119, 162, 184, 186, 189; Beatles at, 193–95, *197*; history of, 191; Kane, L., on, 198; Lennon, J., at, 195–96; Segregation at, 191–92
Gaye, Marvin, 166
Gaynor, Mitzi, 58, 70
Gerry and the Pacemakers, 13
Get Back, 53
Glass, Barbara, 27–29; McCartney, P., and, 52
Glass, Ian, 30, 195
Gleason, Jackie, 15, 38
Goldwater, Barry, 193
Gomel, Bob, 42–43, 49, 72
Grand Ol' Opry, 57, 202–3
Green Cove Springs, 115
Gross, Terry, 183
Group, the, 113
Gunther, Curt, 49

Hamburg, 181
Hank Ballard and the Midnighters, 37
Hanzman, Michael, 206
Harben, Kathy, 111–12, 116, 196
Harben, Keith, 6–7, 109
A Hard Day's Night, 30, 76, 96, 118–19, 183–84, *197*, 202; release of, 143–44
Hard Rock Café, 102–3
Hard Rock Vault, *102*

Harrison, George, 7, 9, 13, 18–20, 27–28,
50, 57, 116–17, 159; on audience rela-
tionship, 37; Dresner, L., and, 96–97;
at Dresner dinner, 88–89; on Hur-
ricane Dora, 192; Kane, L., and, 173;
Young, R., and, 153–55, 174
Hayling, Robert, 121, 127–28, 140
"Heartbreak Hotel," 91
Hearts and Flowers, 115
Hell House, 114–15
Help, 202
Hemingway, Ernest, 169, 176
Henry, Clarence, 122, 174, 194
"Here Today," 183
Herman's Hermits, 105
Hill, Tom, 60–61
Hillman, Chris, 113, 115
Hi Records, 174
Hoffman, Dezo, 26, 49, 52, 57–58, 74; on
Beatles' stardom, 92; on McCartney,
P., 88–89
Hollies, the, 13
Honey Fitz, 41, 50
Hurricane Cleo, 164–65
Hurricane Dora, 164, 210; Beatles tour
impacted by, 165–66; Brennan-Bar-
toletti on, 187–88; destruction from,
186–87, *187*; federal aid for, 189–90;
Harrison on, 192; Oliver on, 185–86

"If I Fell," 143, 197, 201
"In My Life," 201
"I Saw Her Standing There," 7
"I Should Have Known Better," 143
"It Don't Come Easy," 202
"I Want to Hold Your Hand," 3–4, 7, 9,
11–12, 18, 43, 104, 110, 183–84

The Jackie Gleason Show, 35
Jackson, Peter, 53
Jacksonville, 118–19, 164–65
Jacksonville Times-Union, 193
Jacobs, David, 104–5
Jacobson, Bud, 171

Jim Crow laws, 4–5, 120, 130, 136, 140,
142, 193
Joca, Mary Ann, 189, *190*
Joey Dee and the Starlighters, 37
John Lennon (Lennon, J.), 178
"Johnny B. Goode," 116
Johnson, Carol, 153
Johnson, Lyndon B., 120, 139, 143, 189,
190
Jones, Jack, 3
Jourard, Marty, 109
Joy, Ron, 178–79

Kane, Larry, 14–15, 23–25, 30, 69, 136,
160, 181; Epstein and, 123–25, 161–62;
on Gator Bowl, 198; Harrison and,
172; Lennon, J., and, 145–48, 150,
155–56, 195, 205; McCartney, P., and,
152–53; rapport with Beatles, 143,
151–52, 159–62, 168–69, 184; on southern tour, 123–25; Starr and, 159
Kane, Mildred, 124–25, 181
Kaufman, Murray, 27–28, 37, 42, 56,
73–74, 91
Kelly, Freda, 88
Kelly, Grace, 42, 45
Kennedy, Jackie, 18, 41, 76
Kennedy, John F., 1–2, 11, 16, 18, 22–23,
49, 65, 120; assassination of, 121, 145
Key West, 1, 3, 168, 169, 170–71; Beatles
in, 173–77, 181–82
Key West Citizen, 171
Key Wester resort, 179–80, *180*, 182,
207–8
King, Martin Luther, Jr., 6, 84, 144,
180, 192; arrests of, *134*, 136, 137–39,
198–99; Beatles and, 199–200; Carr
and, 120–21; "I Have a Dream" speech,
136; Nobel Peace Prize of, 199; Price
and, 130–32; in St. Augustine, 127–35,
137–42; in Tallahassee, 122
Kingston Trio, 111
Kinks, the, 13, 154
Kramer, Billy J., 154

Bob Kealing is the author of five books. A historic preservationist, Kealing is a founder of the Jack Kerouac House in Orlando, Gram Parsons Derry Down in Winter Haven, and Birthplace of the Allman Brothers Band in Jacksonville. A retired reporter, Kealing is a six-time Regional Emmy Award recipient, and two-time recipient of the Edward R. Murrow Award. In more recent years, Kealing has served as public affairs administrator for Seminole County sheriff Dennis Lemma. He is a contributor to the Florida Humanities' *Forum* magazine, *Winter Park* magazine, and WUCF-TV. Kealing and his wife, Karen, have two adult children, Kristen and William.